The publication of the first part of Bertrand Russell's three-volume autobiography was a literary event of the greatest importance, and the praise it received was universal.

The second part carries the reader from the outbreak of the First World War till almost the end of the Second. It was a period of the greatest significance both in the author's life and in world history. As he says himself, 'My life before 1910 and my life after 1914 were as sharply separated as Faust's life before and after he met Mephistopheles.' During these years, Russell's whole conception of human nature changed. He joined energetically in the campaign for peace. After the war he travelled widely. He married a second and a third time, founded a school, established a family. And he wrote a whole series of famous books, including *The Principles of Social Reconstruction*, *Marriage and Morals*, and *The History of Western Philosophy*.

This book, like the first volume, is peopled with some of the most eminent figures of the time, and continues the story of Bertrand Russell's persistent struggle to protest his beliefs.

THE AUTOBIOGRAPHY OF BERTRAND RUSSELL

VOLUME II

THE
AUTOBIOGRAPHY
OF
BERTRAND
RUSSELL

1914–1944

(VOLUME II)

LONDON

GEORGE ALLEN AND UNWIN LTD

RUSKIN HOUSE   MUSEUM STREET

FIRST PUBLISHED IN 1968
SECOND IMPRESSION 1968
THIS EDITION 1971

ISBN 0 04 921009 2 *Cased*
0 04 921013 0 *Paper*

PRINTED IN GREAT BRITAIN
BY OFFSET LITHOGRAPHY
BY BILLING & SONS LIMITED
GUILDFORD AND LONDON

ACKNOWLEDGEMENTS

ACKNOWLEDGEMENTS are due to the following for permission to include certain letters in this volume: Les Amis d'Henri Barbusse; Margaret Cole, for the letter of Beatrice Webb; John Conrad, through J. M. Dent & Sons, for the letters of Joseph Conrad; Valerie Eliot, for the letters of T. S. Eliot; the Estate of Albert Einstein; the Executors of the H. G. Wells Estate (© 1968 George Philip Wells and Frank Wells); Pearn, Pollinger & Higham, with the concurrence of William Heinemann Ltd., for passages from the letters of D. H. Lawrence; the Public Trustee and the Society of Authors, for the letters of Bernard Shaw; the Trustees of the Will of Mrs Bernard Shaw; and the Council of Trinity College, Cambridge. Facsimiles of Crown-copyright records in the Public Record Office appear by permission of the Controller of H.M. Stationery Office. The above list includes only those who requested formal acknowledgement; many others have kindly granted permission to publish letters.

The Defiled Sanctuary
by William Blake

I saw a chapel all of gold
    That none did dare to enter in,
And many weeping stood without,
    Weeping, mourning, worshipping.

I saw a serpent rise between
    The white pillars of the door,
And he forced and forced and forced
    Till down the golden hinges tore:

And along the pavement sweet,
    Set with pearls and rubies bright,
All his shining length he drew,—
    Till upon the altar white

Vomited his poison out
    On the bread and on the wine.
So I turned into a sty,
    And laid me down among the swine.

CONTENTS

CHAPTER I

THE FIRST WAR

THE PERIOD FROM 1910 to 1914 was a time of transition. My life before 1910 and my life after 1914 were as sharply separated as Faust's life before and after he met Mephistopheles. I underwent a process of rejuvenation, inaugurated by Ottoline Morrell and continued by the War. It may seem curious that the War should rejuvenate anybody, but in fact it shook me out of my prejudices and made me think afresh on a number of fundamental questions. It also provided me with a new kind of activity, for which I did not feel the staleness that beset me whenever I tried to return to mathematical logic. I have therefore got into the habit of thinking of myself as a non-supernatural Faust for whom Mephistopheles was represented by the Great War.

During the hot days at the end of July, I was at Cambridge, discussing the situation with all and sundry. I found it impossible to believe that Europe would be so mad as to plunge into war, but I was persuaded that, if there was war, England would be involved. I felt strongly that England ought to remain neutral, and I collected the signatures of a large number of professors and Fellows to a statement which appeared in the *Manchester Guardian* to that effect. The day War was declared, almost all of them changed their minds. Looking back, it seems extraordinary that one did not realize more clearly what was coming. On Sunday, August 2nd, as mentioned in the earlier volume of this autobiography, I met Keynes hurrying across the Great Court of Trinity to borrow his brother-in-law's motor-bicycle to go up to London.[1] I presently discovered that the Government had sent for him to give them financial advice. This made me realize the imminence of our participation in the War. On the Monday morning I decided to go to London. I lunched with the Morrells at Bedford Square, and found Ottoline entirely of my way of thinking. She agreed with Philip's determination to make a pacifist speech in the House. I went down to the House in the hope of hearing Sir Edward Grey's famous statement,

[1] His brother-in-law was A. V. Hill, eminent in scientific medicine. He had rooms on the next staircase to mine.

but the crowd was too great, and I failed to get in. I learned, however, that Philip had duly made his speech. I spent the evening walking round the streets, especially in the neighbourhood of Trafalgar Square, noticing cheering crowds, and making myself sensitive to the emotions of passers-by. During this and the following days I discovered to my amazement that average men and women were delighted at the prospect of war. I had fondly imagined, what most pacifists contended, that wars were forced upon a reluctant population by despotic and Machiavellian governments. I had noticed during previous years how carefully Sir Edward Grey lied in order to prevent the public from knowing the methods by which he was committing us to the support of France in the event of war. I naïvely imagined that when the public discovered how he had lied to them, they would be annoyed; instead of which, they were grateful to him for having spared them the moral responsibility.

On the morning of August 4th, I walked with Ottoline up and down the empty streets behind the British Museum, where now there are University buildings. We discussed the future in gloomy terms. When we spoke to others of the evils we foresaw, they thought us mad; yet it turned out that we were twittering optimists compared to the truth. On the evening of the 4th, after quarrelling with George Trevelyan along the whole length of the Strand, I attended the last meeting of a neutrality committee of which Graham Wallas was chairman. During the meeting there was a loud clap of thunder, which all the older members of the committee took to be a German bomb. This dissipated their last lingering feeling in favour of neutrality. The first days of the War were to me utterly amazing. My best friends, such as the White-heads, were savagely warlike. Men like J. L. Hammond, who had been writing for years against participation in a European War, were swept off their feet by Belgium. As I had long known from a military friend at the Staff College that Belgium would inevitably be involved, I had not supposed important publicists so frivolous as to be ignorant on this vital matter. The *Nation* newspaper used to have a staff luncheon every Tuesday, and I attended the luncheon on August 4th. I found Massingham, the editor, vehemently opposed to our participation in the war. He welcomed enthusiastically my offer to write for his newspaper in that sense. Next day I got a letter from him, beginning: 'Today is not yesterday . . .', and stating that his opinion had completely changed. Nevertheless, he printed a long letter from me protesting against the War in his next issue.[1] What changed his opinion I do not know. I know that one of Asquith's daughters saw him descending the steps of the German Embassy late on the afternoon of August 4th, and I have some suspicion that he was consequently warned of the unwisdom of a

[1] The full text is reproduced on page 42.

lack of patriotism in such a crisis. For the first year or so of the War he remained patriotic, but as time went on he began to forget that he had ever been so. A few pacifist M.P.s, together with two or three sympathizers, began to have meetings at the Morrells' house in Bedford Square. I used to attend these meetings, which gave rise to the Union of Democratic Control. I was interested to observe that many of the pacifist politicians were more concerned with the question which of them should lead the anti-war movement than with the actual work against the War. Nevertheless, they were all there was to work with, and I did my best to think well of them.

Meanwhile, I was living at the highest possible emotional tension. Although I did not foresee anything like the full disaster of the War, I foresaw a great deal more than most people did. The prospect filled me with horror, but what filled me with even more horror was the fact that the anticipation of carnage was delightful to something like ninety per cent of the population. I had to revise my views on human nature. At that time I was wholly ignorant of psycho-analysis, but I arrived for myself at a view of human passions not unlike that of the psycho-analysts. I arrived at this view in an endeavour to understand popular feeling about the War. I had supposed until that time that it was quite common for parents to love their children, but the War persuaded me that it is a rare exception. I had supposed that most people liked money better than almost anything else, but I discovered that they liked destruction even better. I had supposed that intellectuals frequently loved truth, but I found here again that not ten per cent of them prefer truth to popularity. Gilbert Murray, who had been a close friend of mine since 1902, was a pro-Boer when I was not. I therefore naturally expected that he would again be on the side of peace; yet he went out of his way to write about the wickedness of the Germans, and the super-human virtue of Sir Edward Grey. I became filled with despairing tenderness towards the young men who were to be slaughtered, and with rage against all the statesmen of Europe. For several weeks I felt that if I should happen to meet Asquith or Grey I should be unable to refrain from murder. Gradually, however, these personal feelings disappeared. They were swallowed up by the magnitude of the tragedy, and by the realization of the popular forces which the statesmen merely let loose.

In the midst of this, I was myself tortured by patriotism. The successes of the Germans before the Battle of the Marne were horrible to me. I desired the defeat of Germany as ardently as any retired colonel. Love of England is very nearly the strongest emotion I possess, and in appearing to set it aside at such a moment, I was making a very difficult renunciation. Nevertheless, I never had a moment's doubt as to what

I must do. I have at times been paralyzed by scepticism, at times I have been cynical, at other times indifferent, but when the War came I felt as if I heard the voice of God. I knew that it was my business to protest, however futile protest might be. My whole nature was involved. As a lover of truth, the national propaganda of all the belligerent nations sickened me. As a lover of civilization, the return to barbarism appalled me. As a man of thwarted parental feeling, the massacre of the young wrung my heart. I hardly supposed that much good would come of opposing the War, but I felt that for the honour of human nature those who were not swept off their feet should show that they stood firm. After seeing troop trains departing from Waterloo, I used to have strange visions of London as a place of unreality. I used in imagination to see the bridges collapse and sink, and the whole great city vanish like a morning mist. Its inhabitants began to seem like hallucinations, and I would wonder whether the world in which I thought I had lived was a mere product of my own febrile nightmares.[1] Such moods, however, were brief, and were put an end to by the need of work.

Throughout the earlier phases of the War, Ottoline was a very great help and strength to me. But for her, I should have been at first completely solitary, but she never wavered either in her hatred of war, or in her refusal to accept the myths and falsehoods with which the world was inundated.

I found a minor degree of comfort in the conversation of Santayana, who was at Cambridge at that time. He was a neutral, and in any case he had not enough respect for the human race to care whether it destroyed itself or not. His calm, philosophical detachment, though I had no wish to imitate it, was soothing to me. Just before the Battle of the Marne, when it looked as if the Germans must soon take Paris, he remarked in a dreamy tone of voice: 'I think I must go over to Paris. My winter underclothes are there, and I should not like the Germans to get them. I have also another, though less important, reason, which is that I have there a manuscript of a book on which I have been working for the last ten years, but I do not care so much about that as about the underclothes.' He did not, however, go to Paris, because the Battle of the Marne saved him the trouble. Instead, he remarked to me one day: 'I am going to Seville tomorrow because I wish to be in a place where people do not restrain their passions.'

With the beginning of the October Term, I had to start again lecturing on mathematical logic, but I felt it a somewhat futile occupation. So I took to organizing a branch of the Union of Democratic Control among the dons, of whom at Trinity quite a number were at first sympathetic. I also addressed meetings of undergraduates who were quite willing to

[1] I spoke of this to T. S. Eliot, who put it into *The Waste Land*.

listen to me. I remember in the course of a speech, saying: 'It is all nonsense to pretend the Germans are wicked', and to my surprise the whole room applauded. But with the sinking of the *Lusitania*, a fiercer spirit began to prevail. It seemed to be supposed that I was in some way responsible for this disaster. Of the dons who had belonged to the Union of Democratic Control, many had by this time got commissions. Barnes (afterwards Bishop of Birmingham) left to become Master of the Temple. The older dons got more and more hysterical, and I began to find myself avoided at the high table.

Every Christmas throughout the War I had a fit of black despair, such complete despair that I could do nothing except sit idle in my chair and wonder whether the human race served any purpose. At Christmas time in 1914, by Ottoline's advice, I found a way of making despair not unendurable. I took to visiting destitute Germans on behalf of a charitable committee to investigate their circumstances and to relieve their distress if they deserved it. In the course of this work, I came upon remarkable instances of kindness in the middle of the fury of war. Not infrequently in the poor neighbourhoods landladies, themselves poor, had allowed Germans to stay on without paying any rent, because they knew it was impossible for Germans to find work. This problem ceased to exist soon afterwards, as the Germans were all interned, but during the first months of the War their condition was pitiable.

One day in October 1914 I met T. S. Eliot in New Oxford Street. I did not know he was in Europe, but I found he had come to England from Berlin. I naturally asked him what he thought of the War. 'I don't know,' he replied, 'I only know that I am not a pacifist.' That is to say, he considered any excuse good enough for homicide. I became great friends with him, and subsequently with his wife, whom he married early in 1915. As they were desperately poor, I lent them one of the two bedrooms in my flat, with the result that I saw a great deal of them.[1] I was fond of them both, and endeavoured to help them in their troubles until I discovered that their troubles were what they enjoyed. I held some debentures nominally worth £3,000, in an engineering firm, which during the War naturally took to making munitions. I was much puzzled in my conscience as to what to do with these debentures, and at last I gave them to Eliot. Years afterwards, when the War was finished and he was no longer poor, he gave them back to me.

During the summer of 1915 I wrote *Principles of Social Reconstruction*, or *Why Men Fight* as it was called in America without my consent. I had had no intention of writing such a book, and it was totally unlike

---

[1] The suggestion sometimes made, however, that one of us influenced the other is without foundation.

anything I had previously written, but it came out in a spontaneous manner. In fact I did not discover what it was all about until I had finished it. It has a framework and a formula, but I only discovered both when I had written all except the first and last words. In it I suggested a philosophy of politics based upon the belief that impulse has more effect than conscious purpose in moulding men's lives. I divided impulses into two groups, the possessive and the creative, considering the best life that which is most built on creative impulses. I took, as examples of embodiments of the possessive impulses, the State, war and poverty; and of the creative impulses, education, marriage and religion. Liberation of creativeness, I was convinced, should be the principle of reform. I first gave the book as lectures, and then published it. To my surprise, it had an immediate success. I had written it with no expectation of its being read, merely as a profession of faith, but it brought me in a great deal of money, and laid the foundation for all my future earnings.

These lectures were in certain ways connected with my short friendship with D. H. Lawrence. We both imagined that there was something important to be said about the reform of human relations, and we did not at first realize that we took diametrically opposite views as to the kind of reform that was needed. My acquaintance with Lawrence was brief and hectic, lasting altogether about a year. We were brought together by Ottoline, who admired us both and made us think that we ought to admire each other. Pacifism had produced in me a mood of bitter rebellion, and I found Lawrence equally full of rebellion. This made us think, at first, that there was a considerable measure of agreement between us, and it was only gradually that we discovered that we differed from each other more than either differed from the Kaiser.

There were in Lawrence at that time two attitudes to the war: on the one hand, he could not be whole-heartedly patriotic, because his wife was German; but on the other hand, he had such a hatred of mankind that he tended to think both sides must be right in so far as they hated each other. As I came to know these attitudes, I realized that neither was one with which I could sympathize. Awareness of our differences, however, was gradual on both sides, and at first all went merry as a marriage bell. I invited him to visit me at Cambridge and introduced him to Keynes and a number of other people. He hated them all with a passionate hatred and said they were 'dead, dead, dead'. For a time I thought he might be right. I liked Lawrence's fire, I liked the energy and passion of his feelings, I liked his belief that something very fundamental was needed to put the world right. I agreed with him in thinking that politics could not be divorced from individual psychology. I felt him to be a man of a certain imaginative genius, and, at first, when I felt inclined to disagree with him, I thought that perhaps his insight into human nature was deeper than mine. It was only gradually that I came to feel him a positive force for evil and that he came to have the same feeling about me.

I was at this time preparing the course of lectures which was afterwards published as *Principles of Social Reconstruction*. He, also, wanted to lecture, and for a time it seemed possible that there might be some sort of loose collaboration between us. We exchanged a number of letters, of which mine are lost but his have been published. In his letters the gradual awareness of the consciousness of our fundamental disagreements can be traced. I was a firm believer in democracy, whereas he had developed the whole philosophy of Fascism before the politicians had thought of it. 'I don't believe', he wrote, 'in democratic control. I think the working man is fit to elect governors or overseers for his immediate circumstances, but for no more. You must utterly revise the electorate. The working man shall elect superiors for the things that concern him immediately, no more. From the other classes, as they rise, shall be elected the higher governors. The thing must culminate in one real head, as every organic thing must—no foolish republic with foolish presidents, but an elected King, something like Julius Caesar.' He, of course, in his imagination, supposed that when a dictatorship was established he would be the Julius Caesar. This was part of the dream-like quality of all his thinking. He never let himself bump into reality. He would go into long tirades about how one must proclaim 'the Truth' to the multitude, and he seemed to have no doubt that the multitude would listen. I asked him what method he was going to adopt. Would he put his political philosophy into a book? No: in our corrupt society the written word is always a lie. Would he go into Hyde Park and proclaim 'the Truth' from a soap box? No: that would be far too dangerous (odd streaks of prudence emerged in him from time to time). Well, I said, what would you do? At this point he would change the subject.

Gradually I discovered that he had no real wish to make the world better, but only to indulge in eloquent soliloquy about how bad it was. If anybody overheard the soliloquies, so much the better, but they were designed at most to produce a little faithful band of disciples who could sit in the deserts of New Mexico and feel holy. All this was conveyed to me in the language of a Fascist dictator as what I *must* preach, the 'must' having thirteen underlinings.

His letters grew gradually more hostile. He wrote, 'What's the good of living as you do anyway? I don't believe your lectures *are* good. They are nearly over, aren't they? What's the good of sticking in the damned ship and haranguing the merchant pilgrims in their own language? Why don't you drop overboard? Why don't you clear out of the whole

show? One must be an outlaw these days, not a teacher or preacher.'
This seemed to me mere rhetoric. I was becoming more of an outlaw
than he ever was and I could not quite see his ground of complaint
against me. He phrased his complaint in different ways at different
times. On another occasion he wrote: 'Do stop working and writing
altogether and become a creature instead of a mechanical instrument.
Do clear out of the whole social ship. Do for your very pride's sake
become a mere nothing, a mole, a creature that feels its way and doesn't
think. Do for heavens sake be a baby, and not a savant any more. Don't
do anything more—but for heavens sake begin to *be*—Start at the very
beginning and be a perfect baby: in the name of courage.

'Oh, and I want to ask you, when you make your will, do leave me
enough to live on. I want you to live for ever. But I want you to make
me in some part your heir.'

The only difficulty with this programme was that if I adopted it
I should have nothing to leave.

He had a mystical philosophy of 'blood' which I disliked. 'There is',
he said, 'another seat of consciousness than the brain and nerves. There
is a blood-consciousness which exists in us independently of the ordinary
mental consciousness. One lives, knows and has one's being in the
blood, without any reference to nerves and brain. This is one half of
life belonging to the darkness. When I take a woman, then the blood-
percept is supreme. My blood-knowing is overwhelming. We should
realize that we have a blood-being, a blood-consciousness, a blood-soul
complete and apart from a mental and nerve consciousness.' This
seemed to me frankly rubbish, and I rejected it vehemently, though I
did not then know that it led straight to Auschwitz.

He always got into a fury if one suggested that anybody could possibly have kindly feelings towards anybody else, and when I objected to
war because of the suffering that it causes, he accused me of hypocrisy.
'It isn't in the least true that you, your basic self, want ultimate peace.
You are satisfying in an indirect, false way your lust to jab and strike.
Either satisfy it in a direct and honourable way, saying "I hate you all,
liars and swine, and am out to set upon you", or stick to mathematics,
where you can be true—But to come as the angel of peace—no, I prefer
Tirpitz a thousand times in that role.'

I find it difficult now to understand the devastating effect that this
letter had upon me. I was inclined to believe that he had some insight
denied to me, and when he said that my pacifism was rooted in blood-
lust I supposed he must be right. For twenty-four hours I thought that I
was not fit to live and contemplated suicide. But at the end of that time,
a healthier reaction set in, and I decided to have done with such morbidness. When he said that I *must* preach his doctrines and not mine I

rebelled, and told him to remember that he was no longer a school-master and I was not his pupil. He had written, 'the enemy of all mankind you are, full of the lust of enmity. It is *not* a hatred of falsehood which inspires you, it is the hatred of people of flesh and blood, it is a perverted mental blood-lust. Why don't you own it? Let us become strangers again. I think it is better.' I thought so too. But he found a pleasure in denouncing me and continued for some months to write letters containing sufficient friendliness to keep the correspondence alive. In the end, it faded away without any dramatic termination.

Lawrence, though most people did not realize it, was his wife's mouthpiece. He had the eloquence, but she had the ideas. She used to spend part of every summer in a colony of Austrian Freudians at a time when psycho-analysis was little known in England. Somehow, she imbibed prematurely the ideas afterwards developed by Mussolini and Hitler, and these ideas she transmitted to Lawrence, shall we say, by blood-consciousness. Lawrence was an essentially timid man who tried to conceal his timidity by bluster. His wife was not timid, and her denunciations have the character of thunder, not of bluster. Under her wing he felt comparatively safe. Like Marx, he had a snobbish pride in having married a German aristocrat, and in *Lady Chatterley* he dressed her up marvellously. His thought was a mass of self-deception masquerading as stark realism. His descriptive powers were remarkable, but his ideas cannot be too soon forgotten.

What at first attracted me to Lawrence was a certain dynamic quality and a habit of challenging assumptions that one is apt to take for granted. I was already accustomed to being accused of undue slavery to reason, and I thought perhaps that he could give me a vivifying dose of unreason. I did in fact acquire a certain stimulus from him, and I think the book that I wrote in spite of his blasts of denunciation was better than it would have been if I had not known him.

But this is not to say that there was anything good in his ideas. I do not think in retrospect that they had any merit whatever. They were the ideas of a sensitive would-be despot who got angry with the world because it would not instantly obey. When he realized that other people existed, he hated them. But most of the time he lived in a solitary world of his own imaginings, peopled by phantoms as fierce as he wished them to be. His excessive emphasis on sex was due to the fact that in sex alone he was compelled to admit that he was not the only human being in the universe. But it was so painful that he conceived of sex relations as a perpetual fight in which each is attempting to destroy the other.

The world between the wars was attracted to madness. Of this attraction Nazism was the most emphatic expression. Lawrence was a suitable exponent of this cult of insanity. I am not sure whether the cold inhuman sanity of Stalin's Kremlin was any improvement.[1]

With the coming of 1916, the War took on a fiercer form, and the position of pacifists at home became more difficult. My relations with Asquith had never become unfriendly. He was an admirer of Ottoline's before she married, and I used to meet him every now and then at Garsington, where she lived. Once when I had been bathing stark naked in a pond, I found him on the bank as I came out. The quality of dignity which should have characterized a meeting between the Prime Minister and a pacifist was somewhat lacking on this occasion. But at any rate, I had the feeling that he was not likely to lock me up. At the time of the Easter Rebellion in Dublin, thirty-seven conscientious objectors were condemned to death and several of us went on a deputation to Asquith to get their sentences reduced. Although he was just starting for Dublin, he listened to us courteously, and took the necessary action. It had been generally supposed, even by the Government, that conscientious objectors were not legally liable to the death penalty, but this turned out to be a mistake, and but for Asquith a number of them would have been shot.

Lloyd George, however, was a tougher proposition. I went once with Clifford Allen (chairman of the No Conscription Fellowship) and Miss Catherine Marshall, to interview him about the conscientious objectors who were being kept in prison. The only time that he could see us was at lunch at Walton Heath. I disliked having to receive his hospitality, but it seemed unavoidable. His manner to us was pleasant and easy, but he offered no satisfaction of any kind. At the end, as we were leaving, I made him a speech of denunciation in an almost Biblical style, telling him his name would go down to history with infamy. I had not the pleasure of meeting him thereafter.

With the coming of conscription, I gave practically my whole time and energies to the affairs of the conscientious objectors. The No Conscription Fellowship consisted entirely of men of military age, but it accepted women and older men as associates. After all the original committee had gone to prison, a substitute committee was formed, of which I became the acting chairman. There was a great deal of work to do, partly in looking after the interests of individuals, partly in keeping a watch upon the military authorities to see that they did not send conscientious objectors to France, for it was only after they had been sent to France that they became liable to the death penalty. Then there was a great deal of speaking to be done up and down the country. I spent three weeks in the mining areas of Wales, speaking sometimes in halls, sometimes out-of-doors. I never had an interrupted meeting, and always

[1] See also my letters to Ottoline with reference to Lawrence on page 53.

found the majority of the audience sympathetic so long as I confined myself to industrial areas. In London, however, the matter was different.

Clifford Allen,[1] the chairman of the No Conscription Fellowship, was a young man of great ability and astuteness. He was a Socialist, and not a Christian. There was always a certain difficulty in keeping harmonious relations between Christian and Socialist pacifists, and in this respect he showed admirable impartiality. In the summer of 1916, however, he was court-martialled and sent to prison. After that, throughout the duration of the War, I only saw him during the occasional days between sentences. He was released on grounds of health (being, in fact, on the point of death) early in 1918, but shortly after that I went to prison myself.

It was at Clifford Allen's police court case when he was first called up that I first met Lady Constance Malleson, generally known by her stage name of Colette O'Niel. Her mother, Lady Annesley, had a friendship with Prince Henry of Prussia which began before the War and was resumed when the War was over. This, no doubt, gave her some bias in favour of a neutral attitude, but Colette and her sister, Lady Clare Annesley, were both genuine pacifists, and threw themselves into the work of the No Conscription Fellowship. Colette was married to Miles Malleson, the actor and playwright. He had enlisted in 1914, but had had the good luck to be discharged on account of a slight weakness in one foot. The advantageous position which he thus secured, he used most generously on behalf of the conscientious objectors, having after his enlistment become persuaded of the truth of the pacifist position. I noticed Colette in the police court, and was introduced to her. I found that she was one of Allen's friends and learned from him that she was generous with her time, free in her opinions, and whole-hearted in her pacifism. That she was young and very beautiful, I had seen for myself. She was on the stage, and had had a rapid success with two leading parts in succession, but when the War came she spent the whole of the daytime in addressing envelopes in the office of the No Conscription Fellowship. On these data, I naturally took steps to get to know her better.

My relations with Ottoline had been in the meantime growing less intimate. In 1915, she left London and went to live at the Manor House at Garsington, near Oxford. It was a beautiful old house which had been used as a farm, and she became absorbed in restoring all its potentialities. I used to go down to Garsington fairly frequently, but found her comparatively indifferent to me.[2] I sought about for some

---

[1] Afterwards Lord Allen of Hurtwood.

[2] Some of my letters to Lady Ottoline, written during the early years of the War and reflecting the state of my mind at that time, are to be found on pages 51–67.

other woman to relieve my unhappiness, but without success until I met Colette. After the police court proceedings I met Colette next at a dinner of a group of pacifists. I walked back from the restaurant with her and others to the place where she lived, which was 43 Bernard Street, near Russell Square. I felt strongly attracted, but had no chance to do much about it beyond mentioning that a few days later I was to make a speech in the Portman Rooms, Baker Street. When I came to make the speech, I saw her on one of the front seats, so I asked her after the meeting to come to supper at a restaurant, and then walked back with her. This time I came in, which I had not done before. She was very young, but I found her possessed of a degree of calm courage as great as Ottoline's (courage is a quality that I find essential in any woman whom I am to love seriously). We talked half the night, and in the middle of talk became lovers. There are those who say that one should be prudent, but I do not agree with them. We scarcely knew each other, and yet in that moment there began for both of us a relation profoundly serious and profoundly important, sometimes happy, sometimes painful, but never trivial and never unworthy to be placed alongside of the great public emotions connected with the War. Indeed, the War was bound into the texture of this love from first to last. The first time that I was ever in bed with her (we did not go to bed the first time we were lovers, as there was too much to say), we heard suddenly a shout of bestial triumph in the street. I leapt out of bed and saw a Zeppelin falling in flames. The thought of brave men dying in agony was what caused the triumph in the street. Colette's love was in that moment a refuge to me, not from cruelty itself, which was unescapable, but from the agonizing pain of realizing that that is what men are. I remember a Sunday which we spent walking on the South Downs. At evening we came to Lewes Station to take the train back to London. The station was crowded with soldiers, most of them going back to the Front, almost all of them drunk, half of them accompanied by drunken prostitutes, the other half by wives or sweethearts, all despairing, all reckless, all mad. The harshness and horror of the war world overcame me, but I clung to Colette. In a world of hate, she preserved love, love in every sense of the word from the most ordinary to the most profound, and she had a quality of rock-like immovability, which in those days was invaluable.

After the night in which the Zeppelin fell I left her in the early morning to return to my brother's house in Gordon Square where I was living. I met on the way an old man selling flowers, who was calling out: 'Sweet lovely roses!' I bought a bunch of roses, paid him for them, and told him to deliver them in Bernard Street. Everyone would suppose that he would have kept the money and not delivered the roses, but it was not so, and I knew it would not be so. The words, 'Sweet lovely roses', were ever since a sort of refrain to all my thoughts of Colette.

We went for a three days' honeymoon (I could not spare more from work) to the 'Cat and Fiddle' on the moors above Buxton. It was bitterly cold and the water in my jug was frozen in the morning. But the bleak moors suited our mood. They were stark, but gave a sense of vast freedom. We spent our days in long walks and our nights in an emotion that held all the pain of the world in solution, but distilled from it an ecstasy that seemed almost more than human.

I did not know in the first days how serious was my love for Colette. I had got used to thinking that all my serious feelings were given to Ottoline. Colette was so much younger, so much less of a personage, so much more capable of frivolous pleasures, that I could not believe in my own feelings, and half supposed that I was having a light affair with her. At Christmas I went to stay at Garsington, where there was a large party. Keynes was there, and read the marriage service over two dogs, ending, 'Whom man hath joined, let not dog put asunder.' Lytton Strachey, was there and read us the manuscript of *Eminent Victorians*. Katherine Mansfield and Middleton Murry were also there. I had just met them before, but it was at this time that I got to know her well. I do not know whether my impression of her was just, but it was quite different from other people's. Her talk was marvellous, much better than her writing, especially when she was telling of things that she was going to write, but when she spoke about people she was envious, dark, and full of alarming penetration in discovering what they least wished known and whatever was bad in their characteristics.[1] She hated Ottoline because Murry did not. It had become clear to me that I must get over the feeling that I had had for Ottoline, as she no longer returned it sufficiently to give me any happiness. I listened to all that Katherine Mansfield had to say against her; in the end I believed very little of it, but I had become able to think of Ottoline as a friend rather than a lover. After this I saw no more of Katherine, but was able to allow my feeling for Colette free scope.

The time during which I listened to Katherine was a time of dangerous transition. The War had brought me to the verge of utter cynicism, and I was having the greatest difficulty in believing that anything at all was worth doing. Sometimes I would have fits of such despair as to spend a number of successive days sitting completely idle in my chair with no occupation except to read Ecclesiastes occasionally. But at the end of this time the spring came, and I found myself free of the doubts and hesitations that had troubled me in relation to Colette. At the height of my winter despair, however, I had found one thing to do, which

[1] See also my letter to Lady Ottoline on page 53.

27

turned out as useless as everything else, but seemed to me at the moment not without value. America being still neutral, I wrote an open letter to President Wilson, appealing to him to save the world. In this letter I said:

Sir,

You have an opportunity of performing a signal service to mankind, surpassing even the service of Abraham Lincoln, great as that was. It is in your power to bring the war to an end by a just peace, which shall do all that could possibly be done to allay the fear of new wars in the near future. It is not yet too late to save European civilization from destruction; but it may be too late if the war is allowed to continue for the further two or three years with which our militarists threaten us.

The military situation has now developed to the point where the ultimate issue is clear, in its broad outlines, to all who are capable of thought. It must be obvious to the authorities in all the belligerent countries that no victory for either side is possible. In Europe, the Germans have the advantage; outside Europe, and at sea, the Allies have the advantage. Neither side is able to win such a crushing victory as to compel the other to sue for peace. The war inflicts untold injuries upon the nations, but not such injuries as to make a continuance of fighting impossible. It is evident that however the war may be prolonged, negotiations will ultimately have to take place on the basis of what will be substantially the present balance of gains and losses, and will result in terms not very different from those which might be obtained now. The German Government has recognized this fact, and has expressed its willingness for peace on terms which ought to be regarded at least as affording a basis for discussion, since they concede the points which involve the honour of the Allies. The Allied Governments have not had the courage to acknowledge publicly what they cannot deny in private, that the hope of a sweeping victory is one which can now scarcely be entertained. For want of this courage, they are prepared to involve Europe in the horrors of a continuance of the war, possibly for another two or three years. This situation is intolerable to every humane man. You, Sir, can put an end to it. Your power constitutes an opportunity and a responsibility; and from your previous actions I feel confident that you will use your power with a degree of wisdom and humanity rarely to be found among statesmen.

The harm which has already been done in this war is immeasurable. Not only have millions of valuable lives been lost, not only have an even greater number of men been maimed or shattered in health, but the whole standard of civilization has been lowered. Fear has invaded men's inmost being, and with fear has come the ferocity that always attends it.

Hatred has become the rule of life, and injury to others is more desired than benefit to ourselves. The hopes of peaceful progress in which our earlier years were passed are dead, and can never be revived. Terror and savagery have become the very air we breathe. The liberties which our ancestors won by centuries of struggle were sacrificed in a day, and all the nations are regimented to the one ghastly end of mutual destruction.

But all this is as nothing in comparison with what the future has in store for us if the war continues as long as the announcements of some of our leading men would make us expect. As the stress increases, and weariness of the war makes average men more restive, the severity of repression has to be continually augmented. In all the belligerent countries, soldiers who are wounded or home on leave express an utter loathing of the trenches, a despair of ever achieving a military decision, and a terrible longing for peace. Our militarists have successfully opposed the granting of votes to soldiers; yet in all the countries an attempt is made to persuade the civilian population that war-weariness is confined to the enemy soldiers. The daily toll of young lives destroyed becomes a horror almost too terrible to be borne; yet everywhere, advocacy of peace is rebuked as treachery to the soldiers, though the soldiers above all men desire peace. Everywhere, friends of peace are met with the diabolical argument that the brave men who have died must not have shed their blood in vain. And so every impulse of mercy towards the soldiers who are still living is dried up and withered by a false and barren loyalty to those who are past our help. Even the men hitherto retained for making munitions, for dock labour, and for other purposes essential to the prosecution of the war, are gradually being drafted into the armies and replaced by women, with the sinister threat of coloured labour in the background. There is a very real danger that, if nothing is done to check the fury of national passion, European civilization as we have known it will perish as completely as it perished when Rome fell before the Barbarians.

It may be thought strange that public opinion should appear to support all that is being done by the authorities for the prosecution of the war. But this appearance is very largely deceptive. The continuance of the war is actively advocated by influential persons, and by the Press, which is everywhere under the control of the Government. In other sections of Society feeling is quite different from that expressed by the newspapers, but public opinion remains silent and uninformed, since those who might give guidance are subject to such severe penalties that few dare to protest openly, and those few cannot obtain a wide publicity. From considerable personal experience, reinforced by all that I can learn from others, I believe that the desire for peace is almost universal, not only among the soldiers, but throughout the wage-earning classes, and especially in industrial districts, in spite of high wages and steady employment. If a plebiscite of the nation were taken on the question whether negotiations should be initiated, I am confident that an overwhelming majority would be in favour of this course, and that the same is true of France, Germany, and Austria-Hungary.

Such acquiescence as there is in continued hostilities is due entirely to fear. Every nation believes that its enemies were the aggressors, and may make war again in a few years unless they are utterly defeated. The United States Government has the power, not only to compel the European Governments to make peace, but also to reassure the populations by making itself the guarantor of the peace. Such action, even if it were resented by the Governments, would be hailed with joy by the populations. If the German Government, as now seems likely, would not only restore conquered territory, but also give its adherence to the League to Enforce Peace or some similar method of settling disputes without war, fear would be allayed, and it is almost certain that an offer of mediation from you would give rise to an irresistible movement in favour of negotiations. But the deadlock is such that no near end to the war is likely except through the mediation of an outside Power, and such mediation can only come from you.

Some may ask by what right I address you. I have no formal title; I am not any part of the machinery of government. I speak only because I must; because others, who should have remembered civilization and human brotherhood, have allowed themselves to be swept away by national passion; because I am compelled by their apostacy to speak in the name of reason and mercy, lest it should be thought that no-one in Europe remembers the work which Europe has done and ought still to do for mankind. It is to the European races, in Europe and out of it, that the world owes most of what it possesses in thought, in science, in art, in ideals of government, in hope for the future. If they are allowed to destroy each other in futile carnage, something will be lost which is more precious than diplomatic prestige, incomparably more valuable than a sterile victory which leaves the victors themselves perishing. Like the rest of my countrymen I have desired ardently the victory of the Allies; like them, I have suffered when victory has been delayed. But I remember always that Europe has common tasks to fulfil; that a war among European nations is in essence a civil war; that the ill which we think of our enemies they equally think of us; and that it is difficult in time of war for a belligerent to see facts truly. Above all, I see that none of the issues in the war are as important as peace; the harm done by a peace which does not concede all that we desire is as nothing in comparison to the harm done by the continuance of the fighting. While all who have power in Europe speak for what they falsely believe to be the interests of their separate nations, I am compelled by a profound conviction to speak for all the nations in the name of Europe. In the name of Europe I appeal to you to bring us peace.

The censorship in those days made it difficult to transmit a document of this sort, but Helen Dudley's sister, Katherine, who had been visiting her, undertook to take it back with her to America. She found an ingenious method of concealing it, and duly delivered it to a committee of American pacifists through whom it was published in almost every newspaper in America. As will be seen in this account, I thought, as most people did at that time, that the War could not end in a victory for either party. This would no doubt have been true if America had remained neutral.

From the middle of 1916 until I went to prison in May 1918, I was very busy indeed with the affairs of the No Conscription Fellowship. My times with Colette were such as could be snatched from pacifist work, and were largely connected with the work itself. Clifford Allen would be periodically let out of prison for a few days, to be court-martialled again as soon as it became clear that he still refused to obey military orders. We used to go together to his courts-martial.

When the Kerensky Revolution came, a great meeting of sympathizers with it was held in Leeds. I spoke at this meeting, and Colette and her husband were at it. We travelled up in the train with Ramsay MacDonald, who spent the time telling long stories of pawky Scotch humour so dull that it was almost impossible to be aware when the point had been reached. It was decided at Leeds to attempt to form organizations in the various districts of England and Scotland with a view to promoting workers' and soldiers' councils on the Russian model. In London a meeting for this purpose was held at the Brotherhood Church in Southgate Road. Patriotic newspapers distributed leaflets in all the neighbouring public houses (the district is a very poor one) saying that we were in communication with the Germans and signalled to their aeroplanes as to where to drop bombs. This made us somewhat unpopular in the neighbourhood, and a mob presently besieged the church. Most of us believed that resistance would be either wicked or unwise, since some of us were complete non-resisters, and others realized that we were too few to resist the whole surrounding slum population. A few people, among them Francis Meynell, attempted resistance, and I remember his returning from the door with his face streaming with blood. The mob burst in led by a few officers; all except the officers were more or less drunk. The fiercest were viragos who used wooden boards full of rusty nails. An attempt was made by the officers to induce the women among us to retire first so that they might deal as they thought fit with the pacifist men, whom they supposed to be all cowards. Mrs Snowden behaved on this occasion in a very admirable manner. She refused point-blank to leave the hall unless the men were allowed to leave at the same time. The other women present agreed with her. This rather upset the officers in charge of the roughs, as they did not particularly wish to assault women. But by this time the mob had its blood up, and pandemonium broke loose. Everybody had to escape as best they could while the police looked on calmly. Two of the drunken viragos began to attack me with their boards full of nails. While I was wondering how one defended oneself against this type of attack, one of the ladies among us went up to the police and suggested that they should defend me. The police, however, merely shrugged their shoulders. 'But he is an eminent philosopher', said the lady, and the police still shrugged. 'But he is famous all over the world as a man of learning', she continued. The police remained unmoved. 'But he is the brother of an earl', she finally cried. At this, the police rushed to my assistance. They were, however, too late to be of any service, and I owe my life to a young woman whom I did not know, who interposed herself between me and the viragos long enough for me to make my escape. She, I am happy to say, was not attacked. But quite a number of people, including several women, had their clothes torn off their backs as they left the building. Colette was present on this occasion, but there was a heaving mob between me and her, and I was unable to reach her until we were both outside. We went home together in a mood of deep dejection.

The clergyman to whom the Brotherhood Church belonged was a pacifist of remarkable courage. In spite of this experience, he invited me on a subsequent occasion to give an address in his church. On this occasion, however, the mob set fire to the pulpit and the address was not delivered. These were the only occasions on which I came across personal violence; all my other meetings were undisturbed. But such is the power of Press propaganda that my non-pacifist friends came to me and said: 'Why do you go on trying to address meetings when all of them are broken up by the mob?'

By this time my relations with the Government had become very bad. In 1916, I wrote a leaflet[1] which was published by the No Conscription Fellowship about a conscientious objector who had been sentenced to imprisonment in defiance of the conscience clause. The leaflet appeared without my name on it, and I found rather to my surprise, that those who distributed it were sent to prison. I therefore wrote to *The Times* to state that I was the author of it. I was prosecuted

[1] The full text will be found on page 63.

at the Mansion House before the Lord Mayor, and made a long speech in my own defence. On this occasion I was fined £100. I did not pay the sum, so that my goods at Cambridge were sold to a sufficient amount to realize the fine. Kind friends, however, bought them in and gave them back to me, so that I felt my protest had been somewhat futile. At Trinity, meanwhile, all the younger Fellows had obtained commissions, and the older men naturally wished to do their bit. They therefore deprived me of my lectureship. When the younger men came back at the end of the War I was invited to return, but by this time I had no longer any wish to do so.

Munition workers, oddly enough, tended to be pacifists. My speeches to munition workers in South Wales, all of which were inaccurately reported by detectives, caused the War Office to issue an order that I should not be allowed in any prohibited area.[1] The prohibited areas were those into which it was particularly desired that no spies should penetrate. They included the whole sea-coast. Representations induced the War Office to state that they did not suppose me to be a German spy, but nevertheless I was not allowed to go anywhere near the sea for fear I should signal to the submarines. At the moment when the order was issued I had gone up to London for the day from Bosham in Sussex, where I was staying with the Eliots. I had to get them to bring up my brush and comb and tooth-brush, because the Government objected to my fetching them myself. But for these various compliments on the part of the Government, I should have thrown up pacifist work, as I had become persuaded that it was entirely futile. Perceiving, however, that the Government thought otherwise, I supposed I might be mistaken, and continued. Apart from the question whether I was doing any good, I could not well stop when fear of consequences might have seemed to be my motive.

At the time, however, of the crime for which I went to prison, I had finally decided that there was nothing further to be done, and my brother had caused the Government to know my decision. There was a little weekly newspaper called *The Tribunal*, issued by the No Conscription Fellowship, and I used to write weekly articles for it. After I had ceased to be editor, the new editor, being ill one week, asked me at the last moment to write the weekly article. I did so, and in it I said that American soldiers would be employed as strike-breakers in England, an occupation to which they were accustomed when in their own country.[2] This statement was supported by a Senate Report which I quoted. I was sentenced for this to six months' imprisonment. All this, however,

[1] See my statement concerning my meeting with General Cockerill of the War Office on page 72.
[2] The full text is reproduced on pages 79–81.

was by no means unpleasant. It kept my self-respect alive, and gave me something to think about less painful than the universal destruction. By the intervention of Arthur Balfour, I was placed in the first division, so that while in prison I was able to read and write as much as I liked, provided I did no pacifist propaganda. I found prison in many ways quite agreeable. I had no engagements, no difficult decisions to make, no fear of callers, no interruptions to my work. I read enormously; I wrote a book, *Introduction to Mathematical Philosophy*, a semi-popular version of *The Principles of Mathematics*, and began the work for *Analysis of Mind*. I was rather interested in my fellow-prisoners, who seemed to me in no way morally inferior to the rest of the population, though they were on the whole slightly below the usual level of intelligence, as was shown by their having been caught. For anybody not in the first division, especially for a person accustomed to reading and writing, prison is a severe and terrible punishment; but for me, thanks to Arthur Balfour, this was not so. I owe him gratitude for his intervention although I was bitterly opposed to all his policies. I was much cheered, on my arrival, by the warder at the gate, who had to take particulars about me. He asked my religion and I replied 'agnostic'. He asked how to spell it, and remarked with a sigh: 'Well, there are many religions, but I suppose they all worship the same God.' This remark kept me cheerful for about a week. One time, when I was reading Strachey's *Eminent Victorians*, I laughed so loud that the warder came round to stop me, saying I must remember that prison was a place of punishment. On another occasion Arthur Waley, the translator of Chinese poetry, sent me a translated poem that he had not yet published called 'The Red Cockatoo'.[1] It is as follows:

> Sent as a present from Annam—
> A red cockatoo.
> Coloured like the peach-tree blossom,
> Speaking with the speech of men.
> And they did to it what is always done
> To the learned and eloquent.
> They took a cage with stout bars
> And shut it up inside.

I had visits once a week, always of course in the presence of a warder, but nevertheless very cheering. Ottoline and Colette used to come alternately, bringing two other people with them. I discovered a method of smuggling out letters by enclosing them in the uncut pages of books. I could not, of course, explain the method in the presence of the warder,

[1] Now included in *Chinese Poems* (London, George Allen & Unwin Ltd.).

so I practised it first by giving Ottoline the *Proceedings of the London Mathematical Society*, and telling her that it was more interesting than it seemed. Before I invented this device, I found another by which I could incorporate love-letters to Colette into letters which were read by the Governor of the prison. I professed to be reading French Revolutionary Memoirs, and to have discovered letters from the Girondin Buzot to Madame Roland. I concocted letters in French, saying that I had copied them out of a book. His circumstances were sufficiently similar to my own to make it possible to give verisimilitude to these letters. In any case, I suspect that the Governor did not know French, but would not confess ignorance.

The prison was full of Germans, some of them very intelligent. When I once published a review of a book about Kant, several of them came up to me and argued warmly about my interpretation of that philosopher. During part of my time, Litvinov was in the same prison, but I was not allowed any opportunity of speaking to him, though I used to see him in the distance.

Some of my moods in prison are illustrated by the following extracts from letters to my brother, all of which had to be such as to be passed by the Governor of the prison:

(May 6, 1918) . . . 'Life here is just like life on an Ocean Liner; one is cooped up with a number of average human beings, unable to escape except into one's own state-room. I see no sign that they are worse than the average, except that they probably have less will-power, if one can judge by their faces, which is all I have to go by. That applies to debtors chiefly. The only real hardship of life here is not seeing one's friends. It was a great delight seeing you the other day. Next time you come, I hope you will bring two others—I think you and Elizabeth both have the list. I am anxious to see as much of my friends as possible. You seemed to think I should grow indifferent on that point but I am certain you were wrong. Seeing the people I am fond of is not a thing I should grow indifferent to, though thinking of them is a great satisfaction. I find it comforting to go over in my mind all sorts of occasions when things have been to my liking.

'Impatience and lack of tobacco do not as yet trouble me as much as I expected, but no doubt they will later. The holiday from responsibility is really delightful, so delightful that it almost outweighs everything else. Here I have not a care in the world: the rest to nerves and will is heavenly. One is free from the torturing question: What more might I be doing? Is there any effective action that I haven't thought of? Have I a right to let the whole thing go and return to philosophy? Here, I *have* to let the whole thing go, which is far more restful than choosing to let it go and doubting if one's choice is justified. Prison has some of the advantages of the Catholic Church. . . .'

(May 27, 1918) . . . 'Tell Lady Ottoline I have been reading the two books on the Amazon: Tomlinson I *loved*; Bates bores me while I am reading him, but leaves pictures in my mind which I am glad of afterwards. Tomlinson owes much to *Heart of Darkness*. The contrast with Bates is remarkable: one sees how our generation, in comparison, is a little mad, because it has allowed itself glimpses of the truth, and the truth is spectral, insane, ghastly: the more men see of it, the less mental health they retain. The Victorians (dear souls) were sane and successful because they never came anywhere near truth. But for my part I would rather be mad with truth than sane with lies. . . .'

(June 10, 1918) . . . 'Being here in these conditions is not as disagreeable as the time I spent as attaché at the Paris Embassy, and not in the same world of horror as the year and a half I spent at a crammer's. The young men there were almost all going into the Army or the Church, so they were at a much lower moral level than the average. . . .'

(July 8, 1918) . . . 'I am not fretting at all, on the contrary. At first I thought a good deal about my own concerns, but not (I think) more than was reasonable; now I hardly ever think about them, as I have done all I can. I read a great deal, and think about philosophy quite fruitfully. It is odd and irrational, but the fact is my spirits depend on the military situation as much as anything: when the Allies do well I feel cheerful, when they do badly, I worry over all sorts of things that seem quite remote from the War. . . .'

(July 22, 1918) . . . 'I have been reading about Mirabeau. His death is amusing. As he was dying he said *"Ah! si j'eusse vécu, que j'eusse donné de chagrin à ce Pitt!"* which I prefer to Pitt's words (except in Dizzy's version). They were not however quite the *last* words Mirabeau uttered. He went on: *"Il ne reste plus qu'une chose à faire: c'est de se parfumer, de se couronner de fleurs et de s'environner de musique, afin d'entrer agréablement dans ce sommeil dont on ne se réveille plus. Legrain, qu'on se prépare à me raser, à faire ma toilette toute entière."* Then, turning to a friend who was sobbing, *"Eh bien! êtes-vous content, mon cher connaisseur en belles morts?"* At last, hearing some guns fired, *"Sont-ce déjà les funérailles d'Achille?"* After that, apparently, he held his tongue, thinking, I suppose, that any further remark would be an anti-climax. He illustrates the thesis I was maintaining to you last Wednesday, that all unusual energy is inspired by an unusual degree of vanity. There is just one other motive: love of power. Philip II of Spain and Sidney Webb of Grosvenor Road are not remarkable for vanity.'

There was only one thing that made me mind being in prison, and that was connected with Colette. Exactly a year after I had fallen in love with her, she fell in love with someone else, though she did not wish it to make any difference in her relations with me. I, however, was bitterly jealous.[1] I had the worst opinion of him, not wholly without reason. We had violent quarrels, and things were never again quite the same between us. While I was in prison, I was tormented by jealousy the whole time, and driven wild by the sense of impotence. I did not think myself justified in feeling jealousy, which I regarded as an abominable emotion, but none the less it consumed me. When I first had occasion to feel it, it kept me awake almost the whole of every night for a fortnight, and at the end I only got sleep by getting a doctor to prescribe sleeping-draughts. I recognize now that the emotion was wholly foolish, and that Colette's feeling for me was sufficiently serious to persist through any number of minor affairs. But I suspect that the philosophical attitude which I am now able to maintain in such matters is due less to philosophy than to physiological decay. The fact was, of course, that she was very young, and could not live continually in the atmosphere of high serious-ness in which I lived in those days. But although I know this now, I allowed jealousy to lead me to denounce her with great violence, with the natural result that her feelings towards me were considerably chilled. We remained lovers until 1920, but we never recaptured the perfection of the first year.

I came out of prison in September 1918, when it was already clear that the War was ending. During the last weeks, in common with most other people, I based my hopes upon Woodrow Wilson. The end of the War was so swift and dramatic that no-one had time to adjust feelings to changed circumstances. I learned on the morning of November 11th, a few hours in advance of the general public, that the Armistice was coming. I went out into the street, and told a Belgian soldier, who said: "Tiens, c'est chic!" I went into a tobacconist's and told the lady who served me. 'I am glad of that', she said, 'because now we shall be able to get rid of the interned Germans.' At eleven o'clock, when the Armistice was announced, I was in Tottenham Court Road. Within two minutes everybody in all the shops and offices had come into the street. They commandeered the buses, and made them go where they liked. I saw a

---

[1] Later I recognized the fact that my feeling sprang not only from jealousy, but also, as is often the case in so deeply serious a relationship as I felt ours to be, from a sense both of collaboration broken and, as happened so often and in so many ways during these years, of the sanctuary defiled.

man and woman, complete strangers to each other, meet in the middle of the road and kiss as they passed.

Late into the night I stayed alone in the streets, watching the temper of the crowd, as I had done in the August days four years before. The crowd was frivolous still, and had learned nothing during the period of horror, except to snatch at pleasure more recklessly than before. I felt strangely solitary amid the rejoicings, like a ghost dropped by accident from some other planet. True, I rejoiced also, but I could find nothing in common between my rejoicing and that of the crowd. Throughout my life I have longed to feel that oneness with large bodies of human beings that is experienced by the members of enthusiastic crowds. The longing has often been strong enough to lead me into self-deception. I have imagined myself in turn a Liberal, a Socialist, or a Pacifist, but I have never been any of these things, in any profound sense. Always the sceptical intellect, when I have most wished it silent, has whispered doubts to me, has cut me off from the facile enthusiasms of others, and has transported me into a desolate solitude. During the War, while I worked with Quakers, non-resisters, and socialists, while I was willing to accept the unpopularity and the inconvenience belonging to unpopular opinions, I would tell the Quakers that I thought many wars in history had been justified, and the socialists that I dreaded the tyranny of the State. They would look askance at me, and while continuing to accept my help would feel that I was not one of them. Underlying all occupations and all pleasures I have felt since early youth the pain of solitude. I have escaped it most nearly in moments of love, yet even there, on reflection, I have found that the escape depended partly upon illusion.[1] I have known no woman to whom the claims of intellect were as absolute as they are to me, and wherever intellect intervened, I have found that the sympathy I sought in love was apt to fail. What Spinoza calls 'the intellectual love of God' has seemed to me the best thing to live by, but I have not had even the somewhat abstract God that Spinoza allowed himself to whom to attach my intellectual love. I have loved a ghost, and in loving a ghost my inmost self has itself become spectral. I have therefore buried it deeper and deeper beneath layers of cheerfulness, affection, and joy of life. But my most profound feelings have remained always solitary and have found in human things no companionship. The sea, the stars, the night wind in waste places, mean more to me than even the human beings I love best, and I am conscious that human affection is to me at bottom an attempt to escape from the vain search for God.

The War of 1914–18 changed everything for me. I ceased to be academic and took to writing a new kind of books. I changed my whole

[1] This and what follows is no longer true (1967).

conception of human nature. I became for the first time deeply convinced that Puritanism does not make for human happiness. Through the spectacle of death I acquired a new love for what is living. I became convinced that most human beings are possessed by a profound unhappiness venting itself in destructive rages, and that only through the diffusion of instinctive joy can a good world be brought into being. I saw that reformers and reactionaries alike in our present world have become distorted by cruelties. I grew suspicious of all purposes demanding stern discipline. Being in opposition to the whole purpose of the community, and finding all the everyday virtues used as means for the slaughter of Germans, I experienced great difficulty in not becoming a complete Antinomian. But I was saved from this by the profound compassion which I felt for the sorrows of the world. I lost old friends and made new ones. I came to know some few people whom I could deeply admire, first among whom I should place E. D. Morel. I got to know him in the first days of the War, and saw him frequently until he and I were in prison. He had single-minded devotion to the truthful presentation of facts. Having begun by exposing the iniquities of the Belgians in the Congo, he had difficulty in accepting the myth of 'gallant little Belgium'. Having studied minutely the diplomacy of the French and Sir Edward Grey in regard to Morocco, he could not view the Germans as the sole sinners. With untiring energy and immense ability in the face of all the obstacles of propaganda and censorship, he did what he could to enlighten the British nation as to the true purposes for which the Government was driving the young men to the shambles. More than any other opponent of the War, he was attacked by politicians and the press, and of those who had heard his name ninety-nine per cent believed him to be in the pay of the Kaiser. At last he was sent to prison for the purely technical offence of having employed Miss Sidgwick, instead of the post, for the purpose of sending a letter and some documents to Romain Rolland. He was not, like me, in the first division, and he suffered an injury to his health from which he never recovered. In spite of all this, his courage never failed. He often stayed up late at night to comfort Ramsay MacDonald, who frequently got 'cold feet', but when MacDonald came to form a government, he could not think of including anyone so tainted with pro-Germanism as Morel. Morel felt his ingratitude deeply, and shortly afterwards died of heart disease, acquired from the hardships of prison life.

There were some among the Quakers whom I admired very greatly, in spite of a very different outlook. I might take as typical of these the treasurer of the No Conscription Fellowship, Mr Grubb. He was, when I first knew him, a man of seventy, very quiet, very averse from publicity, and very immovable. He took what came without any visible sign of emotion. He acted on behalf of the young men in prison with a complete absence of even the faintest trace of self-seeking. When he and a number of others were being prosecuted for a pacifist publication, my brother was in court listening to his cross-examination. My brother, though not a pacifist, was impressed by the man's character and integrity. He was sitting next to Matthews, the Public Prosecutor, who was a friend of his. When the Public Prosecutor sat down at the end of his cross-examination of Mr Grubb, my brother whispered to him: 'Really, Matthews, the role of Torquemada does not suit you!' My brother's remark so angered Matthews that he would never speak to him again.

One of the most curious incidents of the War, so far as I was concerned, was a summons to the War Office to be kindly reasoned with. Several Red Tabs with the most charming manners and the most friendly attitude, besought me to acquire a sense of humour, for they held that no-one with a sense of humour would give utterance to unpopular opinions. They failed, however, and afterwards I regretted that I had not replied that I held my sides with laughter every morning as I read the casualty figures.

When the War was over, I saw that all I had done had been totally useless except to myself. I had not saved a single life or shortened the War by a minute. I had not succeeded in doing anything to diminish the bitterness which caused the Treaty of Versailles. But at any rate I had not been an accomplice in the crime of all the belligerent nations, and for myself I had acquired a new philosophy and a new youth. I had got rid of the don and the Puritan. I had learned an understanding of instinctive processes which I had not possessed before, and I had acquired a certain poise from having stood so long alone. In the days of the Armistice men had high hopes of Wilson. Other men found their inspiration in Bolshevik Russia. But when I found that neither of these sources of optimism was available for me, I was nevertheless able not to despair. It is my deliberate expectation that the worst is to come,[1] but I do not on that account cease to believe that men and women will ultimately learn the simple secret of instinctive joy.

[1] This passage was written in 1931.

LETTERS

From Norbert Wiener

> Bühlstr. 28
> Göttingen
> Germany
> [*c*. June or July, 1914]

My dear Mr Russell

At present I am studying here in Göttingen, following your advice. I am hearing a course on the Theory of Groups with Landau, a course on Differential Equations with Hilbert (I know it has precious little to do with Philosophy but I wanted to hear Hilbert), and three courses with Husserl, one on Kant's ethical writings, one on the principles of Ethics, and the seminary on Phenomenology. I must confess that the intellectual contortions through which one must go before one finds oneself in the true Phenomenological attitude are utterly beyond me. The applications of Phenomenology to Mathematics, and the claims of Husserl that no adequate account can be given of the foundations of Mathematics without starting out from Phenomenology seem to me absurd.

Symbolic logic stands in little favor in Göttingen. As usual, the Mathematicians will have nothing to do with anything so philosophical as logic, while the philosophers will have nothing to do with anything so mathematical as symbols. For this reason, I have not done much original work this term: it is disheartening to try to do original work where you know that not a person with whom you talk about it will understand a word you say.

During the Pfingsten holidays, I called on Frege up at Brunnshaupten in Mecklenburg, where he spends his holidays. I had several interesting talks with him about your work.

A topic which has interested me of late is the question whether one can obtain a simpler set of postulates for Geometry by taking the convex solid & relations between convex solids as indefinable, and defining points as you define instants. I have obtained five or six sets of *definitions* of the fundamental Geometrical concepts in this manner, but I am utterly at a loss for a method to simplify the postulates of Geometry in this manner: e.g. the triangle-transversal postulate offers almost insuperable difficulties if one attempts to simplify it by resolving it into a proposition about arbitrary convex surfaces.

I thank you very much for your interest in my article & discovery. I have some material now that might go with my work on sensation-intensities to make a new article: I would like to ask you what I should do with it. It is an extension of my work on time to polyadic relations having some of the properties of series: for example, to the 'between' relation among the points of a given straight line. . . .[1]

I herewith send you my reprints, and offer my apologies to you for not having sent them sooner. The reason is this: I sent all of my articles destined

[1] The central part of this letter has been omitted as being too technical for general interest.

for distribution in America to father, with directions to 'sow them where they would take root'. Father probably imagined that I had sent your copies to you direct.

I am very glad to hear that you had such an enjoyable time with us, and I shall certainly spend next year studying under you in Cambridge. I am just beginning to realise what my work under you there has ment [*sic*] for me.

Yours very respectfully
Norbert Wiener

To the London *Nation* for August 15, 1914
Sir

Against the vast majority of my countrymen, even at this moment, in the name of humanity and civilization, I protest against our share in the destruction of Germany.

A month ago Europe was a peaceful comity of nations; if an Englishman killed a German, he was hanged. Now, if an Englishman kills a German, or if a German kills an Englishman, he is a patriot, who has deserved well of his country. We scan the newspapers with greedy eyes for news of slaughter, and rejoice when we read of innocent young men, blindly obedient to the word of command, mown down in thousands by the machine-guns of Liège. Those who saw the London crowds, during the nights leading up to the Declaration of War, saw a whole population, hitherto peaceable and humane, precipitated in a few days down the steep slope to primitive barbarism, letting loose, in a moment, the instincts of hatred and blood lust against which the whole fabric of society has been raised. 'Patriots' in all countries acclaim this brutal orgy as a noble determination to vindicate the right; reason and mercy are swept away in one great flood of hatred; dim abstractions of unimaginable wickedness—Germany to us and the French, Russia to the Germans—conceal the simple fact that the enemy are men, like ourselves, neither better nor worse—men who love their homes and the sunshine, and all the simple pleasures of common lives; men now mad with terror in the thought of their wives, their sisters, their children, exposed, with our help, to the tender mercies of the conquering Cossack.

And all this madness, all this rage, all this flaming death of our civilization and our hopes, has been brought about because a set of official gentlemen, living luxurious lives, mostly stupid, and all without imagination or heart, have chosen that it should occur rather than that any one of them should suffer some infinitesimal rebuff to his country's pride. No literary tragedy can approach the futile horror of the White Paper. The diplomatists, seeing from the first the inevitable end, mostly wishing to avoid it, yet drifted from hour to hour of the swift crisis, restrained by punctilio from making or accepting the small concessions that might have saved the world, hurried on at last by blind fear to loose the armies for the work of mutual butchery.

And behind the diplomatists, dimly heard in the official documents, stand vast forces of national greed and national hatred—atavistic instincts, harmful to mankind at its present level, but transmitted from savage and half-animal ancestors, concentrated and directed by Governments and the Press, fostered by the upper class as a distraction from social discontent, artificially nourished by the sinister influence of the makers of armaments, encouraged by a whole foul literature of 'glory', and by every text-book of history with which the minds of children are polluted.

England, no more than other nations which participate in this war, can be absolved either as regards its national passions or as regards its diplomacy.

For the past ten years, under the fostering care of the Government and a portion of the Press, a hatred of Germany has been cultivated and a fear of the German Navy. I do not suggest that Germany has been guiltless; I do not deny that the crimes of Germany have been greater than our own. But I do say that whatever defensive measures were necessary should have been taken in a spirit of calm foresight, not in a wholly needless turmoil of panic and suspicion. It is this deliberately created panic and suspicion that produced the public opinion by which our participation in the war has been rendered possible.

Our diplomacy, also, has not been guiltless. Secret arrangements, concealed from Parliament and even (at first) from almost all the Cabinet, created, in spite of reiterated denials, an obligation suddenly revealed when the war fever had reached the point which rendered public opinion tolerant of the discovery that the lives of many, and the livelihood of all, had been pledged by one man's irresponsible decisions. Yet, though France knew our obligations, Sir E. Grey refused, down to the last moment, to inform Germany of the conditions of our neutrality or of our intervention. On August 1st he reports as follows a conversation with the German Ambassador (No. 123):

'He asked me whether, if Germany gave a promise not to violate Belgian neutrality, we would engage to remain neutral. I replied that I could not say that; our hands were still free, and we were considering what our attitude should be. All I could say was that our attitude would be determined largely by public opinion here, and that the neutrality of Belgium would appeal very strongly to public opinion here. I did not think that we could give a promise of neutrality on that condition alone. The Ambassador pressed me as to whether I could not formulate conditions on which we would remain neutral. He even suggested that the integrity of France and her colonies might be guaranteed. I said I felt obliged to refuse definitely any promise to remain neutral on similar terms, and I could only say that we must keep our hands free.'

It thus appears that the neutrality of Belgium, the integrity of France and her colonies, and the naval defence of the northern and western coasts of France, were all mere pretexts. If Germany had agreed to our demands in all these respects, we should still not have promised neutrality.

I cannot resist the conclusion that the Government has failed in its duty to the nation by not revealing long-standing arrangements with the French, until, at the last moment, it made them the basis of an appeal to honour; that it has failed in its duty to Europe by not declaring its attitude at the beginning of the crisis; and that it has failed in its duty to humanity by not informing Germany of conditions which would insure its non-participation in a war which, whatever its outcome, must cause untold hardship and the loss of many thousands of our bravest and noblest citizens.

Yours, etc.

August 12, 1914   *Bertrand Russell*

From Lord Morley[1]

Flowermead
Princes Road
Wimbledon Park, S.W.
Aug. 7. 16 ['14]

Dear Mr. Russell

Thank you for telling me that you and I are in accord on this breakdown of right and political wisdom. The approval of a man like you is of real value, and I value it sincerely.

Yours
M
[Morley]

From C. P. Sanger

Cote Bank
Westbury-on-Trym
Bristol
Friday 7th Aug. 1914

Dear Bertie

It was very kind of you to write. I feel overwhelmed by the horror of the whole thing. As you know I have always regarded Grey as one of the most wicked and dangerous criminals that has ever disgraced civilization, but it is awful that a liberal Cabinet should have been parties to engineering a war to destroy Teutonic civilization in favour of Servians and the Russian autocracy. I pray that the economic disturbance may be so great as to compel peace fairly soon, but it looks as bad as can be.

Yours fraternally
C. P. Sanger

From F. C. S. Schiller

Esher House
Esher, Surrey
19/8/14

Dear Russell

I have just read first your admirable letter in the *Nation* and then the White Book, with special attention to the sequence of events which culminated in the passage you quote from No.123. As a result I must express to you not only my entire agreement with your sentiments (which are those of every civilized man) but also with your argument. It seems to me clear on his own evidence that Sir E. Grey must bear a large share of the catastrophe, whether he acted as he did consciously or stupidly. He steadily refused to give Germany any assurance of neutrality on any conditions, until he produced a belief that he meant England to fight, and Germany thereupon ran 'amok'. But the evidence shows that she was willing to bid high for our neutrality.

First (No. 85) she promised the integrity of France proper and of Belgium (tho leaving her neutrality contingent). When Grey said that wasn't enough (No. 101) and demanded a pledge about Belgian neutrality (No. 114), the German Secretary of State explained, stupidly but apparently honestly, what

[1] I wrote to congratulate him on having resigned from the Government on the outbreak of war.

the difficulty was (No. 122), and said he must consult the Chancellor and Kaiser. This the papers have represented as a refusal to give the pledge, whereas it is obvious that Lichnowsky's conversation with Grey (No. 123) next day *was* the answer. And I don't see how anything more could have been conceded. Belgian neutrality and the integrity of France and her colonies, with a hint of acceptance of any conditions Grey would impose if only he would state them. Of course, that would have reduced the war with France to a farce, and meant presumably that France would not be (seriously) attacked at all, but only contained. One gets the impression throughout that Germany really wanted to fight *Russia* and had to take on France because of the system of alliances. Also that Russia had been goading Austria into desperation, (No. 118 s.f.), was willing to fight, (109, 139), was lying, or suspected of lying by Germany (112, 121, 139 p. 72 top of 144). It is sickening to think that this deluge of blood has been let loose all in order that the tyranny of the Tsar shall be extended over all the world. As regards the question of Grey's good faith, have you noted that the abstract of the despatches gives no hint of the important contents of No. 123? That was presumably the reason why none of the papers at first noticed it. As for the *Nation* Editor's reply to you, he simply distorts the time order. Lichnowsky's offer to respect Belgian neutrality came *after* Grey's inquiry and answered it. Grey's answers seem mere 'fencing', and if he had really wanted to be neutral he would surely have said to L's. offers 'are these firm pledges?'. But he did not respond at all.

However it is no use crying over spilt milk, and not much to consider as yet how European civilization can be saved; I fear this horror will go on long enough to ruin it completely. But I suspect that not much will be left of the potentates, statesmen and diplomats who have brought about this catastrophy, when the suffering millions have borne it 6 months.

> *Ever sincerely yours*
> *F. C. S. Schiller*

To and from J. L. Hammond   5 Sept. 1914
Dear Hammond

I am glad Norman Angell is replying and am very satisfied to be displaced by him.

As regards Belgium, there are some questions I should like to ask you, not in a controversial spirit, but because I wish, if possible, to continue to feel some degree of political respect for the *Nation*, with which in the past I have been in close agreement.

I. Were the *Nation* ignorant of the fact, known to all who took any interest in military matters, that the Germans, for many years past, had made no secret of their intention to attack France through Belgium in the next war?

II. Did the *Nation* in former years regard the violation of Belgium, if it should occur, as a just ground for war with Germany?

III. If so, why did they never give the slightest hint of this opinion, or ask the Government to make this view clear to Germany? If the object was to save Belgium, this was an obvious duty.

IV. Why did the *Nation* in the past protest against Continental entanglements, when the alleged duty of protecting Belgium already involved all the trouble that could arise from an alliance with France and Russia?

It seems to me that in the past, as in the present, the policy of the *Nation* has been sentimental, in the sense that it has refused to face facts which went against its policy. I do not see, at any rate, how it can be absolved from the charge of either having been thoughtless in the past, or being hysterical now.

If there is an answer, I should be very grateful for it.

Yours sincerely
Bertrand Russell

Oatfield
19 Oct. 1914

Dear Russell

Your letter—accusing my handwriting of a certain obscurity—was a great shock, but less than it would have been had I not already received a similar intimation, less tactfully conveyed, from the printers. I had therefore already addressed myself to the painful task of reform, with the result that you see.

My letter was in answer to one from you asking why if the *Nation* thought we should fight over Belgium it had not let its readers know that this was its opinion, and why if it took this view, it objected to foreign entanglements. (I send your letter as the simplest way.) First of all I must ask you—in justice to the *Nation*—to distinguish between the *Nation* and me. I have had no responsibility for the paper's line on foreign policy (or on Armaments) with which I have not associated myself. I agreed with the *N.* entirely on Persia. I am therefore not quite the right person to answer your questions; but I think the *Nation* could clear itself of inconsistency.

1. I don't know whether the *Nation* was aware of this or not. (Personally I was not. I always thought Germany might develop designs on Belgium and Holland and in the last article on Foreign Policy that I wrote in the *Speaker* I said we could not look idly on if she attacked them.)

2. The *Nation* drew attention to our obligation to Belgium in April 1912, March 1913, and the week before the war.

3. I imagine that they did not call upon the Government to impress this on Germany because they imagined that it was generally known that an English Government would consider the obligation binding.

4. The *Nation* argued that the entente with France and Russia made a general war more probable, and that if we were quite independent we could more easily protect Belgium. 'Germany would not violate the neutrality of Belgium for the sake of some small military advantage if she might otherwise reckon on our neutrality' (March 1.1913). They may have been wrong, their general criticisms of Grey may have been right or wrong and their idea that it was possible to build up an Anglo-French-German entente may have been impracticable, but there seems to be no inconsistency in working for that policy for some years and in thinking that it is Germany that has wrecked it. Massingham's view is that Germany 1) would make no concessions during the last fortnight for the Peace of Europe 2) insisted on invading Belgium.

If you say that you think the *Nation* has not allowed enough for the warlike forces in Germany in the past I agree. I think that has been the mistake of all the Peace people. In his book—in many respects admirable—on *The War of Steel and Gold* Brailsford was entirely sceptical, predicting that there would never be a great war in Europe again.

Yours
J. L. Hammond

From Helen Dudley   [1914]

Thank you so much for the flowers. They are a great comfort to me and your letter also—I have read it many times. It was terrible the other evening—yet if we had not seen each other it might have been infinitely more terrible—I might have come to feel that I could never see you again. That is all past now—I do understand how it is with you and I feel more than ever that a profound and lasting friendship will be possible—I hope very soon—as soon as I get back my strength. Nothing that has happened makes any difference finally—it was and still is of the very best.

Goodbye now and if one may speak of peace in this distracted world—peace be with you.

H.
[Helen Dudley]

To Geo. Turner, Esq.   Trinity College
                                                       Cambridge
                                                       26 April 1915

Dear Sir

I am sorry to say I cannot renew my subscription to the Cambridge Liberal Association, and I do not wish any longer to be a member of it. One of my chief reasons for supporting the Liberal Party was that I thought them less likely than the Unionists to engage in a European war. It turns out that ever since they have been in office they have been engaged in deceiving their supporters, and in secretly pursuing a policy of which the outcome is abhorrent to me. Under these circumstances I can do nothing directly or indirectly to support the present Government.

Yours faithfully
Bertrand Russell

The writer of the following letter was a distinguished explorer and soldier. He was in command of the British Expedition to Tibet in 1903–4. He was a very delightful and liberal-minded man, for whom I had a great regard. We travelled together on the 'Mauritania' in 1914.

From Sir Francis Younghusband   London
                                                       May 11 1915

My dear Russell

I am so distressed at what you say about feeling a sense of isolation because of your views regarding the war. It should be all the other way round. You

47

ought to be feeling the pride your friends feel in you for your independence and honesty of thought. Vain and conceited cranks may well be abominated by their friends. But unfortunately it is not they who have the sense of isolation which you feel. They are too satisfied with themselves to have any such feelings. It is only men like you would have the feeling.

But do please remember this that your friends admire and are helped by you even though they may not agree. It is everything that at such a time as this you should have said what you thought. For you know more about the Germans and other continental countries than most of us and you have also made a special study of the first principles of action. And in these times it is of the utmost importance and value that there should be men like you by whom the rest of us can test themselves. I knew scarcely anything of Germany until the war came on. And I am by heredity inclined to take the soldier's view. So I approached this question from quite a different standpoint to what you did. I was all the more interested in knowing what you thought, and tried to get my ideas straight and just by yours.

From my own experience of Government action and of military attitudes I should say that it was almost impossible for any one outside the inner Government circle to get a true view at the first start off. The crisis came so suddenly to the outside public. Underneath the surface it had been brewing up but we knew nothing of it—or very little. Then suddenly it breaks and we have to form the best opinion we can. And as regards the military attitude I know from experience how frightfully dangerous it is when you have the physical means of enforcing your own point of view—how apt you are to disregard any one else's. I have seen that with military commanders on campaign and probably I have been pretty bad myself. This it seems to me is what Germany is suffering from. She certainly had accumulated tremendous power and this made her utterly inconsiderate of the feelings and rights of others. And what I take it we have to drive into her is the elementary fact that it does not pay to disregard these rights and feelings—that she *must* regard them.

Yours very sincerely
Francis Younghusband

A specimen typical of many:

Ryde
Sept. 20 '15

It may be perfectly true, and happily so, that you are not a Fellow of Trinity, —but your best friends, if you have any, would not deny that you are a silly ass. And not only a silly ass,—but a mean-spirited and lying one at that,—for you have the sublime impertinence and untruthfulness to talk about 'no doubt atrocities have occurred on both sides'. You, together with your friends (?) Pigou, Marshall, Walter G. Bell, A. R. Waller, Conybeare, etc. know perfectly well that to charge the British Army with atrocities is a pernicious lie of which only an English Boche traitor could be guilty,—and your paltry attempt to introduce the Russians stamps you for what you are!

Yours
J. Bull

The occasion of the following letter was my taking the chair for Shaw at a meeting to discuss the War:

From G. B. Shaw

10 Adelphi Terrace
[London]W.C.
16th October. 1915

Dear Bertrand Russell

You had better talk it over with the Webbs. As far as I am concerned, do exactly as the spirit moves you. If you wish to reserve your fire, it is quite easy to open the meeting by simply stating that it is a Fabian meeting, and that the business of the Fabian Society is, within human limits, the dispassionate investigation of social problems, and the search for remedies for social evils; that war is a social problem like other social problems and needs such investigation side by side with recruiting demonstrations and patriotic revivals; that the subject of this evenings lecture is the psychological side of war; and that you have pleasure in calling upon etc etc etc etc.

I am certainly not going to be obviously politic, conciliatory and bland. I mean to get listened to, and to make the lecture a success; and I also mean to *encourage* the audience if I can; but I shall do it with as much ostensible defiance of the lightning as possible. The important thing is that the meeting should be good humoured and plucky; for what is really the matter with everybody is funk. In the right key one can say anything: in the wrong key, nothing: the only delicate part of the job is the establishment of the key.

I have no objection on earth to the lines you indicate; and before or after my speech is the same to me. Our job is to make people serious about the war. It is the monstrous triviality of the damned thing, and the vulgar frivolity of what we imagine to be patriotism, that gets at my temper.

Yours ever
G.B.S.

P.S. As this will not be delivered until late afternoon (if then) I send it to Webb's.

The occasion of the following letter was my pamphlet on the policy of the Entente, in which I criticized Gilbert Murray's defence of Grey.

To Gilbert Murray

34, Russell Chambers
Bury Street, W.C.
28th December 1915

Dear Gilbert

Thank you for your letter. I am very sorry I gave a wrong impression about your connection with the F.O. I certainly thought you had had more to do with them.

I agree with all you say about the future. I have no wish to quarrel with those who stand for liberal ideas, however I may disagree about the war. I thought it necessary to answer you, just as you thought it necessary to write your pamphlet, but I did not mean that there should be anything offensive in my answer; if there was, I am sorry. I feel our friendship still lives in the eternal world, whatever may happen to it here and now. And I too can say God bless you.

Yours ever
B. Russell

The following letter should have been included in Volume I had it been available at the time of the publication of Volume I. As it was not, I add it here to other letters from Santayana.

From George Santayana
Queen's Acre
Windsor
Feb. 8. 1912

Dear Russell

Many thanks for your message, which came this morning in a letter from your brother. I am going to spend Sunday with him at Telegraph House, but expect to go up to Cambridge on Monday or Tuesday of next week, and count on seeing you. Meantime I have a proposal to make, or rather to renew, to you on behalf of Harvard College. Would it be possible for you to go there next year, from October 1912 to June 1913, in the capacity of professor of philosophy? Royce is to be taking a holiday, I shall be away, and Palmer will be there only for the first half of the academic year. Perry, Münsterberg, and two or three young psychologists will be alone on hand. What they have in mind is that you should give a course—three hours a week, of which one may be delegated to the assistant which would be provided for you, to read papers, etc.—in logic, and what we call a 'Seminary' or 'Seminar' in anything you liked. It would also be possible for you to give some more popular lectures if you liked, either at Harvard, or at the Lowell Institute in Boston. For the latter there are separate fees, and the salary of a professor is usually $4000 (£800). We hope you will consider this proposal favourably, as there is no one whom the younger school of philosophers in America are more eager to learn of than of you. You would bring new standards of precision and independence of thought which would open their eyes, and probably have the greatest influence on the rising generation of professional philosophers in that country.

There is no particular urgency in receiving your answer, so that you needn't write to me at all, but wait until I see you next week, unless your decision is absolutely clear and unalterable, in which case you might send me a line to Telegraph House. My permanent address is

c/o Brown Shipley & Co.
123 Pall Mall, S.W.

Yours sincerely
G. Santayana

P.S. I didn't mean to decline your kind offer to put me up, when I go to Cambridge, but as I am going in the middle of the week, I don't know whether it would be equally convenient for you to do so.

Oxford, May 5th [1915]

I read this about 'war babies' in a Spanish newspaper: 'Kitchener, in creating an army, has created love. This is a great change in a country where only marriage was known before.'

G. Santayana

[Dec. '17]

The situation is certainly bad from a military point of view, or for those who are angry because the war interferes with their private or political machinations. It may last a long time yet; or else be renewed after a mock peace. But, looking at it all calmly, like a philosopher, I find nothing to be pessimistic about. When I go to Sandford to lunch, which is often, it does my heart good to see so many freshly ploughed fields: England is becoming a cultivated country, instead of being a land of moors and fens, like barbarous North Germany. That alone seems to me more than a compensation for all losses: it is setting the *foundations* right. As for Russia, I rather like Lenin, (not that fatuous Kerensky!); he has an ideal he is willing to fight for, and it is a profoundly anti-German ideal. If he remains in power, he may yet have to fight the Germans, and it will be with very poisonous gas indeed. Besides, I think their plans at Berlin have profoundly miscarried, and that the Prussian educational-industrial-military domination we were threatened with is undermined at home. Military victory would not now do, because the more peoples they rope in, the more explosives they will be exploding under their own establishment.

As for deaths and loss of capital, I don't much care. The young men killed would grow older if they lived, and then they would be good for nothing; and after being good for nothing for a number of years they would die of catarrh or a bad kidney or the halter or old age—and would that be less horrible? I am willing, almost glad, that the world should be poorer: I only wish the population too could become more sparse; and I am perfectly willing to live on a bread-ticket and a lodging-ticket and be known only by a number instead of a baptismal name, provided all this made an end of living on lies, and really cleared the political air. But I am afraid the catastrophe won't be great enough for that, and that some false arrangement will be patched up—in spite of Lenin—so that we shall be very much as we were before. People are not intelligent. It is very unreasonable to expect them to be so, and that is a fate my philosophy reconciled me to long ago. How else could I have lived for forty years in America?

All this won't interest you, but since it is written I will let it go.

[*G. Santayana*]

To Ottoline Morrell [Cambridge]
1915

Did you see in to-day's *Morning Post* a letter from an American, dated 'Ritz Hotel', expressing his horrified bewilderment to find, in New College Chapel, a tablet inscribed 'Pro Patria', on which are being inscribed the names of New College men who have been killed in the war, among the rest *three*

Germans! He expressed his horror to the verger, who replied 'They died for *their* country. I knew them—they were very fine men.' It is creditable to New College. The worthy American thinks it necessary to give us a lesson in how to be patriots.

'Elizabeth' [my sister-in-law] expressed regret at the fact that her 5 German nephews in the war are all still alive. She is a true patriot. The American would like her.

I could come to you Tues. & Wed. 15th and 16th, if it suited you. I should like to see [D. H.] Lawrence. . . .

> [Cambridge]
> Sunday evg.
> [Postmark 10 May '15]

I am feeling the weight of the war much more since I came back here—one is made so terribly aware of the waste when one is here. And Rupert Brooke's death brought it home to me. It is deadly to be here now, with all the usual life stopped. There will be other generations—yet I keep fearing that something of civilization will be lost for good, as something was lost when Greece perished in just this way. Strange how one values civilization—more than all one's friends or anything—the slow achievement of men emerging from the brute—it seems the ultimate thing one lives for. I don't live for human *happiness*, but for some kind of struggling emergence of mind. And here, at most times, that is being helped on—and what has been done is given to new generations, who travel on from where we have stopped. And now it is all arrested, and no one knows if it will start again at anything like the point where it stopped. And all the elderly apostates are overjoyed.

> 34 Russell Chambers
> Wed. night
> [Postmark 27 My. '15]

I am only just realizing how Cambridge oppressed me. I feel far more alive here, and far better able to face whatever horrors the time may bring. Cambridge has ceased to be a home and a refuge to me since the war began. I find it unspeakably painful being thought a traitor. Every casual meeting in the Court makes me quiver with sensitive apprehension. One ought to be more hardened.

My Dearest, forgive me that I have been so horrid lately. But really I have had rather a bad time, and I have been haunted by horrors, and I didn't want to speak all that was in my mind until it had subsided, because it was excessive and mad. So I got stiff and dull.

> Friday
> [Postmark 11 Ju '15]

I think I will make friends with the No-Conscription people. The U.D.C. is too mild and troubled with irrelevancies. It will be all right after the war, but not now. I wish good people were not so mild. The non-resistance people I know here are so Sunday-schooly—one feels they don't know the volcanic side of human nature, they have little humour, no intensity of will, nothing of what makes men effective. They would never have denounced the Pharisees or turned out the money-changers. How passionately I long that one could break through the prison walls in one's own nature. I feel now-a-days so much as if some great force for good were imprisoned within me by scepticism and cynicism and lack of faith. But those who have no such restraint always seem ignorant and a little foolish. It all makes one feel very lonely.

I can't make head or tail of Lawrence's philosophy. I dread talking to him about it. It is not sympathetic to me.

July 1915

Lawrence took up my time from morning till 10.30, so I couldn't write yesterday. We had a terrific argument but not a disastrous one. He attacks me for various things that I don't feel to blame about—chiefly, in effect, for having a scientific temper and a respect for fact. I will send you his written comments on my syllabus. I shall be glad to know what you think of them. He took me to see a Russian Jew, Kotiliansky, and [Middleton] Murry and Mrs. Murry [Katherine Mansfield]—they were all sitting together in a bare office high up next door to the Holborn Restaurant, with the windows shut, smoking Russian cigarettes without a moment's intermission, idle and cynical. I thought Murry *beastly* and the whole atmosphere of the three dead and putrefying.

Then we went to the Zoo—the baboon gave me much cynical satisfaction: he looked long and deliberately at everybody, and then slowly showed his teeth and snarled, with inconceivable hatred and disgust. Swift would have loved him. Then we went up to Hampstead, to the Radfords, where Mrs. Lawrence was staying. I was dead tired after the first hour, as we began arguing at once. I told Lawrence that I thought we ought to be independent of each other, at any rate at first, and not try to start a school. When he talks politics he seems to me so wild that I could not formally work with him. I hope he won't be hurt. He did not seem to be, as I put it very carefully. He is undisciplined in thought, and mistakes his wishes for facts. He is also muddle-headed. He says 'facts' are quite unimportant, only 'truths' matter. London is a 'fact' not a 'truth'. But he wants London pulled down. I tried to make him see that that would be absurd if London were unimportant, but he kept reiterating that London doesn't really exist, and that he could easily make people see it doesn't, and then they would pull it down. He was so confident of his powers of persuasion that I challenged him to come to Trafalgar Square at once and begin preaching. That brought him to earth and he began to shuffle. His attitude is a little mad and not quite honest, or at least very muddled. He has not learnt the lesson of individual impotence. And he regards all my attempts to make him acknowledge facts as mere timidity, lack of courage to think boldly, self-indulgence in pessimism. When one gets a glimmer of the facts into his head, as I did at last, he gets discouraged, and says he will go to the South Sea Islands, and bask in the sun with 6 native wives. He is tough work. The trouble with him is a tendency to mad exaggeration.

July 1915
Tuesday

Yes, the day Lawrence was with me was horrid. I got filled with despair, and just counting the moments till it was ended. Partly that was due to liver, but not wholly. Lawrence is very like Shelley—just as fine, but with a similar impatience of fact. The revolution he hopes for is just like Shelley's prophecy of banded anarchs fleeing while the people celebrate a feast of love. His psychology of people is amazingly good up to a point, but at a certain point he gets misled by love of violent colouring.

Friday evg. I dined with my Harvard pupil, [T. S.] Eliot, and his bride. I expected her to be terrible, from his mysteriousness; but she was not so bad. She is light, a little vulgar, adventurous, full of life—an artist I think he said, but I should have thought her an actress. He is exquisite and listless; she says she married him to stimulate him, but finds she can't do it. Obviously he married in order to be stimulated. I think she will soon be tired of him. She refuses to go to America to see his people, for fear of submarines. He is ashamed of his marriage, and very grateful if one is kind to her. He is the Miss Sands type of American. [Miss Sands was a highly-cultivated New Englander, a painter and a friend of Henry James and Logan Pearsall Smith.]

Hatch
Kingsley Green
Haslemere
Thurs. mg.
[Postmark 9 Sp. '15]

My Darling

I was very glad of your letter this morning—such a dear letter. I wish I could avoid getting unhappy. I can, if I have interests away from you and do not stay on and on in the family atmosphere—but otherwise the feeling of being a mere superfluous ghost, looking on but not participating, grows too strong to be borne. By spending some days in town each week it will be all right. The Lady[1] has been explaining the situation to me, and is going to do so further today, as she is taking me out for a picnic, while Mrs. Waterlow [her sister] goes to town. She says—and I believe her—that she was unguarded with my brother at first, because she looked upon him as safely married, and therefore suitable as a lover. Suddenly, without consulting her, he wrote and said he was getting divorced. It took her breath away, and rather flattered her; she drifted, said nothing definite, but allowed him tacitly to assume everything. Now she is feeling very worried, because the inexorable moment is coming when his divorce will be absolute and she will have to decide. Her objections to him are the following:

(*a*) He sleeps with 7 dogs on his bed. She couldn't sleep a wink in such circumstances.[2]

(*b*) He reads Kipling aloud.

[1] 'Elizabeth', my brother's third wife.
[2] I told her about Josephine's dog biting Napoleon. What Emperors have borne, she may. [Josephine's dog bit Napoleon in the calf on their wedding-night.]

(*c*) He loves Telegraph House, which is hideous.

I daresay other objections might be found if one searched long enough, they are all three well chosen to appeal to me. She is a flatterer, and has evidently set herself to the task of getting me to be not against her if she breaks with him. But it is an impossible task. I am too fond of my brother, and shall mind his suffering too much, to forgive her inwardly even if she has a perfectly good case. She says she is still in great uncertainty, but I don't think she will marry him. She would be *delighted* to go on having him for a lover, but I feel sure he will never agree to that.

I must finish, as this must be posted in a moment.

Don't worry about me. It will be all right as long as I don't let my thoughts get too concentrated on what I can't have. I *loved* the children's picnic, because for once I was not a ghost. I can't enter into the family life when you are present, partly because you absorb my attention, partly because in your presence I am always paralyzed with terror, stiff and awkward from the sense of your criticism. I know that some things I do or don't do annoy you, for reasons I don't understand, and it makes it impossible for me to be natural before you, though sometimes it makes me exaggerate the things you hate. But when I am not tired, I can surmount all those things. Owing to being constrained and frightened when I am with you, my vitality doesn't last long at Garsington, and when it is gone I become defenceless against thoughts I want to keep at a distance.

Thursday night
[Postmark London,
29 October '15]

My Darling

I *was* glad to get your letter. I had begun to feel anxious. I am glad Lawrence was so wonderful. I have no doubt he is right to go, but I couldn't desert England. I simply *cannot bear* to think that England is entering on its autumn of life—it is too much anguish. I will not believe it, and I will believe there is health and vigour in the nation somewhere. It is all hell now, and shame—but I believe the very shame will in the end wake a new spirit. The more England goes down and down, the more profoundly I want to help, and the more I feel tied to England for good or ill. I cannot write of other things, they seem so small in comparison.

Your
B.

Wednesday
[Postmark Nov. 10, '15]

Eliot had a half holiday yesterday and got home at 3.30. It is quite funny how I have come to love him, as if he were my son. He is becoming much more of a man. He has a profound and quite unselfish devotion to his wife, and she is really very fond of him, but has impulses of cruelty to him from time to time. It is a Dostojevsky type of cruelty, not a straightforward every-day kind. I am every day getting things more right between them, but I can't let them alone at present, and of course I myself get very much interested. She is a person who lives on a knife-edge, and will end as a criminal or a saint—I don't know which yet. She has a perfect capacity for both.

[1915] Wed.

My Darling

I don't know what has come over me lately but I have sunk again into the state of lethargy that I have had at intervals since the war began. I am sure I ought to live differently, but I have utterly lost all will-power. I want someone to take me in hand and order me about, telling me where to live and what to do and leaving me no self-direction at all. I have never felt quite like that before. It is all mental fatigue I am sure, but it is very intense, and it leaves me with no interest in anything, and not enough energy to get into a better frame of mind by my own efforts. In fact I should fight against anything that might be suggested to do me good. My impulse is just to sit still and brood.

I can't do much till my lectures are over but that won't be long now. If I could get some one like Desmond [MacCarthy] to come to the country with me then and make me walk a lot, I should get better. But everyone is busy and I haven't the energy to arrange things. I don't do any work. I shall have to get to work for Harvard some time but the thought of work is a nightmare. I am sure something ought to be done or I shall go to pieces.

Irene [Cooper Willis] has just been here scolding me about Helen [Dudley] —someone told her the whole story lately—that hasn't made me any more cheerful than I was before. Sense of Sin is one of the things that trouble me at these times. The state of the world is at the bottom of it I think, and the terrible feeling of impotence. I thought I had got over it but it has come back worse than ever. Can you think of anything that would help me? I *should* be grateful if you could. My existence just now is really too dreadful.

I know now that it is just an illness and it doesn't any longer make me critical of you or of anybody. It is my will that is gone. I have used it too much and it has snapped.

You have enough burdens already—but if you know anyone who could look after me for a while and order me about it would make a difference.

Your
B.

Sat. [1916]

I enclose a letter from Captain White. You will see that he feels the same sort of hostility or antagonism to me that Lawrence feels—I think it is a feeling that seems to exist in most of the people with whom I feel in sympathy on the spiritual side—probably the very same thing which has prevented you from caring for me as much as you thought you would at first. I wish you could find out and tell me what it is. It makes one feel very isolated. People with whom I have intellectual sympathy hardly ever have any spiritual life, or at any rate have very little; and the others seem to find the intellectual side of me unbearable. You will think I am lapsing into morbidness again, but that is not so; I simply want to get to the bottom of it so as to understand it; if I can't get over it, it makes it difficult to achieve much.

I had told White I was troubled by the fact that my audiences grow, and that people who ought to be made uncomfortable by my lectures[1] are not—notably Mrs. Acland [whose husband was in the Government], who sits enjoying herself, with no feeling that what I say is a condemnation of the Government. I thought after my last lecture I would point the moral practically.

I feel I know very little of what you have been thinking and feeling lately. I have been so busy that my letters have been dull, so I can't complain. But it will be a relief to see you and to find out something of what has been going on in you. Ever since the time when I was at Garsington last, I have been quite happy as far as personal things are concerned. Do you remember that at the time when you were seeing Vittoz [a Swiss physician who treated her] I wrote a lot of stuff about Theory of Knowledge, which Wittgenstein criticized with the greatest severity? His criticism, tho' I don't think you realized it at the time, was an event of first-rate importance in my life, and affected everything I have done since. I saw he was right, and I saw that I could not hope ever again to do fundamental work in philosophy. My impulse was shattered, like a wave dashed to pieces against a breakwater. I became filled with utter despair,[2] and tried to turn to you for consolation. But you were occupied with Vittoz and could not give me time. So I took to casual philandering, and that increased my despair. I *had* to produce lectures for America, but I took a metaphysical subject although I was and am convinced that all fundamental work in philosophy is logical. My reason was that Wittgenstein persuaded me that what wanted doing in logic was too difficult for me. So there was no really vital satisfaction of my philosophical impulse in that work, and philosophy lost its hold on me. That was due to Wittgenstein more than to the war. What the war has done is to give me a new and less difficult ambition, which seems to me quite as good as the old one. My lectures have persuaded me that there is a possible life and activity in the new ambition. So I want to work quietly, and I feel more at peace as regards work then I have ever done since Wittgenstein's onslaught.

From Stanley Unwin

40, Museum Street
London, W.C.
November 29th, 1915

Dear Sir

I notice with very great interest in the current number of *The Cambridge Magazine* that you are planning to give a Course of Lectures on 'The Principles of Social Reconstruction'.

If it is your intention that the Lectures should subsequently be published in book form, I hope we may have the pleasure of issuing them for you.

---

[1] These lectures afterwards became *Principles of Social Reconstruction*.
[2] I soon got over this mood.

We enclose a prospectus of *Towards a Lasting Settlement*, a volume in which we know you are interested. We hope to publish the book on December 6th.

> *Yours faithfully*
> *Stanley Unwin*

[This was the beginning of my connection with Allen & Unwin.]

From T. S. Eliot   Tuesday
                                                 [Jan. 1916.]

Dear Bertie

This is wonderfully kind of you—really the last straw (so to speak) of generosity. I am very sorry you have to come back—and Vivien says you have been an angel to her—but of course I shall jump at the opportunity with the utmost gratitude. I am sure you have done *everything* possible and handled her in the very best way—better than I—I often wonder how things would have turned out but for you—I believe we shall owe her life to you, even.

I shall take the 10.30, and look forward to a talk with you before you go. Mrs. Saich[1] is expecting you. She has made me very comfortable here.

> *Affectionately*
> *Tom*

From Charlotte C. Eliot   4446 Westminster Place
                                                 May 23rd, 1916

Dear Mr Russell

Your letter relative to a cablegram sent us, was received some little time ago. I write now to thank you for the affection that inspired it. It was natural you should feel as you did with the awful tragedy of the Sussex of such recent occurrence. Mr. Eliot did not believe it possible that even the Germans, (a synonym for all that is most frightful,) would attack an American liner. It would be manifestly against their interest. Yet I am aware there is still a possibility of war between Germany and America. The more we learn of German methods, open and *secret*, the greater is the moral indignation of many Americans. I am glad all our ancestors are English with a French ancestry far back on one line. I am sending Tom copy of a letter written by his Great-great-grandfather in 1811, giving an account of his grandfather (*one* of them) who was born about 1676—in the county of Devon, England—Christopher Pearse.

I am sure your influence in every way will confirm my son in his choice of Philosophy as a life work. Professor Wood speaks of his thesis as being of exceptional value. I had hoped he would seek a University appointment next

---

[1] The charwoman at my flat. She said I was 'a very percentric gentleman'. Once when the gasman came and turned out to be a socialist, she said 'he talked just like a gentleman'. She had supposed only 'gentlemen' were socialists.

Mrs. Eliot was ill and needed a holiday. Eliot at first could not leave London, so I went first with her to Torquay, and Eliot replaced me after a few days.

year. If he does not I shall feel regret. I have absolute faith in his Philosophy but not in the vers libres.

Tom is very grateful to you for your sympathy and kindness. This gratitude I share.

> *Sincerely yours*
> *Charlotte C. Eliot*
> [T. S. Eliot's mother]

To Lucy Martin Donnelly,
Professor of English at Bryn Mawr College

> 34 Russell Chambers
> Bury St., W.C.
> 10 Feb. 1916

My dear Lucy

I was glad to hear from you at Kyoto—as for Continents, there are so far only 3 in which I have written to you—it is your plain duty to go to Africa & Australia in order to complete your collection.

I *do* hope you will manage to come to England by the Siberian Railway. It would be a great pleasure to see you, & I am sure that I could make you sympathize with the point of view which I & most of my friends take about the war.

You needn't have been afraid about my lectures. Helen [Flexner] wrote me quite a serious remonstrance, which amused me. I should have thought she would have known by this time that social caution in the expression of opinion is not my strong point. If she had known Christ before he delivered the Sermon on the Mount she would have begged him to keep silence for fear of injuring his social position in Nazareth. People who count in the world are oblivious of such things. As a matter of fact, my lectures are a great success—they are a rallying-ground for the intellectuals, who are coming daily more to my way of thinking not only as regards the war but also as regards general politics. All sorts of literary & artistic people who formerly despised politics are being driven to action, as they were in France by the Dreyfus case. In the long run, their action will have a profound effect. It is primarily to them that I am speaking.—I have given up writing on the war because I have said my say & there is nothing new to say.—My ambitions are more vast & less immediate than my friends' ambitions for me. I don't care for the applause one gets by saying what others are thinking; I want actually to *change* people's thoughts. Power over people's minds is the main personal desire of my life; & this sort of power is not acquired by saying popular things. In philosophy, when I was young, my views were as unpopular & strange as they could be; yet I have had a very great measure of success. Now I have started on a new career, & if I live & keep my faculties, I shall probably be equally successful. Harvard has invited me to give a course of lectures 12 months hence on the sort of things I am now lecturing on, & I have agreed to go. As soon as the war is over, people here will want just that sort of thing. When you once understand what my ambitions are, you will see that I go the right way about to realize them. In any large undertaking, there are rough times to go through, & of course success may not come till after one is dead—but those things don't matter if one is in earnest. I have something important to say on the philosophy of life & politics, something appropriate to the times. People's general outlook here has changed with extraordinary rapidity during the last 10 years; their beliefs are disintegrated, & they want a new doctrine. But those who will mould the future won't *listen* to anything that retains old superstitions & conventions. There is a sharp cleavage between old & young; after a gradual development, I have come down on the side of the young. And because I am on their side, I can contribute something of experience which they are willing to respect when it is not merely criticism.—Let me hear again soon—I am interested by your impressions of the Far East.

Yrs affly
B Russell

Have you read Romain Rolland's Life of Michel Angelo? It is a wonderful book.

To Ottoline Morrell   Sunday aft.

[Postmark London 30 Jan. '16.]

I have read a good deal of Havelock Ellis on sex. It is full of things that everyone ought to know, very scientific and objective, most valuable and interesting. What a folly it is the way people are kept in ignorance on sexual matters, even when they think they know everything. I think almost all civilised people are in some way what would be thought abnormal, and they suffer because they don't know that really ever so many people are just like them. One so constantly hears of things going wrong when people marry, merely through not knowing the sort of things that are likely to happen, and through being afraid to talk frankly. It seems clear to me that marriage ought to be constituted by children, and relations not involving children ought to be ignored by the law and treated as indifferent by public opinion. It is only through children that relations cease to be a purely private matter. The whole traditional morality I am sure is superstitious. It is not true that the very best things are more likely to come to those who are very restrained—they either grow incapable of letting themselves go, or when they do, they become too violent and headlong. Do you agree?

Goodbye my darling. I am as happy as one can be in these times, and very full of love. It *will* be a joy to see you again if you come up.

Your
B.

Trin. Coll.
Feb. 27 1916

My Darling

I believe I forgot to tell you I was coming here for the week-end. I came to speak to the 'Indian Majliss' a Club of Indian students here. They were having their annual dinner, about 100 of them, and they asked me to propose the toast of 'India'. Your friend Sarawadi (?) was there, and spoke extraordinarily well. They had asked me because of the line I have taken about the war—at least I suppose so. But when I came to speak an odd sense of responsibility came over me. I remembered that after all I don't want the Germans to win, and I don't want India to rebel at this moment. I said that if I were a native of India I did not think I should desire a German victory. This was received in dead silence, and subsequent speeches said that was the only thing in my speech that they disagreed with. Their nationalism was impressive. They spoke of unity between Moslems and Hindoos, of the oppressiveness of England, of sharp defeat as the only way of checking tyrants. Many of them were able, very earnest, quite civilised. The man who spoke last was a biologist, full of passion for science, just going to return to India. 'I am going', he said, 'from this land of prosperity to the land of plague and famine, from this land of freedom to the land where if I am truthful I am disloyal, if I am honest I am seditious; from this land of enlightenment to the land of religious bigotry, the land that I love, my country. A man must be more than human to love such a country; but those who would serve it have become more than human.' What a waste to make such men fight political battles! In a happier world, he would probably discover preventives for cholera; as it is, his life will be full of strife and bitterness, resisting evil, not creating good. All of them were fearless and thoughtful; most of them were very bitter. Mixed in with it all was an odd strain of undergraduate fun and banter, jibes about the relative merits of Oxford and Cambridge, and such talk as amuses the English youth in quiet times. The mixture, which was in each separate speech, was very curious.

Tonight I meet them again, or some of them, and give them my lecture on education. I am very glad indeed to have got to know their point of view and their character. It must be appallingly tragic to be civilised and educated and belong to such a country as India.

Helen [Dudley] is coming to lunch. I hope I shall see Nicod; also Armstrong[1]. Yesterday I lunched with Waterlow[2] which was dull.

I spoke to the Indians for half an hour, entirely without preparation or any scrap of notes. I believe I speak better that way, more spontaneously and less monotonously.

Trinity College
Sunday evening 19 Mar. '16

My Darling

The melancholy of this place now-a-days is beyond endurance—the Colleges are dead, except for a few Indians and a few pale pacifists and bloodthirsty old men hobbling along victorious in the absence of youth. Soldiers are billeted in the courts and drill on the grass; bellicose parsons preach to them in stentorian tones from the steps of the Hall. The town at night is plunged in a darkness compared to which London is a blaze of light. All that one has cared for is dead, at least for the present; and it is hard to believe that it will ever revive. No one thinks about learning or feels it of any importance. And from the outer deadness

---

[1] Armstrong was a man whom I came to know as an under-graduate at Cambridge. He enlisted at the beginning of the war, lost a leg and became a pacifist.

[2] Afterwards Sir Sidney. He was a nephew of Elizabeth, and in the Foreign Office. We had many common friends at Cambridge.

my thoughts travel to the deadness in myself—I look round my shelves at the books of mathematics and philosophy that used to seem full of hope and interest, and now leave me utterly cold. The work I have done seems so little, so irrelevant to this world in which we find we are living. And in everything except work I have failed so utterly. All the hopes of five years ago come before me like ghosts. I struggle to banish them from my mind but I can't. All our happy times are in my memory, though I know it is better not to think of them. I know I must work and think and learn to be interested in mental things, but utter weariness overwhelms me in the thought. It is no use to keep on running away from spectres. I must let them catch me up and then face them. When I have learnt to work properly again, I shall feel more inward independence, and things will be better. Ever since I knew you, I have tried to get from you what one ought to get out of oneself.

46 Gordon Square
Bloomsbury
Tuesday night
[1916]

My Darling

I have not heard from you since the letter you wrote on Friday, but as I only get my letters once a day now (when I call for them, in the morning) it is not surprising.

I had a queer adventure today. Lloyd George was led to think he might as well find out at first hand about the conscientious objectors, so he had Clifford Allen and Miss Marshall and me to lunch at his place near Reigate, fetching us and sending us back in his own motor. He was very unsatisfactory, and I think only wanted to exercise his skill in trying to start a process of bargaining. Still, it was worth something that he should see Allen and know the actual man. It will make him more reluctant to have him shot.

I feel convinced the men will have to suffer a good deal before public opinion and Government will cease to wish to persecute them. I got the impression that Ll. George expects the war to go on for a long time yet; also that he thinks the whole situation very black. He seemed *quite* heartless. Afterwards I saw Anderson [a Labour M.P.] at the House: he is an oily humbug.

It is quite private about L.G. I suppose.

The first thing that wants doing is to overhaul the whole of the decisions of the Tribunals and have all conscience cases re-heard. No doubt a good many are cowards: people are unspeakably cruel about cowardice—some have gone mad, some have committed suicide, and people merely shrug their shoulders and remark that they had no pluck. Nine-tenths of the human race are incredibly hateful.

From Bernard Shaw

10 Adelphi Terrace. W.C.
18th April 1916

Dear Bertrand Russell

Yeats wrote to me about Chappelow, enclosing a letter from a lady, a cousin of his. But I really dont see what is to be done. The Act has been passed;

and he must either serve or go through with his martyrdom. There is no ground on which exemption can be demanded for him: he seems to have just let things slide, like a child unable to conceive that the law had anything to do with him personally, instead of appealing or taking advice. I have no private influence; and exfluence, which I probably have, would not help him.

His letter is not that of a man made of martyr-stuff. He seems to be, like many literary people, helpless in practical affairs and the army is in some ways the very place for him; for he will be trained to face the inevitable, and yet have no responsibilities. He will be fed and clothed and exercised and told what to do; and he will have unlimited opportunities for thinking about other things. He will not be asked to kill anybody for a year to come; and if he finds his conscience insuperably averse, he can throw down his arms and take his two years hard labor then if he must, and be in much better condition for it. But by that time he will either have been discharged as unfit for service or else have realized that a man living in society must act according to the collective conscience under whatever protest his individual conscience may impel him to make. I think that is what we are bound to tell all the pacific young men who apply to us. Martyrdom is a matter for the individual soul: you cant advise a man to undertake it.

I do not blame any intelligent man for trying to dodge the atrocious boredom of soldiering if it can be dodged; but Chappelow seems to have been too helpless to make any attempt to dodge it: he simply stood gaping in the path of the steamroller. I am sorry for him; but I can only advise him to serve. Can you suggest anything better?

Yours ever
G. Bernard Shaw

Postscript

It would hardly help him to say 'I don't mind being bound by the conscience of England, or by my own conscience; but I don't feel at home with the conscience of Lord Northcliffe, Sir Edward Carson, and General Robertson, who naturally thinks there is nothing like leather'.

P.P.S.

Influence can work only in the direction of letting the prisoner out after he is sentenced on some pretext or other.

The following is the leaflet for which I, in common with those who distributed it, was prosecuted:

TWO YEARS' HARD LABOUR FOR
REFUSING TO DISOBEY THE
DICTATES OF CONSCIENCE.

This was the sentence passed on Ernest F. Everett, of 222, Denton's Green Lane, St. Helens, by a Court Martial held on April 10th [1916].

Everett was a teacher at St. Helens, and had been opposed to all war since the age of 16. He appealed as a Conscientious Objector before the Local and Appeal Tribunals, both of which treated him very unfairly, going out of their way to recommend his dismissal from school. They recognised his conscientious claim only so far as to award him non-combatant service. But as the purpose of such service is to further the prosecution of the war, and to release others for the trenches, it was impossible for him to accept the decision of the Tribunals.

On March 31st he was arrested as an absentee, brought before the magistrates, fined £2, and handed over to the Military Authorities. By them he was taken under escort to Warrington Barracks, where he was compelled to put on uniform. On April 1st he was taken to Abergele, where he was placed in the Non-Combatant Corps, which is part of the Army.

He adopted consistently a policy of passive resistance to all military orders. The first morning, April 2, when the men were ordered to fall in for fatigue duty, he refused, saying: 'I refuse to obey any order given by any military authority.' According to the Corporal, who gave the order, Everett 'said it in quite a nice way'.

The Corporal informed the Lieutenant, who repeated the order, and warned Everett of the seriousness of his conduct. Everett still answered politely, but explained why he could not obey. The Lieutenant ordered the Conscientious Objector to the guard-room, where he remained all night.

The Captain visited the prisoner, who stated that 'he was not going to take orders'. The Captain ordered him to be brought before the Commanding Officer on a charge of disobedience.

Everett was next brought before the Colonel, who read aloud to him Section 9 of the Army Act, and explained the serious consequences of disobedience. But Everett remained firm, saying 'He could not and would not obey any military order.'

The result was that he was tried by Court Martial on April 10th. He stated in evidence in his own defence: 'I am prepared to do work of national importance which does not include military service, so long as I do not thereby release some other man to do what I am not prepared to do myself.'

The sentence was two years' hard labour. Everett is now suffering this savage punishment solely for refusal to go against his conscience. He is fighting the old fight for liberty and against religious persecution in the same spirit in which martyrs suffered in the past. Will you join the persecutors? Or will you stand for those who are defending conscience at the cost of obloquy and pain of mind and body?

Forty other men are suffering persecution for conscience sake in the same way as Mr. Everett. Can you remain silent whilst this goes on?

Issued by the No-Conscription Fellowship, 8, Merton House, Salisbury Court, Fleet Street, London, E.C.

From *The Times* of May 17th, 1916

ADSUM QUI FECI.[1]

To the Editor of *The Times*

Sir, A leaflet was lately issued by the No-Conscription Fellowship dealing with the case of Mr. Everett, a conscientious objector, who was sentenced to

[1] The heading to this letter was added by *The Times*.

two years' hard labour by Court-martial for disobedience to the military authorities. Six men have been condemned to varying terms of imprisonment with hard labour for distributing this leaflet. I wish to make it known that I am the author of this leaflet, and that if anyone is to be prosecuted I am the person primarily responsible.

Yours faithfully
Bertrand Russell

From A. N. Whitehead   June 4th [1916]

Dearest Bertie
Good luck to you in every way. Let me know if and how I can help or shew any office of friendship. You know well enough that the mere fact that I think your views of state policy and of private duty in relation to it to be mistaken, do not diminish affection.

Yours affectionately
A. N. Whitehead

I am just going to commence my address for Section A at Newcastle in September—I will shew it you in ms.

From Cecil Spring Rice   British Embassy
[British Ambassador in   Washington
Washington]   8 June 1916

My dear Mr President[1]
I am sorry to say that Russell has been convicted under 'defence of the realm act' for writing an undesirable pamphlet. Under these circumstances it would be impossible to issue a passport to him to leave the country.

I am sorry, and Sir Edward Grey is sorry, that it is impossible to meet your wishes but I trust that you will understand the necessity in which my government is placed.

Oddly enough I was at the Berlin Embassy when we got into trouble owing to Russell's attitude when on a visit to Berlin as the German government strongly objected to his language.[2]

Yours sincerely
Cecil Spring Rice

To Professor James H. Woods,
of the Harvard Department of Philosophy   34 Russell Chambers
                                            30 July 1916
Dear Professor Woods
Your letter and the Ambassador's were not wholly a surprise to me. I cabled to you on receiving them, but I doubt if the cable ever reached you. Your letter was most kind. The allusion to my doings in Berlin was misleading. I was there in 1895 for the purpose of writing a book on German Socialism;

[1] The President of Harvard University.
[2] It was not my language, but my attending Socialist meetings, that was objected to.

this led me to associate with Socialists, and therefore to be excluded from the Embassy. I did nothing publicly all the time I was there. The Kaiser was having Socialists imprisoned in large numbers for their opinions, which gave me a hatred for him that I retain to this day. But unless in quite private conversations I never expressed my feelings all the time I was there. I have never been in Berlin since 1895.

I should be glad to know whether you have seen or received the verbatim report of my trial. It has been sent you, but may have been stopped by the Censor, who is anxious that America should not know the nature of my crime. You will have heard that I have been turned out of Trinity for the same offence. The sum-total of my crime was that I said two years' hard labour in prison was an excessive punishment for the offence of having a conscientious objection to participation in war. Since then, the same offence has been punished by the death-sentence, commuted to 10 years' penal servitude. Anyone who thinks that I can be made to hold my tongue when such things are being done is grossly mistaken. And the Government only advertizes its own errors by trying ineffectually to punish those of us who won't be silent. Working men are sent to prison when they commit the crime that I committed. And when they come out, no one will employ them, so that they are reduced to living on charity. This is a war for liberty.

This letter will no doubt never reach you, but it may be found interesting by the Censor. If it does reach you, please let me know by return of post. It is a matter of some public interest to know what is allowed to pass, and if I don't hear from you within 6 weeks I shall assume that this letter has been stopped.

These are fierce times. But there is a new spirit abroad, and good will come out of it all in the end. I wish your country had not embarked upon the career of militarism.

> *Yours ever gratefully*
> B.R.

To Ottoline Morrell

[June 1916]

My Darling

A 1000 thanks for your dear dear letter which I have just got. I am grateful for it.

This prosecution is the very thing I wanted. I have a very good case morally —as good as possible. I think myself that the legal case is good tho' no doubt they will convict, and I rather hope they will. I have seen the solicitor (George Baker) and arranged to defend myself without a barrister in the 1st Court on Monday. Then I shall appeal,[1] and employ a barrister the 2nd time. The 2nd time is not till the autumn, so I shall be able to go round the country in the summer as I had planned. That is not at all a wild scheme—apart from any good it may do, I shall learn a lot that I want to know.

I saw Miss Marshall and Allen and a number of the others—they were all delighted and hoping I should get a savage sentence. It is all great fun, as well as a magnificent opportunity. The sort of opportunity I have longed for—and

[1] I appealed and was again convicted.

I have come by it legitimately, without going out of my way. I am going back to Cambridge now, coming up again Friday and staying here till Monday. Think of me Monday 11.30. I hope I shall be worthy of the occasion.

Goodbye my Darling Love. Your love and sympathy do help far more than you know.

Your
B.

Monday evg. [1916]

Today I had lunch and a country walk with the Rev. Morgan Jones, a prominent pacifist here [in South Wales] and a real saint. Then I went to a neighbouring town for a meeting—it was to have been in the school, but that was refused at the last moment, so we had it in the open air. A Unitarian Minister spoke who has a son a C.O. It is wonderful what the C.Os. have done for the cause of peace—the heroism is no longer all on the side of war.

I ought to have gone into more hostile districts. Here it is merely a picnic and I feel I should be better employed in town. After the 23rd I shall be back in town—by then most of our Nat. Committee will be gone.

I am *longing* to know how Allen's visit went off. I am so terribly afraid it will have been a failure.

Speaking is a great nervous strain. I feel very slack all the rest of the time. But I sleep well and my mind is at peace so I don't get really tired. I never have any fundamental worries now-a-days.

I shall be very poor, having lost America and probably Trinity. I shall have to find some other way of making money. I think if Trinity turns me out I shall advertise academic lectures in London on philosophical subjects. It would be delightful if they succeeded, as they wouldn't interfere with political work. I have often dreamt of having an independent school like Abelard. It might lead to great things. I feel I am only on the threshold of life—the rest has been preparation—I mean as far as work is concerned. Quite lately I have somehow found myself—I have poise and sanity—I no longer have the feeling of powers unrealized within me, which used to be a perpetual torture. I don't care what the authorities do to me, they can't stop me long. Before, I have felt either wicked or passively resigned—now I feel fully active and contented with my activity—I have no inward discords any more—and nothing ever really troubles me.

I realize that as soon as the worst of the stress is over I shall want some more intellectual occupation. But I see room for endless work on political theory. And it will have the advantage that it will involve seeing all sorts of people and getting to know all sorts of human facts—it won't leave half of me unsatisfied as abstract work does. The only doubt is whether I shan't some day be suddenly overwhelmed by the passion for the things that are eternal and perfect, like mathematics. Even the most abstract political theory is terribly mundane and temporary. But that must be left to the future.

It is very sad seeing you so seldom. I feel as if we should lose intimacy and get out of the way of speaking of personal things—it would be a great loss if that happened. I know extraordinarily little of your inner life now-a-days, and

I wish I knew more, but I don't know how to elicit it. My own existence has become so objective that I hardly have an inner life any more for the present —but I should have if I had leisure.

My Dearest, I am full of love to you—visions are always in my mind of happy days after the war, when we shall get back to poetry and beauty and summer woods, and the vision of things outside this earth. But the war keeps one tied to earth. And sometimes I wonder if we have both grown so impersonal that it has become difficult to give oneself to personal love—it always was difficult for you. It is a great loss if it is so. I hope it isn't. Do write a full letter when you can, and tell me something of your inward life.

From the Trinity College Council

Trinity College
Cambridge
11 July 1916

Dear Russell

It is my duty to inform you that the following resolution was unanimously passed by the College Council today:

'That, since Mr. Russell has been convicted under the Defence of the Realm Act, and the conviction has been affirmed on appeal, he be removed from his Lectureship in the College.'

Yours sincerely
H. McLeod Innes

From S. Alexander

24, Brunswick Road
Withington
M/C
16.7.16

Dear Russell

I feel indignant about the action of Trinity, which disgraces them (as well as making them ridiculous). I don't share your views about War (as I think you may know) and I can't well judge the effect of your action—though I have hated the bungling and injustice of the treatment of Conscientious Objectors. But sensible people, even if they don't know and admire you personally, respect honest convictions; and Trinity's action is both intolerant and impertinent. It matters to all of us at Universities (and elsewhere) more perhaps than it matters to you.

Yours sincerely
S. Alexander
[The distinguished philosopher]
I have only the Trinity address, and must send that way.

From my brother Frank

Telegraph House
Chichester
16 July 1916

My dear Bertie

I have seen the Trinity announcement in the paper, and whatever you may say, I very much regret it. No doubt these stuffy old dons were very uncongenial to you, and were also unfriendly on account of your views, but still, I always thought you well suited to an academic life, and a personality of great value to the young—in stirring their ideas. I think as time goes on you will miss it more than you realize and probably regret it.

I can't attempt to shape your career for you—you must be the only guide and the only judge of your own actions—but don't finally cut yourself off too rashly and above all beware of popular audiences. The average [man] is such a fool that any able man who can talk can sway him for a time. What the world wants of first class intellects like yours is not action—for which the ordinary politician or demagogue is good enough—but thought, a much more rare quality. Think out our problems, embody the result in writing, and let it slowly percolate through the teachers of the next generation. And don't suppose the people you meet are as earnest, as deep or as sincere as you are.

As mere experience and learning about human beings what you are doing now may have its value, but you see what I am trying to say is that you are *wasting* yourself. You are not making the best use for the world of your talents. As soon as you come to see that you will change your activities.

Well—I don't preach to you often, because as a rule you don't need it, but at the moment I think you are a little (or rather, a great deal) carried away.

It's a long time to Feb. 1—why not go to America sooner?—they ought to be glad to get rid of you!

Come and see us when you are in London and try and spend a few placid days here with us in August.

Yours affectionately
F

From F. M. Cornford[1]

Burrows Hill
Gomshall
Surrey
23 July 1916

Dear Russell

I have only today received an account of the College Council's action and a report of your trial before the Mayor.

I must tell you that I think your case was as unanswerable as it was unanswered, and the decision, so far as I can see, was utterly unwarranted by the evidence.

I was glad you said you could respect your friends who are not pacifists in quite the same sense that you are. What you think of me I don't know: but I have admired the fight you have put up.

As for the College Council, you know too much to confuse it with the College. The older dons, last time I saw them, seemed to me to be in various stages of insanity. Something will have to be done when the younger ones come back. I am sure there would have been a majority of the whole body against the Council, if it had come before a full College meeting.

---

[1] Cornford was a Fellow of Trinity, and a distinguished writer on ancient philosophy. His wife was Frances Cornford the poet. His son was killed in the Spanish Civil War. I was very fond of both him and his wife.

I feel very bitterly that the Council has disgraced us. When you and Moore came back[1], I was delighted that we had recovered you both, and now we have lost one of you, it is a real grief and humiliation.

> *Yours sincerely*
> *F. M. Cornford*

To G. Lowes Dickinson

> 34 Russell Chambers
> Bury Street, W.C.
> Sunday [1916]

Dear Goldie

Thank you very much for your letter in the *Nation*[2], which I read with gratitude. One has a little the sense of reading one's own obituaries[3], a thing I have always wished to be able to do! The Whiteheads are *very* decent about this. I think McT[4]. and Lawrence were the prime movers. I have been sold up, but owing to kind friends I have lost nothing. I don't know who they are—whoever they are, I am most grateful and touched.

Clifford Allen is to be taken tomorrow. Casement[5] is to be shot. I am ashamed to be at large.

> *Yours ever*
> *B.R.*

From C. P. Sanger

> Finches
> Aston Tirrold
> 22 Aug. 1916

Dear Bertie

You will have realised how I feel about all this persecution. Did you ever meet Constable—a young economist who was going to the bar—at our house. He's a Major now and in writing to me from the front says 'I was very glad to see that there have been protests against the action of Trinity with regard to Bertrand Russell. I must say that men I have met out here nearly all agree with me that the College has merely stultified itself.' . . .

Masefield writing up the Dardanelles—has been allowed to see some official documents and so on. It is most disheartening that literary men of standing should try to make a mere calamity 'epic' for American consumption.

> *Yours fraternally*
> *Charles Percy Sanger*

[1] Moore had been invited back from Edinburgh where he had had a post.
[2] Of July 29th, 1916.
[3] I was able to in 1921. The allusion is to my being turned out of Trinity.
[4] McTaggart.
[5] Sir Roger Casement, who first became known for his protests against atrocities in the Congo, was an Irish rebel who sided with the Germans. He was captured, tried and executed.

From James Ward

6, Selwyn Gardens
Cambridge
3.ix.16

Dear Russell

I am amazed and grieved to see how you are being badgered and hounded about. It is most outrageous, and what the motive for it all may be I am quite at a loss to surmise. Are they afraid that you will sneak off to America or is there some rabid fanatic trying to persuade them that you are what the McTaggarts call us—pro-Germans? I see you are announced to lecture in Manchester: is there no danger of your lectures being prohibited? Well you have just got to compose yourself with dignity and patience and there will be voices in your favour to speak out before long.

Since I saw you I have been trying to draw up a statement to justify your action and to serve as a separate preamble to accompany an invitation to protest against the action of the College Council to be sent to all the fellows of the College (exclusive of the Council)[1]. . . .

> *Yours ever*
> *James Ward*

The writer of the following letter was killed not long afterwards. I never met him, but I came to know his fiancée, Dorothy Mackenzie, who, on the news of his death, became blind for three weeks.

From Lieut. A. Graeme West

9th Batt. Oxfordshire &
Buckinghamshire Light
Infantry
Bovington Camp
Wareham
Dorset
Sunday, Sept. 3. 1916

Dear Mr Russell

Seeing the new scene that has been added to this amazing farce of which you are the unfortunate protagonist, I could not help writing to you. Of course you know that such sane men as still live, or have kept their sanity, have nothing but admiration for you, and therefore you may cry that this note is impertinent. Literally, I suppose it is; but not to me.

I cannot resist the joy of communicating directly with one whom I admired so much before the war, as the writer of the clearest and finest philosophical English prose, and whom I admire so much more now when all the intellectuals, except, thank god, Shaw, have lost the use of their reason.

I think there may be some shade of excuse for this liberty at a time when reason and thought are in danger and when you, their ablest champion, are the victim of incompetence and derision: at such a time those who love Justice should speak.

I know you must have many friends in the army, and are aware that it, too, contains men of good-will, though it is through it and its domination that

[1] Nothing came of this.

71

England finds herself as she is; yet one more assurance of complete under-standing and sympathy may not annoy you.

Were I back in the Ranks again—and I wish I were—I could have picked half-a-dozen men of our platoon to have signed with me: here, it is not so.

Thank you, then, for all you are and all you have written, for 'A Free Man's Worship' and *Justice in War Time* and *The Policy of the Entente* and many others; and I hope that I (and you, of course, for we don't know what they mayn't do to you) may live to see you.

> *Yours sincerely*
> *A. Graeme West*
> *2nd Lieut.*

From H. G. Wells
[to Miles Malleson]

52, St. James's Court
Buckingham Gate, S.W.
[1916]

My dear Sir

I think that a small minority of the C.O.'s are sincerely honest men but I believe that unless the path of the C.O. is made difficult it will supply a stam-pede track for every variety of shirker. Naturally a lot of the work of control falls on the hands of clumsy and rough minded men. I really don't feel very much sympathy with these 'martyrs'. I don't feel so sure as you do that all C.O.'s base the objection on love rather than hate. I have never heard either Cannan or Norman speak lovingly of any human being. Their normal attitude has always been one of opposition—to anything. Enthusiasm makes them liverish. And the *Labour Leader* group I believe to be thoroughly dishonest, Ramsey MacDonald, I mean, Morel and the editor. I may be wrong but that is my slow and simple conviction.

> *Very sincerely yours*
> *H. G. Wells*

My statement concerning my meeting with General Cockerill on September 5th, 1916:

I called at the War Office with Sir Francis Younghusband by appointment at 3.15 to see General Cockerill. He had beside him a report of my speeches in S. Wales and drew special attention to a sentence in a speech I made at Cardiff saying there was no good reason why this war should continue another day. He said that such a statement made to miners or munition workers was calculated to diminish their ardour. He said also that I was encouraging men to refuse to fight for their country. He said he would withdraw the order for-bidding me to enter prohibited areas if I would abandon political propaganda and return to mathematics. I said I could not conscientiously give such an undertaking.

He said:

'You and I probably regard conscience differently. I regard it as a still small voice, but when it becomes blatant and strident I suspect it of no longer being a conscience.'

I replied:

'You do not apply this principle to those who write and speak in favour of the war; you do not consider that if they hold their opinions in secret they are conscientious men, but if they give utterance to them in the Press or on the platform they are mere propagandists. There seems some lack of justice in this differentiation.'

He remained silent a long while and then replied:

'Yes, that is true. But', he said, 'you have said your say, can you not rest content with having said it and return to those other pursuits in which'—so he was pleased to add—'you have achieved so much distinction? Do you not think there is some lack of a sense of humour in going on reiterating the same thing?'

I failed to reply that I had observed this lack—if it were one—in *The Times*, the *Morning Post* and other patriotic organs, which appeared to me to be somewhat addicted to reiteration, and that if it would not serve any purpose to repeat myself I failed to see why he was so anxious to prevent me from doing so. But what I did say was that new issues are constantly arising and I could not barter away my right to speak on such issues. I said:
'I appeal to you as a man, would you not feel less respect for me if I agreed to this bargain which you propose?'

After a long hesitation he replied:

'No, I should respect you more; I should think better of your sense of humour if you realized the uselessness of saying the same thing over and over again.'

I told him that I was thinking of delivering lectures on the general principles of politics in Glasgow, Edinburgh and Newcastle. He asked whether these would involve the propaganda he objected to. I said no, not directly, but they would state the general principles out of which the propaganda has grown, and no doubt men with sufficient logical acumen would be able to draw inferences. He then gave it to be understood that such lectures could not be permitted. He wound up with an earnest appeal to me not to make the task of the soldiers more difficult when they were engaged in a life and death struggle.
I told him that he flattered me in supposing my influence sufficient to have any such result, but that I could not possibly cease my propaganda as the result of a threat and that if he had wished his appeal to have weight he ought not to have accompanied it by a threat. I said I was most sincerely sorry to be compelled to do anything which the authorities considered embarrassing, but that I had no choice in the matter.
We parted with mutual respect, and on my side at least, without the faintest feeling of hostility. Nevertheless it was perfectly clear that he meant to proceed to extremities if I did not abandon political propaganda.

To Ottoline Morrell   [September 1916]
                                                       Monday night
My Darling

There seems a good chance that the authorities will relent towards me—I am half sorry! I shall soon have come to the end of the readjustment with Mrs. E. [Mrs. T. S. Eliot] I think it will all be all right, on a better basis. As soon as it is settled, I will come to Garsington. I long to come.

I have been realizing various things during this time. It is odd how one finds out what one really wants, and how very selfish it always is. What I want permanently—not consciously, but deep down—is stimulus, the sort of thing that keeps my brain active and exuberant. I suppose that is what makes me a vampire. I get a stimulus most from the instinctive feeling of success. Failure makes me collapse. Odd things give me a sense of failure—for instance, the way the C.Os. all take alternative service, except a handful. Wittgenstein's criticism gave me a sense of failure. The real trouble between you and me has always been that you gave me a sense of failure—at first, because you were not happy; then, in other ways. To be *really* happy with you, not only momentarily, I should have to lose that sense of failure. I had a sense of success with Mrs. E. because I achieved what I meant to achieve (which was not so very difficult), but now I have lost that, not by your fault in the least. The sense of success helps my work: when I lose it, my writing grows dull and lifeless. I often feel success quite apart from happiness: it depends upon what one puts one's will into. Instinctively, I turn to things in which success is possible, just for the stimulus.

I have always cared for you in yourself, and not as a stimulus or for any self-centred reason; but when I have felt that through caring for you and feeling unsuccessful I have lost energy, it has produced a sort of instinctive resentment. That has been at the bottom of everything—and now that I have at last got to the bottom of it, it won't be a trouble any longer. But unless I can cease to have a sense of failure with you, I am bound to go on looking for stimulus elsewhere from time to time. That would only cease if I ceased to care about work—I am sure all this is the exact truth.

I would set my will in a different direction as regards you, if I knew of any direction in which I *could* succeed. But I don't think it can be done in that way.

The rare moments of mystic insight that I have had have been when I was free from the will to succeed. But they have brought a new kind of success, which I have at once noticed and wanted, and so my will has drifted back into the old ways And I don't believe I should do anything worth doing without that sort of will. It is very tangled.

To Constance Malleson (Colette)   Gordon Square
                                                       September 29, 1916

You are already where I have struggled to be, and without the weariness of long effort. I have hated many people in the past. The language of hate still comes to me easily, but I don't really hate anyone now. It is defeat that makes one hate people—and now I have no sense of defeat anywhere. No one need ever be defeated—it rests with oneself to make oneself invincible. Quite lately

I have had a sense of freedom I never had before . . . I don't like the spirit of socialism—I think freedom is the basis of everything.

* * *

'The keys to an endless peace'—

I am not so great as that, *really* not—I know where peace is—I have seen it, and felt it at times—but I can still imagine misfortunes that would rob me of peace. But there is a world of peace, and one can live in it and yet be active still over all that is bad in the world. Do you know how sometimes all the barriers of personality fall away, and one is free for all the world to come in—the stars and the night and the wind, and all the passions and hopes of men, and all the slow centuries of growth—and even the cold abysses of space grow friendly —'*E il naufragar m'e dolce in questo mare*'. And from that moment some quality of ultimate peace enters into all one feels—even when one feels most passionately. I felt it the other night by the river—I thought you were going to withdraw yourself—I felt that if you did I should lose the most wonderful thing that had ever come to me—and yet an ultimate fundamental peace remained—if it hadn't, I believe I should have lost you then. I cannot bear the littleness and enclosing walls of *purely* personal things—I want to live always open to the world, I want personal love to be like a beacon *fire* lighting up the darkness, not a timid refuge from the cold as it is very often.

London under the stars is strangely moving. The momentariness of the separate lives seems so strange—

In some way I can't put into words, I feel that some of our thoughts and feelings are just of the moment, but others are part of the eternal world, like the stars—even if their actual existence is passing, something—some spirit or essence—seems to last on, to be part of the real history of the universe, not only of the separate person. Somehow, that is how I want to live, so that as much of life as possible may have that quality of eternity. I can't explain what I mean—you will have to know—of course I don't succeed in living that way— but that is 'the shining key to peace'.

Oh, I am happy, happy, happy—

B.

Gordon Square
October 23, 1916

I have meant to tell you many things about my life, and every time the moment has conquered me. I am strangely unhappy because the pattern of my life is complicated, because my nature is hopelessly complicated; a mass of contradictory impulses; and out of all this, to my intense sorrow, pain to you must grow. The centre of me is always and eternally a terrible pain—a curious wild pain—a searching for something beyond what the world contains, something transfigured and infinite—the beatific vision—God—I do not find it, I do not think it is to be found—but the love of it is my life—it's like passionate love for a ghost. At times it fills me with rage, at times with wild despair, it is the source of gentleness and cruelty and work, it fills every passion that I have—it is the actual spring of life within me.

75

I can't explain it or make it seem anything but foolishness—but whether foolish or not, it is the source of whatever is any good in me. I have known others who had it—Conrad especially—but it is rare—it sets one oddly apart and gives a sense of great isolation—it makes people's gospels often seem thin. At most times, now, I am not conscious of it, only when I am strongly stirred, either happily or unhappily. I seek escape from it, though I don't believe I ought to. In that moment with you by the river I felt it most intensely.

'Windows always open to the world' I told you once, but through one's windows one sees not only the joy and beauty of the world, but also its pain and cruelty and ugliness, and the one is as well worth seeing as the other, and one must look into hell before one has any right to speak of heaven.

B.

From Lieut. A. Graeme West   Wednesday night
                                              Dec. 27. 1916

Dear Mr Russell

To-night here on the Somme I have just finished your *Principles of Social Reconstruction* which I found waiting for me when I came out of the line. I had seen a couple of Reviews of it, one in the *Nation*, one in *Land and Water* and from the praise of the former and the thinly veiled contempt of the latter I augured a good book. It encouraged me all the more as the state of opinion in England seems to fall to lower and lower depths of undignified hatred. It is only on account of such thoughts as yours, on account of the existence of men and women like yourself that it seems worth while surviving the war—if one should haply survive. Outside the small circle of that cool light I can discern nothing but a scorching desert.

Do not fear though that the life of the spirit is dying in us, nor that hope or energy will be spent; to some few of us at any rate the hope of helping to found some 'city of God' carries us away from these present horrors and beyond the graver intolerance of thought as we see in it our papers. We shall not faint and the energy and endurance we have used here on an odious task we shall be able to redouble in the creative work that peace will bring to do. We are too young to be permanently damaged in body or spirit, even by these sufferings.

Rather what we feared until your book came was that we would find no one left in England who would build with us. Remember, then, that we are to be relied on to do twice as much afterwards as we have done during the war, and after reading your book that determination grew intenser than ever; it is for you that we would wish to live on.

I have written to you before and should perhaps apologise for writing again, but that seems to me rather absurd: you cannot mind knowing that you are understood and admired and that those exist who would be glad to work with you.

Yours sincerely
A. Graeme West. 2nd Lt.
6th Oxford & Bucks. L.I.
B.E.F.

From the Press:

SECOND LIEUTENANT ARTHUR GRAEME WEST, Oxford and Bucks Light Infantry, whose death is officially announced to-day, was the eldest son of Arthur Birt West, 4 Holly Terrace, Highgate. He fell on April 3 [1917], aged 25.

To Colette   Guildford
                                                December 28, 1916

How can love blossom among explosions and falling Zeppelins and all the surroundings of our love? It has to grow jagged and painful before it can live in such a world. I long for it to be otherwise—but soft things die in this horror, and our love has to have pain for its life blood.

I hate the world and almost all the people in it. I hate the Labour Congress and the journalists who send men to be slaughtered, and the fathers who feel a smug pride when their sons are killed, and even the pacifists who keep saying human nature is essentially good, in spite of all the daily proofs to the contrary. I hate the planet and the human race—I am ashamed to belong to such a species—And what is the good of me in that mood?

                                                B.

From Dorothy Mackenzie   77, Lady Margaret Road
                                                Highgate. N.W.5
                                                June 5th. [1917]

Dear Mr Russel

I am glad you sent Graeme West's letters to the *Cambridge Magazine,* for I am very sure he speaks for a great many, some of whom *will* survive.

When I had read your *Principles of Social Reconstruction,* being a young woman instead of a young man, I had the joy of being able to come and hear you speak at the Nursery of the Fabian Society. And I dared to say you were too gloomy, and that the world was not so spoilt as you thought. It was because West was in my thoughts that I was able to do that, and kindly you smiled at the optimism of youth, but the sadness of your smiling set me fearing.

Now I know that you were right and I was wrong. But I assure you Mr. Russel, that we women want to build, and we unhappily do survive. And I can end my letter as he ended his and say very truly 'it is for you that we would wish to live on'.

It is very difficult to know what to do. I am an elementary teacher, and every class in the school but mine is disciplined by a military method. I have to work as it were by stealth, disguising my ideas as much as possible. Children, as you are aware, do not develop themselves, in our elementary schools. Your chapter on education encouraged me more than anything I have read or heard since I started teaching. I thank you for that encouragement. It is most sad to teach in these days; underpaid, overworked, the man I loved most killed for a cause in which he no longer believed, out of sympathy with most of my friends and relations, I find strength and comfort in you through your book. I feel indeed that you understand.

                                        Dorothy Mackenzie

From A. N. Whitehead

Twelve
Elm Park Gardens
Chelsea. S.W.
Jan. 8th, 17

Dear Bertie

I am awfully sorry, but you do not seem to appreciate my point.

I don't want my ideas propagated *at present* either under my name or anybody else's—that is to say, as far as they are at present on paper. The result will be an incomplete misleading exposition which will inevitably queer the pitch for the final exposition when I want to put it out.

My ideas and methods grow in a different way to yours and the period of incubation is long and the result attains its intelligible form in the final stage, —I do not want you to have my notes which in chapters are lucid, to precipitate them into what I should consider as a series of half-truths. I have worked at these ideas off and on for all my life, and should be left quite bare on one side of my speculative existence if I handed them over to some one else to elaborate. Now that I begin to see day-light, I do not feel justified or necessitated by any view of scientific advantage in so doing.

I am sorry that you do not feel able to get to work except by the help of these notes—but I am sure that you must be mistaken in this, and that there must be the whole of the remaining field of thought for you to get to work on— though naturally it would be easier for you to get into harness with some formed notes to go on. But my reasons are conclusive. I will send the work round to you naturally, when I have got it into the form which expresses my ideas.

Yours affectly
Alfred N. Whitehead

Before the war started, Whitehead had made some notes on our knowledge of the external world and I had written a book on this subject in which I made use with due acknowledgement of ideas that Whitehead had passed on to me. The above letter shows that this had vexed him. In fact, it put an end to our collaboration.

To Lady Emily Lutyens

57, Gordon Square
W.C. (1)
21.III.17

Dear Lady Emily

I have shortened my article by seven lines, which was what seemed needed— six lines close to the end and one in the middle of the last column.

Is it really necessary to say that I am 'heir-presumptive to the present Earl Russell'? I cannot see that my brother's having no children makes my opinions more worthy of respect.

I have corrected a few inaccuracies in the biography.

'Critical detachment' is hardly my attitude to the war. My attitude is one of intense and passionate protest—I consider it a horror, an infamy, an overwhelming and unmitigated disaster, making the whole of life ghastly

Yours very sincerely
Bertrand Russell

To Colette   Gordon Square
                                               March 27, 1917

I cannot express a thousandth part of what is in my heart—our day in the country was so marvellous. All through Sunday it grew and grew, and at night it seemed to pass beyond the bounds of human things. I feel no longer all alone in the world. Your love brings warmth into all the recesses of my being. You used to speak of a wall of separation between us. That no longer exists. The winter is ending, we shall have sunshine and the song of birds, and wild flowers, primroses, bluebells, and then the scent of the may. We will keep joy alive in us. You are strong and brave and free, and filled with passion and love—the very substance of all my dreams come to life.

                                           Gordon Square
                                         September 23, 1917

The whole region in my mind where you lived, seems burnt out.
There is nothing for us both but to try and forget each other.
Goodbye—

                                            B.

From Colette   Mecklenburgh Square
                                         September 26, 1917

I thought, until last night, that our love would grow and grow until it was strong as loneliness itself.

I have gazed down Eternity with you. I have held reins of glory in my two hands—Now, though I will still believe in the beauty of eternal things, they will not be for me. You will put the crown on your work. You will stand on the heights of impersonal greatness. I worship you, but our souls are strangers— I pray that I may soon be worn out and this torture ended.

                                            C.

To Colette   Gordon Square
                                           October 25, 1917

I have known real happiness with you—If I could live by my creed, I should know it still. I feel imprisoned in egotism—weary of effort, too tired to break through into love.

How can I bridge the gulf?

                                            B.

From *The Tribunal.* Thursday, January 3rd, 1918

THE GERMAN PEACE OFFER

by Bertrand Russell

The more we hear about the Bolsheviks, the more the legend of our patriotic press becomes exploded. We were told that they were incompetent, visionary and corrupt, that they must fall shortly, that the mass of Russians were against them, and that they dared not permit the Constituent Assembly to meet. All these statements have turned out completely false, as anyone may see by reading the very interesting despatch from Arthur Ransome in the *Daily News* of December 31st.

Lenin, whom we have been invited to regard as a German Jew, is really a Russian aristocrat who has suffered many years of persecution for his opinions. The social revolutionaries who were represented as enemies of the Bolsheviks have formed a connection with them. The Constituent Assembly is to meet as soon as half its members have reached Petrograd, and very nearly half have already arrived. All charges of German money remain entirely unsupported by one thread of evidence.

The most noteworthy and astonishing triumph of the Bolsheviks is in their negotiations with the Germans. In a military sense Russia is defenceless, and we all supposed it a proof that they were mere visionaries when they started negotiations by insisting upon not surrendering any Russian territory to the Germans. We were told that the Germans would infallibly insist upon annexing the Baltic Provinces and establishing a suzerainty over Poland. So far from this being the case, the German and Austrian Governments have officially announced that they are prepared to conclude a Peace on the Russian basis of no annexations and no indemnities, provided that it is a general Peace, and they have invited the Western Powers to agree to these terms.

This action has placed the Governments of the Western Powers in a most cruel dilemma. If they refuse the German offer, they are unmasked before the world and before their own Labour and Socialist Parties: they make it clear to all that they are continuing the war for purposes of territorial aggrandisement. If they accept the offer, they afford a triumph to the hated Bolsheviks and an object lesson to democratic revolutionaries everywhere as to the way to treat with capitalists, Imperialists and war-mongers. They know that from the patriotic point of view they cannot hope for a better peace by continuing the war, but from the point of view of preventing liberty and universal peace, there is something to be hoped from continuation. It is known that unless peace comes soon there will be starvation throughout Europe. Mothers will be maddened by the spectacle of their children dying. Men will fight each other for possession of the bare necessaries of life. Under such conditions the sane constructive effort required for a successful revolution will be impossible. The American Garrison which will by that time be occupying England and France, whether or not they will prove efficient against the Germans, will no doubt be capable of intimidating strikers, an occupation to which the American Army is accustomed when at home. I do not say that these thoughts are in the mind of the Government. All the evidence tends to show that there are no thoughts whatever in their mind, and that they live from hand to mouth consoling themselves with ignorance and sentimental twaddle. I say only that if they were capable of thought, it would be along such lines as I have suggested that they would have to attempt to justify a refusal to make Peace on the basis of the German offer, if indeed they do decide to refuse.

Some democrats and Socialists are perhaps not unwilling that the war should continue, since it is clear that if it does it must lead to universal revolution. I think it is true that this consequence must follow, but I do not think that we ought on that account to acquiesce in the refusal to negotiate should that be the decision at which our Governments arrive. The kind of revolution with which we shall in that case be threatened will be far too serious and terrible to be a source of good. It would be a revolution full of violence, hatred and bloodshed, driven by hunger, terror and suspicion,—a revolution in which all that is best in Western civilisation is bound to perish. It is this prospect that our rulers ought to be facing. It is this risk that they run for such paltry objects as the annexation of African Colonies and Mesopotamia. Labour's war aims accepted almost unanimously on December 28th are on the whole very sane, and might easily form the basis for the immediate initiation of negotiations. Labour at the moment has enormous power. Is it too much to hope that it will use this power to compel some glimmer of sanity on the part of the blinded and maddened rulers of the Western Powers? Labour holds the key. It can if it chooses secure a just and lasting peace within a month, but if this opportunity is allowed to pass by, all that we hold dear will be swallowed up in universal ruin.

The above article was that for which I was sentenced to prison.

To Professor Gilbert Murray   57, Gordon Square
                                     London, W.C.1
                                     15th February 1918

My dear Gilbert

I am very much touched by the kindness of your letter. It really is good of you to act when our views are so different. Of course if I had known the blaze of publicity that was going to be directed upon that one sentence of the *Tribunal*, I should have phrased it very much more carefully, in such a way as to prevent misunderstanding by a public not used to the tone of exasperated and pugnacious pacifists. Unless the Government had prosecuted, no-one but pacifists would ever have seen the sentence. Certainly it is a thousand to one that no American would ever have seen it. I wrote for the *Tribunal* once a week for a year, generally in great haste in the middle of other work. In the course of this time it was almost unavoidable that I should emit at least one careless sentence—careless that is as to form, for as regards the matter I adhere to it.

So far as I can discover, the immediate cause of the prosecution was the fact that I had ceased to write these articles, or indeed to take any part in pacifist work beyond attending an occasional Committee. I made up my mind to this course last autumn, but it was impossible to carry it out instantly without inconvenience to colleagues. I therefore informed the N.C.F. that I would cease to be their Acting Chairman at the New Year. Accordingly, the last article I wrote for the *Tribunal* appeared on January 10, a week after the article for which I am prosecuted. It seems that the authorities realised that if they wished to punish me they must act at once, as I should not be committing any further crimes. All my plans were made for going back entirely to writing and philosophical lecturing, but whether I shall now be able to resume these plans when I come out of prison is of course doubtful. I do not much dislike the prospect of prison, provided I am allowed plenty of books to read. I think the freedom from responsibility will be rather restful. I cannot imagine anything that there could be to do for me, unless the American Embassy were to take the view that the matter is too trumpery to be worth a prosecution, but I cannot say that I have any great desire to see the prosecution quashed. I think those of us who live in luxury on money which is secured to us by the Criminal Law ought to have some idea of the mechanism by which our happiness is secured, and for this reason I shall be glad to know the inside of a prison.

With my very warmest thanks,

Yours ever affectionately
Bertrand Russell

57 Gordon Square W.C.1
27.3.18

Dear Gilbert

You have been so very kind that I feel I ought to write to you in regard to what is being done in my case. Assuming that the sentence is confirmed, it seems it will be the thing to ask for 1*st* Division. This will need preparing soon, as things move slowly. Hirst is willing to approach Morley, Loreburn, Buckmaster, & Lansdowne, asking them to write to Cave. It seems to me that Asquith & Grey might be willing to; also a certain number of un-political learned men. If you were willing, you could do this better than any one else. If private representations fail (as they probably will) letters to the Press will be necessary. All this will have to be done quickly if it is to be effective.

I saw E. D. Morel yesterday for the first time since he came out, & was impressed by the seriousness of a six months' sentence. His hair is completely white (there was hardly a tinge of white before)—when he first came out, he collapsed completely, physically & mentally, largely as the result of insufficient food. He says one only gets three quarters of an hour for reading in the whole day—the rest of the time is spent on prison work etc. It seems highly probable that if the sentence is not mitigated my mind will not remain as competent as it has been. I should regret this, as I still have a lot of philosophy that I wish to do.

Yrs ever
Bertrand Russell

From E. M. Forster

Alexandria
12-2-18

Dear Russell,

In the middle of a six course dinner at the Club last night I was told that you were in prison. This is to send you my love. I suppose they will let you have it when you come out.

Here all is comfort and calm. One will become very queer indeed if it, and the war, last much longer.

Yours fraternally
E. M. Forster

From Lancelot Hogben   London April 10th. 18

Dear Mr Russell
   I am only writing a little note to tell you how splendid I think your stand
has been. Being an ex convict, I understand a little at what cost you have been
true. It is inspiring to us who are younger men and who see so many of our
own friends succumbing to cynical indifference or academic preoccupation to
know that there is at least one of the Intellectuals of Europe who have not
allowed the life of the mind to kill the life of the spirit. . . . This is rather in-
effective, but well,

                              Good luck
                              Yours very sincerely
                              Lancelot Hogben

From G. Lowes Dickinson   11 Edwardes Square
                                        W. 8. Ap. 19, [1918]
Dear Bertie
   I wish I could have seen you, but I haven't been able to fit it in, and I go
away today for the rest of April. I hope to be there on May 1st. It is difficult
to have any hope. I suppose the best thing that could happen now would be
for you to get first-class imprisonment. If they fine you, you will I suppose be
called up at once, and have to go through the mill as a C.O. The only chance
is that the brute [Lord] Derby has gone from the War Office and I understand
that Milner is more sympathetic to the C.Os. We are governed by men as
base as they are incompetent, and the country, maddened by fear and hate,
continues to will it so. I blush all over to be English, sometimes. Yet one knows
that the individual Englishman is a decent, kindly well-meaning chap. Its the
pack, and its leaders, that are so vile. But what use in words? One can alter
nothing; and human speech seems to have lost all meaning. To change the
subject, I am reading Aristotle on the Soul. Its refreshing to be back at a time
when the questions were being examined freshly by first-class minds. Aristotle's
method of approach might be yours. One sees however, I think, that the
conception of 'substance' has already fixed thought in a certain unconscious
rut. In my old age, owing I suppose to you and others, I find my mind more
disencumbered and active than it was in youth. But the packs of wolves will not
be satisfied until they have killed off every free mind and brave soul. That's the
secret object of the war. So long.

                              G.L.D.
                              [Lowes Dickinson]

From C. P. Sanger   58 Oakley Street
                                        Chelsea, S.W.3
                                        28th April 1918
Dear Bertie
   Although we haven't met much lately, you are constantly in my thoughts.
Its difficult to say what one feels—you have always been so very much to me
and I can't bear the thought that you may go to prison, though I know that

your fortitude and self control will bring you safely through the ordeal. Its a mad world—a nightmare. I sometimes think I shall wake up and find that it was a dream after all. I hope that reality will prove to be better than appearance —if there is anything besides this absurd world of blood and explosives.

But if things can be improved, it is you and those like you who will do it and the younger men—if any of them survive—will look to you.

Yours fraternally
C. P. Sanger

P.S. Daphne[1] directs me to send her love.

From G. B. Shaw

Ayot, St Lawrence
Welwyn, Herts.
18th March 1918

Dear Miss Mackenzie

I am naturally a good deal concerned about Russell; but I can do nothing: he must help himself, and that vigorously, if he is to win his appeal. At his trial there seems to have been no adequate defence: he, or his counsel, should have talked for a week and clamored to the heavens against tyranny and injustice and destruction of popular rights and deuce knows what else in order to make the authorities as sorry as possible that they had stirred up these questions, even if they had obtained the sentence all the same. Russell is not an imbecile who cannot defend himself. He is not a poor man who cannot afford a strong bar. He is practically a nobleman with a tremendous family record on the Whig side as a hereditary defender of popular liberties. Yet the impression left on the public is that he has been disposed of in ten minutes like an ordinary pickpocket. That must be to some extent the fault of himself and his friends. It seems like a repetition of the monstrous mistake of Morell's plea of guilty, which must have been made under silly advice under the impression that guilt is a question of fact, and not of the ethical character of the action in question.

The only matter that is really in doubt is whether Russell should conduct his own case or employ counsel. In his place I should unhesitatingly do the job myself. A barrister will put up some superficially ingenious plea which will give him a good professional chance of shewing off before the Court of Appeal, one which will not compromise him by any suspicion of sympathy with Russell's views, and the failure of which will be a foregone conclusion. Russell will have no preoccupations of that sort; and he can, as an amateur, take liberties with court procedure which a barrister cannot. He is accustomed to public speaking, and therefore not under the necessity of getting another man to speak for him simply through nervousness and inexperience.

His case is not by any means a weak one. To begin with, he can point out that he is being prosecuted for a hypothetical prophecy occupying half a dozen lines in an article containing several positive statements which have since turned out to be entirely wrong and might even have been dangerously misleading. He was wrong about the Bolsheviks, about the Constituent Assembly,

[1] His daughter.

about the German and Austrian Governments. Yet no exception is taken to these errors.

But when he got on to the solider ground taken by Lord Lansdowne, and argued that a continuation of the war must lead inevitably to starvation throughout Europe, a ridiculous pretext is found for attacking him. The war is full of ironies: the belligerents claiming to be the defenders of liberties which they have all been engaged at one time or another in vigorously suppressing. The Germans forget their oppression of Prussian Poland, and denounce England as the oppressor of Ireland, Egypt and India. The French forget Tonquin, Morocco, Algeria and Tunisia, and the Bonapartist regime, and revile the Germans as conquerors and annexationists. Italy forgets Abyssinia and the Tripolitaine, and claims Dalmatia and part of the Austrian Tyrol, whilst driving Austria from the Trentino on nationalist grounds. Finally, America, which has been engaged in conflicts with her own workers which in Colorado and some other States have almost approached the proportions of a civil war, assumes the mission of redeeming the German proletariat from slavery. All these ironies have been pointed out again and again in the bitterest terms by philosophic journalists, except the last which Russell was the first to hint at very mildly in *The Tribunal.* Immediately some foolish censor, knowing nothing about irony or history or anything else except the rule of thumb of his department, pounces on the allusion as something that has not been passed before, and therefore must be challenged.

But the main point is that if Russell, in spite of his social and academic position, is to be savagely punished for writing about the war as a Pacifist and a philosopher, the intimidation of the Press will be carried thereby to a point in England which it has not yet attained in Germany or Austria; and if it be really an advantage to be a free country, that advantage will go to Germany. We are claiming the support of the world in this war solely on the ground that we represent Liberal institutions, and that our enemies represent despotic ones. The enemy retorts that we are the most formidable and arbitary Empire on the face of the earth; and there is so much to be said for this view in consequence of our former conquests that American and Russian public opinion is sorely perplexed about us. Russell can say, 'If you like to persecute me for my Liberal opinions, persecute away and be damned: I am not the first of my family to suffer in that good cause; but if you have any regard for the solidarity of the Alliance, you will take care to proclaim to the world that England is still the place where a man can say the thing he will &c. (peroration ad lib.).

This is the best advice I can give in the matter as Russell's friend.

Yours faithfully
G. *Bernard Shaw*

10 Adelphi Terrace W.C.2
29th April 1917 [1918]

Dear Bertrand Russell

I have an uneasy feeling that you will take legal advice on Wednesday, and go into prison for six months for the sake of allowing your advocate to make a favourable impression on the bench by advancing some ingenious defence, long since worn out in the service of innumerable pickpockets, which they will be able to dismiss (with a compliment to the bar) with owl-like gravity.

I see nothing for it but to make a scene by refusing indignantly to offer any defence at all of a statement that any man in a free country has a perfect right to make, and declaring that as you are not an unknown person, and your case will be reported in every capital from San Francisco east to Tokyo, and will be taken as the measure of England's notion of the liberty she professes to be fighting for, you leave it to the good sense of the bench to save the reputation of the country from the folly of its discredited and panic stricken Government. Or words to that effect. You will gain nothing by being considerate, and (unlike a barrister) lose nothing by remembering that a cat may look at a king, and, *à fortiori*, a philosopher at a judge.

ever
G.B.S.

To my brother Frank   Brixton
                                                          June 3, 1918

Existence here is not disagreeable, but for the fact that one can't see one's friends. The one fact does make it, to me, very disagreeable—but if I were devoid of affection, like many middle aged men, I should find nothing to dislike. One has no responsibilities, and infinite leisure. My time passes very fruitfully. In a normal day, I do four hours philosophical writing, four hours philosophical reading, and four hours general reading—so you can understand my wanting a lot of books. I have been reading Madame Roland's memoirs and have come to the conclusion that she was a very over-rated woman: snobbish, vain, sentimental, envious—rather a German type. Her last days before her execution were spent in chronicling petty social snubs or triumphs of many years back. She was a democrat chiefly from envy of the *noblesse*. Prisons in her day were more cheerful than now: she says if she were not writing her memoirs she would be painting flowers or playing an air. Pianos are not provided in Brixton. On the other hand, one is not guillotined on leaving, which is in some ways an advantage.—During my two hours' exercise I reflect upon all manner of things. It is good to have a time of leisure for reflection and altogether it is a godsend being here. But I don't want too much godsend!

I am quite happy and my mind is very active. I enjoy the sense that the time is fruitful—after giving out all these last years, reading almost nothing and writing very little and having no opportunity for anything civilized, it is a real delight to get back to a civilized existence. But oh I *shall* be glad when it is over! I have given up the bad habit of imagining the war may be over some day. One must compare the time with that of the Barbarian invasion. I feel like Appolinaris Sidonius—The best one could be would be to be like St. Augustine. For the next 1000 years people will look back to the time before 1914 as they did in the Dark Ages to the time before the Gauls sacked Rome. Queer animal, Man!

Your loving brother
Bertrand Russell

To Colette   5th July 1918

Beloved I do long for you—I keep thinking of all the wonderful things we will do together—I think of what we will do when we can go abroad after the war —I long to go with you to Spain: to see the great Cathedral of Burgos, the Velasquez in Madrid—the gloomy Escorial, from which madmen used to spread ruin over the world in the days before madness was universal—Seville in dancing sunlight, all orange groves and fountains—Granada, where the Moors lingered till Ferdinand and Isabella drove them out—Then we could cross the straits, as the Moors did, into Morocco—and come back by Naples and Rome and Siena and Florence and Pisa—Imagine the unspeakable joy of it—the riot of colour and beauty—freedom—the sound of Italian bells—the strange cries, rich, full-throated, and melancholy with all the weight of the ages—the great masses of flowers, inconceivably bright—men with all the beauty of wild animals, very erect, with bright swiftly-glancing eyes—and to step out into the morning sunshine, with blue sea and blue hills—it is all there for us, some day. I long for the madness of the South with you.

The other thing I long for with you—which we can get sooner—is the Atlantic—the Connemara coast—driving mist—rain—waves that moan on the rocks—flocks of sea-birds with wild notes that seem the very soul of the restless sadness of the sea—and gleams of sun, unreal, like glimpses into another world—and wild wild wind, free and strong and fierce—There, there is life—and there, I feel, I could stand with you and let our love commune with the western storm—for the same spirit is in both. My Colette, my Soul, I feel the breath of greatness inspiring me through our love—I want to put the spirit of the Atlantic into words—I must, *I must*, before I die, find *some* way to say the essential thing that is in me, that I have never said yet—a thing that is not love or hate or pity or scorn, but the very breath of life, fierce, and coming from far away, bringing into human life the vastness and the fearful passionless force of non-human things.

                                    10th August [1918]

If I had been in Gladstone's place I would never have let Gordon go to Khartoum, but having let him go I think it was foolish not to back him up, because it was bound to incense people. It started the movement of imperialism which led on to the Boer War and thence to the present horror. It is useless in politics to apply a policy people won't understand. I remember a talk we had in the woods once about what Allen would do if he were Prime Minister, in which this came up.

I didn't realize that the film job you refused was the life of Lloyd George. Certainly you *had* to refuse that. One might as well have expected St John to take employment under Pontius Pilate as official biographer of Judas Iscariot.

What a queer work the Bible is. Abraham (who is a pattern of all the virtues) twice over, when he is going abroad, says to his wife: 'Sarah my dear, you are a very good-looking person, and the King is very likely to fall in love with you. If he thinks I am your husband, he will put me to death, so as to be able to marry you; so you shall travel as my sister, which you are, by the way.' On each occasion the King does fall in love with her, takes her into his harem, and gets diseased in consequence, so he returns her to Abraham. Meanwhile Abraham has a child by the maidservant, whom Sarah dismisses into the wilderness with the new-born infant, without Abraham objecting. Rum tale.

And God has talks with Abraham at intervals, giving shrewd worldly advice. Then later, when Moses begs to see God, God allows him to see his 'hind parts'. There is a terrible fuss, thunder and whirlwind and all the paraphernalia, and then all God has to say is that he wants the Jews to eat *un*leavened bread at the Passover—he says this over and over again, like an old gentleman in his dotage. Queer book.

Some texts are *very* funny. Deut. XXIV, 5: 'When a man hath taken a new wife, he shall not go out to war, neither shall he be charged with any business: but he shall be free at home one year, and shall cheer up his wife which he hath taken.' I should never have guessed 'cheer up' was a Biblical expression. Here is another really inspiring text: 'Cursed be he that lieth with his mother-in-law. And all the people shall say, Amen.' St Paul on marriage: 'I say therefore to the unmarried and widows, It is good for them if they abide even as I. But if they cannot contain, let them marry: for it is better to marry than to burn.' This has remained the doctrine of the Church to this day. It is clear that the Divine purpose in the text 'it is better to marry than to burn' is to make us all feel how *very* dreadful the torments of Hell must be.

Thursday 16th [August 1918]

Dear one, will you be very patient and kind with me the seven weeks that remain, and bear with me if I grow horrid? It has been difficult after the hopes of release. I am very tired, very weary. I am of course tortured by jealousy; I knew I should be. I know so little of your doings that I probably imagine more than the truth. I have grown so nervy from confinement and dwelling on the future that I feel a sort of vertigo, an impulse to destroy the happiness in prospect. *Will you please quite calmly ignore anything I do these next weeks in obedience to this impulse.* As yet, I am just able to see that it is mad, but soon it will seem the only sanity. I shall set to work to hurt you, to make you break with me; I shall say I won't see you when I first come out; I shall pretend to have lost all affection for you. All this is madness—the effect of jealousy and impatience combined. The pain of wanting a thing very much at last grows so great that one has to try not to want it any longer—Now here it is: *I want everything as we planned it—Ashford, then Winchelsea if you can. If later I say I don't want this, please pay no attention.*

To Miss Rinder[1]   30th July, 1918

Many thanks for *Spectator* review. Is it not odd that people can in the same breath praise 'the free man's worship' and find fault with my views on the war? The free man's worship is merely the expression of the pacifist outlook when it was new to me. So many people enjoy rhetorical expressions of fine feelings, but hate to see people perform the actions that must go with the feelings if they are genuine. How could any one, approving the free man's worship, expect me

[1] Miss Rinder worked at the No Conscription Fellowship, and was chiefly concerned with details in the treatment of pacifist prisoners.

to join in the trivial self-righteous moral condemnation of the Germans? All moral condemnation is utterly against the whole view of life that was then new to me but is now more and more a part of my being. I am naturally pugnacious, and am only restrained (when I am restrained) by a realisation of the tragedy of human existence, and the absurdity of spending our little moment in strife and heat. That I, a funny little gesticulating animal on two legs, should stand beneath the stars and declaim in a passion about *my* rights—it seems so laughable, so out of all proportion. Much better, like Archimedes, to be killed because of absorption in eternal things. And when once men get away from their rights, from the struggle to take up more room in the world than is their due, there is such a capacity of greatness in them. All the loneliness and the pain and the eternal pathetic hope—the power of love and the appreciation of beauty—the concentration of many ages and spaces in the mirror of a single mind—these are not things one would wish to destroy wantonly, for any of the national ambitions that politicians praise. There is a possibility in human minds of something mysterious as the night-wind, deep as the sea, calm as the stars, and strong as Death, a mystic contemplation, the 'intellectual love of God'. Those who have known it cannot *believe* in wars any longer, or in any kind of hot struggle. If I could give to others what has come to me in this way, I could make them too feel the futility of fighting. But I do not know how to communicate it: when I speak, they stare, applaud, or smile, but do not understand.

To Ottoline Morrell   August 8th, 1918

All you write about S.S. [Siegfried Sassoon] is interesting and poignant. I know so well the indignation he suffers from—I have lived in it for months, and on the edge of it for years. I think that one way of getting over it is to perceive that others might judge oneself in the same way, unjustly, but with just as good grounds. Those of us who are rich are just like the young women whose sex flourishes on the blood of soldiers. Every motor-tyre is made out of the blood of negroes under the lash, yet motorists are not all heartless villains. When we buy wax matches, we buy a painful and lingering death for those who make them. . . . War is only the final flower of the capitalist system, but with an unusual proletariat. S.S. sees war, not peace, from the point of view of the proletariat. But this is only politics. The fundamental mistake lies in wrong expectations, leading to cynicism when they are not realised. Conventional morality leads us to expect unselfishness in decent people. This is an error. Man is an animal bent on securing food and propagating the species. One way of succeeding in these objects is to persuade others that one is after *their* welfare—but to be really after any welfare but one's own and one's children's is unnatural. It occurs like sadism and sodomy, but is equally against nature. A good social system is not to be secured by making people unselfish, but by making their own vital impulses fit in with other people's. This is feasible. Our present system makes self-preservation only possible at the expense of others. The system is at fault; but it is a weakness to be disgusted with people because they aim at self-preservation. One's idealism needs to be too robust for such weaknesses. It doesn't do to forget or deny the animal in man. The God in man will not be visible, as a rule, while the animal is thwarted. Those who have produced stoic philosophies have all had enough to eat and drink. The sum total of the matter is that one's idealism must be *robust* and must fit in with the facts of nature; and that which is horrible in the actual world is mainly due to a bad system. Spinoza, always, is right in all these things, to my mind.

11th August, 1918

It is quite true what you say, that you have never expressed yourself—but who has, that has anything to express? The things one says are all unsuccessful attempts to say something else—something that perhaps by its very nature cannot be said. I know that I have struggled all my life to say something that I never shall learn how to say. And it is the same with you. It is so with all who spend their lives in the quest of something elusive, and yet omnipresent, and at once subtle and infinite. One seeks it in music, and the sea, and sunsets; at times I have seemed very near it in crowds when I have been feeling strongly what they were feeling; one seeks it in love above all. But if one lets oneself imagine one has found it, some cruel irony is sure to come and show one that it is not really found. (I have come nearest to expressing myself in the chapter on Education in *Social Reconstruction*. But it is a very long way from a really full self-expression. You are hindered by timidity.)

The outcome is that one is a ghost, floating through the world without any real contact. Even when one feels nearest to other people, something in one seems obstinately to belong to God and to refuse to enter into any earthly communion—at least that is how I should express it if I thought there was a God. It is odd isn't it? I care passionately for this world, and many things and people in it, and yet . . . what is it all? There *must* be something more important, one feels, though I don't *believe* there is. I am haunted—some ghost, from some extra-mundane region, seems always trying to tell me something that I am to repeat to the world, but I cannot understand the message. But it is from listening to the ghost that one comes to feel oneself a ghost. I feel I shall find the truth on my deathbed and be surrounded by people too stupid to understand— fussing about medicines instead of searching for wisdom. Love and imagination mingled; that seems the main thing so far.

Your B.

27th August, 1918

I have been reading Marsh[1] on Rupert [Brooke]. It makes me very sad and very indignant. It hurts reading of all that young world now swept away— Rupert and his brother and Keeling and lots of others—in whom one foolishly thought at the time that there was hope for the world—they were full of life and energy and truth—Rupert himself loved life and the world—his hatreds were very concrete, resulting from some quite specific vanity or jealousy, but in the main he found the world lovable and interesting. There was nothing of humbug in him. I feel that after the war-mongers had killed his body in the Dardanelles they have done their best to kill his spirit by ——'s lies. . . . When will people

---

[1] Afterwards Sir Edward. He had been a close friend of mine when we were undergraduates, but became a civil servant, an admirer of Winston Churchill and then a high Tory.

learn the robustness of truth? I do not know who my biographer may be, but I should like him to report 'with what flourish his nature will' something like this: 'I was not a solemn stained glass saint, existing only for purposes of edification; I existed from my own centre, many things that I did were regrettable, I did not respect respectable people, and when I pretended to do so it was humbug. I lied and practised hypocrisy, because if I had not I should not have been allowed to do my work; but there is no need to continue the hypocrisy after my death. I hated hypocrisy and lies: I loved life and real people, and wished to get rid of the shams that prevent us from loving real people as they really are. I believed in laughter and spontaneity, and trusted to nature to bring out the genuine good in people, if once genuineness could come to be tolerated.' Marsh goes building up the respectable legend, making the part of youth harder in the future, so far as lies in his power—I try so hard not to hate, but I do hate respectable liars and oppressors and corruptors of youth—I hate them with all my soul, and the war has given them a new lease of power. The young were shaking them off, but they have secured themselves by setting the young to kill each other. But rage is useless; what is wanted is to carry over into the new time something of the gaiety and civilised outlook and genial expansive love that was growing when the war came. It is useless to add one's quota to the sum of hate—and so I try to forget those whom I cannot but hate when I remember them.

Friday, 30 Aug. 18

My dearest O

It was a *delight* seeing you—tho' you do not seem in very good health—and those times are difficult for talking—letters are really more satisfactory—your letters are the *very greatest joy* to me—To begin with personal things: I do trust my *friends* to do everything possible—no one ever had such kind and devoted friends—I am wonderfully touched by what all of you have done; the people I don't trust are the philosophers (including Whitehead). They are cautious and constitutionally timid; nine out of ten hate me personally (not without reason); they consider philosophical research a foolish pursuit, only excusable when there is money in it. Before the war I fancied that quite a lot of them thought philosophy important; now I know that most of them resemble Professors Hanky and Panky in *Erewhon Revisited*.

I trust G. Murray, on the whole, over this business. If he gets me a post, I hope it will be not *very* far from London—not further than Birmingham say. I don't the least desire a post except as a way of getting round Geddes: what I desire is to do original work in philosophy, but apparently no one in Government circles considers that worth doing. Of course a post will interfere to some extent with research tho' it need not interfere very much. I *must* have *some* complete holiday when I first come out of prison. I do not want *residence* away from London: I would *almost* as soon face another term of imprisonment, for reasons which can't be explained to G. Murray. But I am *most* grateful to him for all the trouble he is taking. I am not *worrying* in the least.

How delightful of you to think of Lulworth too. It was the very place I had been thinking of, before I came upon it in R. Brooke. I was only there once for a moment on a walking-tour (1912) and have always wanted to go back. *Do* stick to the plan—latish October. We can settle exactly when, later. It will be *glorious*.

I wonder whether you quite get at Brett. I am sure her deafness is the main cause of all that you regret in her. She wrote a terrible account of what it means to her the other day in a letter you sent me—I don't know whether you read it. If not I will show it you. I am *very* sorry about Burnley. It is a blow. There will be no revival of pacifism; the war will go on till the Germans admit themselves beaten, which I put end of next year. Then we shall have the League to *Enforce* Peace, which will require conscription everywhere.—Much interested about S.S. and munition factory; all experience may be useful. It would never occur to me to think of it as an 'attitude'.

I was sorry to refuse so many books, and also to give you the trouble of taking so many away. I believe in future I shall be able to send them by Carter Paterson. My cell is small and I *must* keep down the number of books. Between books and earwigs I have hardly had room to turn round.

Please thank Miss Bentinck most warmly for the lovely peaches. I think it *very* kind of her to send them when she thinks me so wicked.—I don't know how long you are staying at Kirkby Lonsdale—All that region is so associated in my mind with Theodore's death.

Oh won't it be glorious to be able to walk across fields and see the horizon and talk freely and be with friends—It is near enough now to believe it will come—I am settled into this existence, and fairly placid, but only because it will end soon. All kinds of delights float before my mind—above all talk, *talk*, TALK. I never knew how one can hunger for it—The time here has done me good, I have read a lot and thought a lot and grown *collected*, I am bursting with energy—but I do long for civilization and civilized talk—And I long for the SEA and wildness and wind—I hate being all tidy like a book in a library where no one reads—Prison is horribly like that—Imagine if you knew you were a delicious book, and some Jew millionaire bought you and bound you uniform with a lot of others and stuck you up in a shelf behind glass, where you merely illustrated the completeness of his System—and no anarchist was allowed to read you—That is what one feels like—but soon now one will be able to insist on being read.—Goodbye—Much much love—and endless thanks for your endless kindness. *Do* stick to Lulworth—

Your B.

P.S. Letter to Brett elsewhere. Please return commonplace books—Wednesday will do. But I run short of them unless they are returned.

To Dorothy Brett   30. 8 18

My dear Brett

Thank you for your letter. It is a kindness writing letters to me when I am here, as they are the only unhampered contact I can have with other people. I think prison, if it lasted, would be worse than your fate, but as mine is so brief it is nothing like as bad as what you have to endure. I do realize how terrible it is. But I believe there are things you could do that would make it less trying, small things mostly. To begin with a *big* thing: practise the mental discipline of not thinking how great a misfortune it is; when your mind begins to run in that direction, stop it violently by reciting a poem to yourself or thinking of the multiplication-table or some such plan. For smaller things: try, as far as possible, not to sit about with people who are having a general conversation; get in a corner with a tête-à-tête; make yourself interesting in the first place by being interested in whoever you are talking with, until things become easy and natural. I suppose you have practised lip-reading? Take care of your inner attitude to people: let it not be satirical or aloof, set yourself to try and get inside their skins and feel the passions that move them and the seriousness of the things that matter to them. Don't judge people morally: however just one's judgment, that is a barren attitude. Most people have a key, fairly simple; if you find it, you can unlock their hearts. Your deafness need not prevent this, if you make a point of tête-à-tête. It has always seemed to me fearfully trying for you at Garsington to spend so much time in the middle of talk and laughter that you cannot understand. Don't do more of that than you must. You *can* be 'included in human life'. But it wants effort, and it wants that you should *give* something that people will value. Though your deafness may make that harder, it doesn't make it impossible. Please don't think all this very impertinent. I have only written it because I can't bear to think how you suffer.

Poor Mr. Green! Tell him to consult me when he wants to make a conquest; I will give him sage advice, which he evidently needs.—Your picture of the 3 women sounds most exciting. I do hope it will be glorious. I hope I shall see you when you return from destroying your fellow-creatures in Scotland—I sympathize with the Chinese philosopher who fished without bait, because he liked fishing but did not like catching fish. When the Emperor found him so employed, he made him Prime Minister. But I fear that won't happen to me.

Yrs.
B.R.

The lady to whom the above letter is addressed was a daughter of Lord Esher but was known to all her friends by her family name of Brett. At the time when I wrote the above letter, she was spending most of her time at Garsington with the Morrells. She went later to New Mexico in the wake of D. H. Lawrence.

To Ottoline Morrell   31/8/18
(For any one whom it may interest)

There never was such a place as prison for crowding images—one after another they come upon me—early morning in the Alps, with the smell of aromatic pines and high pastures glistening with dew—the lake of Garda as one first sees it coming down out of the mountains, just a glimpse far below, dancing and gleaming in the sunlight like the eyes of a laughing, mad, Spanish gypsy—thunderstorm in the Mediterranean, with a dark violet sea, and the mountains of Corsica in sunshine far beyond—the Scilly Isles in the setting sun, enchanted and unreal, so that you think they must have vanished before you can reach them, looking like the Islands of the Blest, not to be achieved during this mortal life—the smell of the bog myrtle in Skye—memories of sunsets long ago, all the way back into childhood—I can hear now as if it were yesterday the street-cry of a man in Paris selling 'artichaux verts et beaux' 24 years ago almost to a day. Quite from childhood I remember a certain row of larches after rain, with a raindrop at the end of every twig—and I can hear the wind in the tree-tops in midnight woods on summer nights—everything free or beautiful comes into my thoughts sooner or later. What is the use of shutting up the body, seeing that the mind remains free? And outside my own life, I have lived, while I have been here, in Brazil and China and Tibet, in the French Revolution, in the souls of animals and even of the lowest animals. In such adventures I have forgotten the prison in which the world is keeping itself at the moment: I am free, and the world shall be.

September 4th, 1918

Dearest O

It is *dreadful* the killing of the people who might have made a better future. As for me: I am *sure* it is a 'sure firm growth'. It is two quite distinct things: some quite good technical ideas, which have come simply because they were due, like cuckoos in April; and a way of feeling towards life and the world, which I have been groping after especially since the war started, but also since a certain moment in a churchyard near Broughton, when you told me to make a place for wildness in my morality, and I asked you what you meant, and you explained. It has been very difficult: my instinctive morality was so much that of self-repression. I used to be afraid of myself and the darker side of my instincts; now I am not. You began that, and the war completed it.

CHAPTER II

RUSSIA

THE ENDING OF THE WAR enabled me to avoid several unpleasant things which would otherwise have happened to me. The military age was raised in 1918, and for the first time I became liable to military service, which I should of course have had to refuse. They called me up for medical examination, but the Government with its utmost efforts was unable to find out where I was, having forgotten that it had put me in prison. If the War had continued I should very soon have found myself in prison again as a conscientious objector. From a financial point of view also the ending of the War was very advantageous to me. While I was writing *Principia Mathematica* I felt justified in living on inherited money, though I did not feel justified in keeping an additional sum of capital that I inherited from my grandmother. I gave away this sum in its entirety, some to the University of Cambridge, some to Newnham College, and the rest to various educational objects. After parting with the debentures that I gave to Eliot, I was left with only about £100 a year of unearned money, which I could not get rid of as it was in my marriage settlement. This did not seem to matter, as I had become capable of earning money by my books. In prison, however, while I was allowed to write about mathematics, I was not allowed to write the sort of book by which I could make money. I should therefore have been nearly penniless when I came out but for the fact that Sanger and some other friends got up a philosophical lectureship for me in London. With the ending of the War I was again able to earn money by writing, and I have never since been in serious financial difficulties except at times in America.

The ending of the War made a difference in my relations with Colette. During the War we had many things to do in common, and we shared all the very powerful emotions connected with the War. After the War things became more difficult and more strained. From time to time we would part for ever, but repeatedly these partings proved unexpectedly temporary. During the three summer months of 1919, Littlewood (the mathematician) and I rented a farmhouse on a hill about a mile outside Lulworth. There were a good many rooms in this farmhouse, and we had a series of visitors throughout the whole summer. The place was extraordinarily beautiful, with wide views along the coast. The bathing was good, and there were places where Littlewood could exhibit his prowess as a climber, an art in which he was very expert. Meantime I had been becoming interested in my second wife. I met her first in 1916 through her friend Dorothy Wrinch. Both were at Girton, and Dorothy Wrinch was a pupil of mine. She arranged in the summer of 1916 a two days' walk with herself, Dora Black, Jean Nicod, and me. Jean Nicod was a young French philosopher, also a pupil of mine, who had escaped the War through being consumptive. (He died of phthisis in 1924.) He was one of the most delightful people that I have ever known, at once very gentle and immensely clever. He had a type of whimsical humour that delighted me. Once I was saying to him that people who learned philosophy should be trying to understand the world, and not only, as in universities, the systems of previous philosophers. 'Yes,' he replied, 'but the systems are so much more interesting than the world.' Dora Black, whom I had not seen before, interested me at once. We spent the evening at Shere, and to beguile the time after dinner, I started by asking everybody what they most desired in life. I cannot remember what Dorothy and Nicod said; I said that I should like to disappear like the man in Arnold Bennett's *Buried Alive*, provided I could be sure of discovering a widow in Putney as he did. Dora, to my surprise, said that she wanted to marry and have children. Until that moment I had supposed that no clever young woman would confess to so simple a desire, and I concluded that she must possess exceptional sincerity. Unlike the rest of us she was not, at that time, a thorough-going objector to the War.

In June 1919, at Dorothy Wrinch's suggestion, I invited her to come to tea with Allen and me at the flat that I shared with him in Battersea. She came, and we embarked on a heated argument as to the rights of fathers. She said that, for her part, if she had children she would consider them entirely her own, and would not be disposed to recognize the father's rights. I replied hotly: 'Well, whoever I have children by, it won't be you!' As a result of this argument, I dined with her next evening, and at the end of the evening we arranged that she should come to Lulworth for a long visit. I had on that day had a more than usually definitive parting from Colette, and I did not suppose that I should ever see her again. However, the day after Littlewood and I got to Lulworth I had a telegram from Colette to say that she was on her way down in a hired car, as there was no train for several hours. Fortunately, Dora was not due for some days, but throughout the summer I had difficulties and awkwardnesses in preventing their times from overlapping.

I wrote the above passage in 1931, and in 1949 I showed it to

Colette. Colette wrote to me, enclosing two letters that I had written to her in 1919, which showed me how much I had forgotten. After reading them I remembered that throughout the time at Lulworth my feelings underwent violent fluctuations, caused by fluctuations in Colette's behaviour. She had three distinct moods: one of ardent devotion, one of resigned determination to part for ever, and one of mild indifference. Each of these produced its own echo in me, but the letters that she enclosed showed me that the echo had been more resounding than I had remembered. Her letter and mine show the emotional unreliability of memory. Each knew about the other, but questions of tact arose which were by no means easy. Dora and I became lovers when she came to Lulworth, and the parts of the summer during which she was there were extraordinarily delightful. The chief difficulty with Colette had been that she was unwilling to have children, and that I felt if I was ever to have children I could not put it off any longer. Dora was entirely willing to have children, with or without marriage, and from the first we used no precautions. She was a little disappointed to find that almost immediately our relations took on all the character of marriage, and when I told her that I should be glad to get a divorce and marry her, she burst into tears, feeling, I think, that it meant the end of independence and light-heartedness. But the feeling we had for each other seemed to have that kind of stability that made any less serious relation impossible. Those who have known her only in her public capacity would scarcely credit the quality of elfin charm which she possessed whenever the sense of responsibility did not weigh her down. Bathing by moonlight, or running with bare feet on the dewy grass, she won my imagination as completely as on her serious side she appealed to my desire for parenthood and my sense of social responsibility.

Our days at Lulworth were a balance of delicious outdoor activities, especially swimming, and general conversations as good as any that I have ever had. The general theory of relativity was in those days rather new, and Littlewood and I used to discuss it endlessly. We used to debate whether the distance from us to the post-office was or was not the same as the distance from the post-office to us, though on this matter we never reached a conclusion. The eclipse expedition which confirmed Einstein's prediction as to the bending of light occurred during this time, and Littlewood got a telegram from Eddington telling him that the result was what Einstein said it should be.

As always happens when a party of people who know each other well is assembled in the country, we came to have collective jokes from which casual visitors were excluded. Sometimes the claims of politeness made these jokes quite painful. There was a lady called Mrs Fiske Warren whom I had known when I lived at Bagley Wood, rich and beautiful and intellectual, highly intellectual in fact. It was for her unofficial benefit that Modern Greats were first invented. Carefully selected dons taught her Greek philosophy without demanding a knowledge of Greek. She was a lady of deep mystical intuitions, and an admirer of Blake. I had stayed at her country house in Massachusetts in 1914, and had done my best to live up to her somewhat rarefied atmosphere. Her husband, whom I had never met, was a fanatical believer in Single Tax, and was in the habit of buying small republics, such as Andorra, with a view to putting Henry George's principles into practice. While we were at Lulworth, she sent me a book of her poems and a book of her husband's on his hobby. At the same time a letter came from her husband, who was in London, saying that he wished to see me. I replied that it was impossible as I was not in London. He telegraphed back to say that he would come to lunch Monday, Tuesday, Wednesday, Thursday, or Friday, whichever suited me, although to do so he had to leave London at six in the morning. I chose Friday, and began hastily cutting the pages of his wife's poems. I found a poem headed 'To One who Sleeps by my Side', in which occurred the line: 'Thou art too full of this world's meat and wine.' I read the poem to the company, and called up the housekeeper, giving orders that the meal should be plentiful and that there should be no deficiency of alcohol. He turned out to be a lean, ascetic, anxious character, too earnest to waste any of the moments of life here below in jokes or frivolities. When we were all assembled at lunch, and I began to offer him food and drink, he replied in a sad voice: 'No, thank you. I am a vegetarian and a teetotaller.' Littlewood hastily made a very feeble joke at which we all laughed much more than its merits warranted.

Summer, the sea, beautiful country, and pleasant company, combined with love and the ending of the War to produce almost ideally perfect circumstances. At the end of the summer I went back to Clifford Allen's flat in Battersea, and Dora went to Paris to pursue the researches which she was making, in her capacity of Fellow of Girton, into the beginnings of French free-thinking philosophy in the seventeenth and eighteenth centuries. I still saw her occasionally, sometimes in London, sometimes in Paris. I was still seeing Colette, and was in a mood of indecision.

At Christmas Dora and I met at the Hague, to which place I went to see my friend Wittgenstein. I knew Wittgenstein first at Cambridge before the War. He was an Austrian, and his father was enormously rich. Wittgenstein had intended to become an engineer, and for that purpose had gone to Manchester. Through reading mathematics he became interested in the principles of mathematics, and asked at Manchester who there was who worked at this subject. Somebody mentioned my name, and he took up his residence at Trinity. He was perhaps the most perfect example I have ever known of genius as traditionally conceived, passionate, profound, intense, and dominating. He had a kind of purity which I have never known equalled except by G. E. Moore. I remember taking him once to a meeting of the Aristotelian Society, at which there were various fools whom I treated politely. When we came away he raged and stormed against my moral degradation in not telling these men what fools they were. His life was turbulent and troubled, and his personal force was extraordinary. He lived on milk and vegetables, and I used to feel as Mrs Patrick Campbell did about Shaw: 'God help us if he should ever eat a beefsteak.' He used to come to see me every evening at midnight, and pace up and down my room like a wild beast for three hours in agitated silence. Once I said to him: 'Are you thinking about logic or about your sins?' 'Both', he replied, and continued his pacing. I did not like to suggest that it was time for bed, as it seemed probable both to him and me that on leaving me he would commit suicide. At the end of his first term at Trinity, he came to me and said: 'Do you think I am an absolute idiot?' I said: 'Why do you want to know?' He replied: 'Because if I am I shall become an aeronaut, but if I am not I shall become a philosopher.' I said to him: 'My dear fellow, I don't know whether you are an absolute idiot or not, but if you will write me an essay during the vacation upon any philosophical topic that interests you, I will read it and tell you.' He did so, and brought it to me at the beginning of the next term. As soon as I read the first sentence, I became persuaded that he was a man of genius, and assured him that he should on no account become an aeronaut. At the beginning of 1914 he came to me in a state of great agitation and said: 'I am leaving Cambridge, I am leaving Cambridge at once.' 'Why?' I asked. 'Because my brother-in-law has come to live in London, and I can't bear to be so near him.' So he spent the rest of the winter in the far north of Norway. In early days I once asked G. E. Moore what he thought of Wittgenstein. 'I think very well of him', he said. I asked why, and he replied: 'Because at my lectures he looks puzzled, and nobody else ever looks puzzled.'

When the War came, Wittgenstein, who was very patriotic, became an officer in the Austrian Army. For the first few months it was still possible to write to him and to hear from him, but before long this became impossible, and I knew nothing of him until about a month after the Armistice, when I got a letter from him written from Monte Cassino, saying that a few days after the armistice he had been taken prisoner by the Italians, but fortunately with his manuscript. It appeared that he had written a book in the trenches, and wished me to read it. He was the kind of man who would never have noticed such small matters as bursting shells when he was thinking about logic. He sent me the manuscript of his book, which I discussed with Nicod and

Dorothy Wrinch at Lulworth. It was the book which was subsequently published under the title *Tractatus Logico-Philosophicus*. It was obviously important to see him and discuss it by word of mouth, and it seemed best to meet in a neutral country. We therefore decided upon the Hague. At this point, however, a surprising difficulty arose. His father, just before the outbreak of the War, had transferred his whole fortune to Holland, and was therefore just as rich at the end as at the beginning. Just about at the time of the Armistice his father had died, and Wittgenstein inherited the bulk of his fortune. He came to the conclusion, however, that money is a nuisance to a philosopher, so he gave every penny of it to his brother and sisters. Consequently he was unable to pay the fare from Vienna to the Hague, and was far too proud to accept it from me. At last a solution of this difficulty was found. The furniture and books which he had had at Cambridge were stored there, and he expressed a willingness to sell them to me. I took the advice of the Cambridge furniture dealer in whose care they were as to their value, and bought them at the figure he suggested. They were in fact worth far more than he supposed, and it was the best bargain I ever made. This transaction made it possible for Wittgenstein to come to the Hague, where we spent a week arguing his book line by line, while Dora went to the Public Library to read the invectives of Salmatius against Milton.

Wittgenstein, though a logician, was at once a patriot and a pacifist. He had a very high opinion of the Russians, with whom he had fraternized at the Front. He told me that once in a village in Galicia, where for the moment he had nothing to do, he found a book-shop, and it occurred to him that there might be a book in it. There was just one, which was Tolstoy on the Gospels. He therefore bought it, and was much impressed by it. He became for a time very religious, so much so that he began to consider me too wicked to associate with. In order to make a living he became an elementary school-master in a country village in Austria, called Trattenbach. He would write to me saying: 'The people of Trattenbach are very wicked.' I would reply: 'Yes, all men are very wicked.' He would reply: 'True, but the men of Trattenbach are more wicked than the men of other places.' I replied that my logical sense revolted against such a proposition. But he had some justification for his opinion. The peasants refused to supply him with milk because he taught their children sums that were not about money. He must have suffered during this time hunger and considerable privation, though it was very seldom that he could be induced to say anything about it, as he had the pride of Lucifer. At last his sister decided to build a house, and employed him as architect. This gave him enough to eat for several years, at the end of which time he returned to Cambridge as a don, where Clive Bell's son wrote poems in heroic couplets against him. He was not always easy to fit into a social occasion. Whitehead described to me the first time that Wittgenstein came to see him. He was shown into the drawing-room during afternoon tea. He appeared scarcely aware of the presence of Mrs Whitehead, but marched up and down the room for some time in silence, and at last said explosively: 'A proposition has two poles. It is *apb*.' Whitehead, in telling me, said: 'I naturally asked what are *a* and *b*, but I found that I had said quite the wrong thing. "*a* and *b* are indefinable," Wittgenstein answered in a voice of thunder.'

Like all great men he had his weaknesses. At the height of his mystic ardour in 1922, at a time when he assured me with great earnestness that it is better to be good than clever, I found him terrified of wasps, and, because of bugs, unable to stay another night in lodgings we had found in Innsbruck. After my travels in Russia and China, I was inured to small matters of that sort, but not all his conviction that the things of this world are of no account could enable him to endure insects with patience. In spite of such slight foibles, however, he was an impressive human being.

I spent almost the whole of the year 1920 in travelling. At Easter, I was invited to lecture at Barcelona at the Catalan University there. From Barcelona I went to Majorca, where I stayed at Soller. The old inn-keeper (the only one in the place) informed me that, as he was a widower, he could not give me any food, but I was at liberty to walk in his garden and pluck his oranges whenever I pleased. He said this with such a courteous air that I felt constrained to express my profound gratitude. In Majorca, I began a great quarrel which raged for many months through many changes of latitude and longitude.

I was planning to go to Russia, and Dora wanted to go with me. I maintained that, as she had never taken much interest in politics, there was no good reason why she should go, and, as typhus was raging, I should not feel justified in exposing her to the risk. We were both adamant, and it was an issue upon which compromise was impossible. I still think I was right, and she still thinks she was right.

Soon after returning from Majorca, my opportunity came. A Labour deputation was going to Russia, and was willing that I should accompany it. The Government considered my application, and after causing me to be interviewed by H. A. L. Fisher, they decided to let me go. The Soviet Government was more difficult to persuade, and when I was already in Stockholm on the way, Litvinov was still refusing permission, in spite of our having been fellow prisoners in Brixton. However, the objections of the Soviet Government were at last overcome. We were a curious party, Mrs Snowden, Clifford Allen, Robert Williams, Tom

Shaw, an enormously fat old Trade Unionist named Ben Turner, who was very helpless without his wife and used to get Clifford Allen to take his boots off for him, Haden Guest as medical attendant, and several Trade Union officials. In Petrograd, where they put the imperial motor-car at our disposal, Mrs Snowden used to drive about enjoying its luxury and expressing pity for the 'poor Czar'. Haden Guest was a theosophist with a fiery temper and a considerable libido. He and Mrs Snowden were very anti-Bolshevik. Robert Williams, I found, was very happy in Russia, and was the only one of our party who made speeches pleasing to the Soviet Government. He always told them that revolution was imminent in England, and they made much of him. I told Lenin that he was not to be trusted, and the very next year, on Black Friday, he ratted. Then there was Charlie Buxton, whose pacifism had led him to become a Quaker. When I shared a cabin with him, he would beg me to stop in the middle of a sentence in order that he might practise silent prayer. To my surprise, his pacifism did not lead him to think ill of the Bolsheviks.

For my part, the time I spent in Russia was one of continually increasing nightmare. I have said in print what, on reflection, appeared to me to be the truth, but I have not expressed the sense of utter horror which overwhelmed me while I was there. Cruelty, poverty, suspicion, persecution, formed the very air we breathed. Our conversations were continually spied upon. In the middle of the night one would hear shots, and know that idealists were being killed in prison. There was a hypocritical pretence of equality, and everybody was called 'tovarisch', but it was amazing how differently this word could be pronounced according as the person addressed was Lenin or a lazy servant. On one occasion in Petrograd (as it was called) four scarecrows came to see me, dressed in rags, with a fortnight's beard, filthy nails, and tangled hair. They were the four most eminent poets of Russia. One of them was allowed by the Government to make his living by lecturing on rhythmics, but he complained that they insisted upon his teaching this subject from a Marxian point of view, and that for the life of him he could not see how Marx came into the matter.

Equally ragged were the Mathematical Society of Petrograd. I went to a meeting of this society at which a man read a paper on non-Euclidean geometry. I could not understand anything of it except the formulae which he wrote on the blackboard, but these were quite the right sort of formulae, so that one may assume the paper to have been competent. Never, in England, have I seen tramps who looked so abject as the mathematicians of Petrograd. I was not allowed to see Kropotkin, who not long afterwards died. The governing classes had a self-confidence quite as great as that produced by Eton and Oxford.

They believed that their formulae would solve all difficulties. A few of the more intelligent knew that this was not the case, but did not dare to say so. Once, in a *tête-à-tête* conversation with a scientific physician named Zalkind, he began to say that climate has a great effect upon character, but instantly he pulled himself up short, and said: 'Of course that is not really the case; only economic circumstances affect character.' I felt that everything that I valued in human life was being destroyed in the interests of a glib and narrow philosophy, and that in the process untold misery was being inflicted upon many millions of people. With every day that I spent in Russia my horror increased, until I lost all power of balanced judgment.

From Petrograd we went to Moscow, which is a very beautiful city, and architecturally more interesting than Petrograd because of the Oriental influence. I was amused by various small ways in which Bolshevik love of mass-production showed itself. The main meal of the day occurred at about four o'clock in the afternoon, and contained among other ingredients the heads of fishes. I never discovered what happened to their bodies, though I suppose they were eaten by the peoples' Komissars. The river Moskwa was chock full of fish, but people were not allowed to catch them, as no up-to-date mechanical method had yet been found to supersede the rod and line. The city was almost starving, but it was felt that fishes' heads, caught by trawlers, were better than fishes' bodies caught by primitive methods.

We went down the Volga on a steamer, and Clifford Allen became extremely ill with pneumonia, which revived the tuberculosis from which he had previously suffered. We were all to leave the boat at Saratov, but Allen was too ill to be moved, so Haden Guest, Mrs Snowden and I remained on the boat to look after him, while it travelled on to Astrakan. He had a very small cabin, and the heat was inconceivable. The windows had to be kept tight shut on account of the malarial mosquitoes, and Allen suffered from violent diarrhoea. We had to take turns nursing him, for although there was a Russian nurse on board, she was afraid to sit with him at night for fear that he might die and his ghost might seize her.

Astrakan seemed to me more like hell than anything I had ever imagined. The town water-supply was taken from the same part of the river into which ships shot their refuse. Every street had stagnant water which bred millions of mosquitoes; every year one third of the inhabitants had malaria. There was no drainage system, but a vast mountain of excrement at a prominent place in the middle of the town. Plague was endemic. There had recently been fighting in the civil war against Denikin. The flies were so numerous that at meal-time a table-cloth had to be put over the food, and one had to insert one's hand underneath and snatch a mouthful quickly. The instant the table-cloth was put down, it became completely black with flies, so that nothing of it remained visible. The place is a great deal below sea-level, and the temperature was 120 degrees in the shade. The leading doctors of the place were ordered by the Soviet officials who accompanied us to hear what Haden Guest had to say about combating malaria, a matter on which he had been engaged for the British Army in Palestine. He gave them an admirable lecture on the subject, at the end of which they said: 'Yes, we know all that, but it is very hot.' I fancy that the next time the Soviet officials came that way those doctors were probably put to death, but of this I have no knowledge. The most eminent of the doctors in question examined Clifford Allen and informed me that he could not possibly live two days. When about a fortnight later we got him out to Reval, the doctor who examined him there again told me that he could not live two days, but by this time I had come to know something of Allen's determination to live, and I was less alarmed. He survived for many years, and became an ornament of the House of Lords.

After I returned to England I endeavoured to express my changing moods, before starting and while in Russia, in the shape of antedated letters to Colette, the last of which I subsequently published in my book about China. As they express my moods at that time better than I can do by anything written now, I will insert them here:

1

London,
April 24, 1920

The day of my departure comes near. I have a thousand things to do, yet I sit here idle, thinking useless thoughts, the irrelevant, rebellious thoughts that well-regulated people never think, the thoughts that one hopes to banish by work, but that themselves banish work instead. How I envy those who *always* believe what they believe, who are not troubled by deadness and indifference to all that makes the framework of their lives. I have had the ambition to be of some use in the world, to achieve something notable, to give mankind new hopes. And now that the opportunity is near, it all seems dust and ashes. As I look into the future, my disillusioned gaze sees only strife and still more strife, rasping cruelty, tyranny, terror and slavish submission. The men of my dreams, erect, fearless and generous, will they ever exist on earth? Or will men go on fighting, killing and torturing to the end of time, till the earth grows cold and the dying sun can no longer quicken their futile frenzy? I cannot tell. But I do know the despair in my soul. I know the great loneliness, as I wander through the world like a ghost, speaking in tones that are not heard, lost as if I had fallen from some other planet.

The old struggle goes on, the struggle between little pleasures and the great pain. I know that the little pleasures are death and yet—I am so tired, so very tired. Reason and emotion fight a deadly war within me, and leave me no energy for outward action. I know that no good thing is achieved without fighting, without ruthlessness and organization and discipline. I know that for collective action the individual must be turned into a machine. But in these things, though my reason may force me to believe them, I can find no inspiration. It is the individual human soul that I love—in its loneliness, its hopes and fears, its quick impulses and sudden devotions. It is such a long journey from this to armies and States and officials; and yet it is only by making this long journey that one can avoid a useless sentimentalism.

All through the rugged years of the War, I dreamed of a happy day after its end, when I should sit with you in a sunny garden by the Mediterranean, filled with the scent of heliotrope, surrounded by cypresses and sacred groves of ilex—and there, at last, I should be able to tell you of my love, and to touch the joy that is as real as pain. The time is come, but I have other tasks, and you have other desires; and to me, as I sit brooding, all tasks seem vain and all desires foolish.

Yet it is not upon these thoughts that I shall act.

2

Petrograd,
May 12, 1920

I am here at last, in this city which has filled the world with history, which has inspired the most deadly hatreds and the most poignant hopes. Will it yield me up its secret? Shall I learn to know its inmost soul? Or shall I acquire only statistics and official facts? Shall I understand what I see, or will it remain an external bewildering show? In the dead of night we reached the empty station, and our noisy motors panted through the sleeping streets. From my window, when I arrived, I looked out across the Neva to the fortress of Peter and Paul. The river gleamed in the early northern dawn; the scene was beautiful beyond all words, magical, eternal, suggestive of ancient wisdom. 'It is wonderful', I said to the Bolshevik who stood beside me. 'Yes,' he replied, 'Peter and Paul is now not a prison, but the Army Headquarters.'

I shook myself. 'Come, my friend,' I thought, 'you are not here as a tourist, to sentimentalize over sunrises and sunsets and buildings starred by Baedeker; you are here as a social investigator, to study economic and political facts. Come out of your dream, forget the eternal things. The men you have come among would tell you they are only the fancies of a bourgeois with too much leisure, and can you be sure they are anything more?' So I came back into the conversation, and tried to learn the mechanism for buying an umbrella at the Soviet Stores, which proved as difficult as fathoming the ultimate mysteries.

The twelve hours that I have so far spent on Russian soil have chiefly afforded material for the imp of irony. I came prepared for physical hardship, discomfort, dirt, and hunger, to be made bearable by an atmosphere of splendid hope for mankind. Our communist comrades, no doubt rightly, have not judged us worthy of such treatment. Since crossing the frontier yesterday afternoon, I have made two feasts and a good breakfast, several first-class cigars, and a night in a sumptuous bedroom of a palace where all the luxury of the *ancien régime* has been preserved. At the stations on the way, regiments of soldiers filled the platform, and the plebs was kept carefully out of sight. It seems I am to live amid the pomp surrounding the government of a great military Empire. So I must readjust my mood. Cynicism is called for, but I am strongly moved, and find cynicism difficult. I come back eternally to the same question: What is the secret of this passionate country? Do the Bolsheviks know its secret? Do they even suspect that it has a secret? I wonder.

3

Petrograd,
May 13, 1920

This is a strange world into which I have come, a world of dying beauty and harsh life. I am troubled at every moment by fundamental questions, the terrible insoluble questions that wise men never ask. Empty palaces and full eating-houses, ancient splendours destroyed, or mummified in museums, while the sprawling self-confidence of returned Americanized refugees spreads throughout the city. Everything is to be systematic: there is to be organization and distributive justice. The same education for all, the same clothes for all, the same kind of houses for all, the same books for all, and the same creed for all—it is very just, and leaves no room for envy, except of the fortunate victims of injustice in other countries.

And then I begin upon the other side of the argument. I remember Dostoevski's *Crime and Punishment*, Gorki's *In the World*, Tolstoy's *Resurrection*. I reflect upon the destruction and cruelty upon which the ancient splendour was built: the poverty, drunkenness, prostitution, in which life and health were uselessly wasted; I think of all the lovers of freedom who suffered in Peter and Paul; I remember the knoutings and pogroms and massacres. By hatred of the old, I become tolerant of the new, but I cannot like the new on its own account.

Yet I reproach myself for not liking it. It has all the characteristics of vigorous beginnings. It is ugly and brutal, but full of constructive energy and faith in the value of what it is creating. In creating a new machinery for social life, it has no time to think of anything beyond machinery. When the body of the new society has been built, there will be time enough to think about giving it a soul—at least, so I am assured. 'We have no time for a new art or a new religion', they tell me with a certain impatience. I wonder whether it is possible to build a body first, and then afterwards inject the requisite amount of soul. Perhaps—but I doubt it.

I do not find any theoretical answer to these questions, but my feelings answer with terrible insistence. I am infinitely unhappy in this atmosphere—stifled by its utilitarianism, its indifference to love and beauty and the life of impulse. I cannot give that importance to man's merely animal needs that is given here by those in power. No doubt that is because I have not spent half my life in hunger and want, as many of them have. But do hunger and want necessarily bring wisdom? Do they make men more, or less, capable of conceiving the ideal society that should be the inspiration of every reformer? I cannot avoid the belief that they narrow the horizon more than they enlarge it. But an uneasy doubt remains, and I am torn in two. . . .

4

On the Volga,
June 2, 1920.

Our boat travels on, day after day, through an unknown and mysterious land. Our company are noisy, gay, quarrelsome, full of facile theories, with glib explanations of everything, persuaded that there is nothing they cannot understand and no human destiny outside the purview of their system. One of us lies at death's door,[1] fighting a grim battle with weakness and terror and the indifference of the strong, assailed day and night by the sounds of loud-voiced love-making and trivial laughter. And all around us lies a great silence, strong as Death, unfathomable as the heavens. It seems that none have leisure to hear the silence, yet it calls to me so insistently that I grow deaf to the harangues of propagandists and the endless information of the well-informed.

Last night, very late, our boat stopped in a desolate spot where there were no houses, but only a great sandbank, and beyond it a row of poplars with the rising moon behind them. In silence I went ashore, and found on the sand a strange assemblage of human beings, half-nomads, wandering from some remote region of famine, each family huddled together surrounded by all its belongings, some sleeping, others silently making small fires of twigs. The flickering flames lighted up

[1] Clifford Allen.

gnarled bearded faces of wild men, strong patient primitive women, and children as sedate and slow as their parents. Human beings they undoubtedly were, and yet it would have been far easier for me to grow intimate with a dog or a cat or a horse than with one of them. I knew that they would wait there day after day, perhaps for weeks, until a boat came in which they could go to some distant place where they had heard—falsely perhaps—that the earth was more generous than in the country they had left. Some would die by the way, all would suffer hunger and thirst and the scorching midday sun, but their sufferings would be dumb. To me they seemed to typify the very soul of Russia, unexpressive, inactive from despair, unheeded by the little set of westernizers who make up all the parties of progress or reaction. Russia is so vast that the articulate few are lost in it as man and his planet are lost in interstellar space. It is possible, I thought, that the theorists may increase the misery of the many by trying to force them into actions contrary to their primeval instincts, but I could not believe that happiness was to be brought to them by a gospel of industrialism and forced labour.

Nevertheless, when morning came, I resumed the interminable discussions of the materialistic conception of history and the merits of a truly popular government. Those with whom I discussed had not seen the sleeping wanderers, and would not have been interested if they had seen them, since they were not material for propaganda. But something of that patient silence had communicated itself to me, something lonely and unspoken remained in my heart through all the comfortable familiar intellectual talk. And at last I began to feel that all politics are inspired by a grinning devil, teaching the energetic and quick-witted to torture submissive populations for the profit of pocket or power or theory. As we journeyed on, fed by food extracted from the peasants, protected by an army recruited from among their sons, I wondered what we had to give them in return. But I found no answer. From time to time I heard their sad songs or the haunting music of the balalaika; but the sound mingled with the great silence of the steppes, and left me with a terrible questioning pain in which occidental hopefulness grew pale.

Sverdlov, the Minister of Transport (as we should call him), who was with us on the steamer on the Volga, was extraordinarily kind and helpful about Allen's illness. We came back on the boat as far as Saratov, and from there to Reval, we travelled all the way in the carriage that had belonged to the Czar's daughters, so that Allen did not have to be moved at any stage. If one might judge from the carriage, some of their habits must have been curious. There was a luxurious sofa of which the seat lifted up, and one then discovered three holes in a row suitable for sanitary purposes. At Moscow on the way home Haden Guest and I had a furious quarrel with Chicherin because he would not allow Allen to leave Moscow until he had been examined by two Soviet doctors, and at first he said that he could not get the Soviet doctors to see him for another two days. At the height of the quarrel, on a staircase, I indulged in a shouting match because Chicherin had been a friend of my Uncle Rollo and I had hopes of him. I shouted that I should denounce him as a murderer. It seemed to us and to Allen vital to get him out of Russia as soon as possible, and we felt that this order to wait for Soviet doctors would endanger his life. At last a compromise was effected by which the doctors saw him at once. One of them was called Popoff; the name of the other I have forgotten. The Soviet Government thought that Allen was friendly to them and that Guest and Mrs Snowden and I were anxious he should die so as to suppress his testimony in their favour.

At Reval I met by accident Mrs Stan Harding, whom I had not known before. She was going into Russia filled with enthusiasm for the Bolsheviks. I did what I could to disenchant her, but without success. As soon as she arrived they clapped her into gaol, and kept her there for eight months. She was finally liberated on the insistent demand of the British Government. The fault, however, lay not so much with the Soviet Government as with a certain Mrs Harrison. Mrs Harrison was an American lady of good family who was with us on the Volga. She was in obvious terror and longing to escape from Russia, but the Bolsheviks kept her under very close observation. There was a spy named Axionev, whom they had taken over from the *ancien régime*, who watched her every movement and listened to her every word. He had a long beard and a melancholy expression, and wrote decadent French verse with great skill. On the night-train he shared a compartment with her; on the boat whenever anybody spoke with her he would creep behind silently. He had extraordinary skill in the art of creeping. I felt sorry for the poor lady, but my sorrow was misplaced. She was an American spy, employed also by the British. The Russians discovered that she was a spy, and spared her life on condition that she became a spy for them. But she sabotaged her work for them, denouncing their friends and letting their enemies go free. Mrs Harding knew that she was a spy, and therefore had to be put away quickly. This was the reason of her denouncing Mrs Harding to the Soviet authorities. Nevertheless, she was a charming woman, and nursed Allen during his illness with more skill and devotion than was shown by his old friends. When the facts about her subsequently came to light, Allen steadfastly refused to hear a word against her.

Lenin, with whom I had an hour's conversation, rather disappointed me. I do not think that I should have guessed him to be a great man, but in the course of our conversation I was chiefly conscious of his intellectual limitations, and his rather narrow Marxian orthodoxy, as well as a distinct vein of impish cruelty. I have told of this interview, as well as of my adventures in Russia, in my book *Practice and Theory of Bolshevism*.

There was at that time no communication with Russia either by letter or telegram, owing to the blockade. But as soon as I reached Reval I began telegraphing to Dora. To my surprise, I got no reply. At last, when I was in Stockholm, I telegraphed to friends of hers in Paris, asking where she was, and received the answer that when last heard of she was in Stockholm. I supposed she had come to meet me, but after waiting twenty-four hours in the expectation of seeing her, I met by chance a Finn who informed me that she had gone to Russia, via the North Cape. I realized that this was a move in our long-drawn-out quarrel on the subject of Russia, but I was desperately worried for fear they would put her in prison, as they would not know why she had come. There was nothing one could do about it, so I came back to England, where I endeavoured to recover some kind of sanity, the shock of Russia having been almost more than I could bear. After a time, I began to get letters from Dora, brought out of Russia by friends, and to my great surprise she liked Russia just as much as I had hated it. I wondered whether we should ever be able to overcome this difference. However, among the letters which I found waiting for me when I got back to England, was one from China inviting me to go there for a year to lecture on behalf of the Chinese Lecture Association, a purely Chinese body which aimed at importing one eminent foreigner each year, and had in the previous year imported Dr Dewey. I decided that I would accept if Dora would come with me, but not otherwise. The difficulty was to put the matter before her, in view of the blockade. I knew a Quaker at Reval, named Arthur Watts, who frequently had to go into Russia in connection with Quaker relief, so I sent him a telegram costing several pounds, explaining the circumstances and asking him to find Dora if he could, and put the matter before her. By a stroke of luck this all worked out. If we were to go, it was necessary that she should return at once, and the Bolsheviks at first supposed that I was playing a practical joke. In the end, however, she managed.

We met at Fenchurch Street on a Sunday, and at first we were almost hostile strangers to each other. She regarded my objections to the Bolsheviks as bourgeois and senile and sentimental. I regarded her love of them with bewildered horror. She had met men in Russia whose attitude seemed to her in every way superior to mine. I had been finding the same consolation with Colette as I used to find during the War. In spite of all this, we found ourselves taking all the necessary steps required for going off together for a year in China. Some force stronger than words, or even than our conscious thoughts, kept us together, so that in action neither of us wavered for a moment. We had to work literally night and day. From the time of her arrival to the time of our departure for China was only five days. It was necessary to buy clothes, to get passports in order, to say goodbye to friends and relations, in addition to all the usual bustle of a long journey; and as I wished to be divorced while in China, it was necessary to spend the nights in official adultery. The detectives were so stupid that this had to be done again and again. At last, however, everything was in order. Dora, with her usual skill, had so won over her parents that they came to Victoria to see us off just as if we had been married. This in spite of the fact that they were completely and entirely conventional. As the train began to move out of Victoria, the nightmares and complications and troubles of recent months dropped off, and a completely new chapter began.

LETTERS

From J. E. Littlewood

> Trinity College
> Cambridge
> [1919]

Dear Russell

Einstein's theory is completely confirmed. The predicted displacement was $1''\cdot72$ and the observed $1''\cdot75 \pm \cdot06$.

> *Yours*
> *J.E.L.*

From Harold J. Laski

> Harvard University
> Cambridge
> August 29, 1919

Dear Mr Russell

I wish I knew how to thank you at all adequately for your letter. When I had finished that book I felt that I cared more for what you and Mr Justice Holmes thought about it than for the opinion of any two living men; and to have you not merely think it worth while, but agree with it is a very big thing to me. So that if I merely thank you abruptly you will realise that it is not from any want of warmth.

I have ventured to send you my first book, which has probably all the vices of the book one writes at twenty-three; but you may be interested in the first chapter and the appendices. And if you'll allow me to, I'd like to send you some more technical papers of mine. But I don't want you to be bothered by their presence, and allow them to interfere with your work.

My interest in liberal Catholicism really dates from 1913 when I read Figgis' *Churches in the Modern State* at Oxford; and while I was writing my first book I came to see that, historically, the church and the State have changed places since the Reformation and that all the evils of unified ecclesiastical control are slowly becoming the technique of the modern State—if they have not already become so: it then struck me that the evil of this sovereignty could be shown fairly easily in the sphere of religion in its state-connection where men might still hesitate to admit it in the economic sphere. The second book tried to bridge the gap; and the book I'm trying now to write is really an attempt to explain the general problem of freedom in institutional terms. If by any lucky chance you have time to write I'd greatly like to send you its plan and have your opinion on it.

There is a more private thing about which I would like you to know in case you think there is a chance that you can help. I know from your *Introduction to Mathematical Logic* that you think well of Sheffer who is at present in the Philosophy Department here. I don't know if you have any personal acquaintance with him. He is a jew and he has married someone of whom the University does not approve; moreover he hasn't the social qualities that Harvard so highly prizes. The result is that most of his department is engaged on a determined effort to bring his career here to an end. Hoernle, who is at present its chairman, is certain that if someone can explain that Sheffer is worth while the talk against him would cease; and he's finished a paper on some aspect of mathematical logic that he himself feels will give him a big standing when it can get published. Myself I think that the whole thing is a combination of anti-semitism and that curious university worship of social prestige which plays so large a part over here. Do you know anyone at Harvard well enough to say (if you so think) that Sheffer ought to have a chance? Of course I write this entirely on my own responsibility but I'm very certain that if Lowell could know your opinion of Sheffer it would make a big difference to his future. And if he left here I think he would find it very difficult to get another post. Please forgive me for bothering you with these details.

I shall wait with immense eagerness for the *Nation*. I owe Massingham many debts; but none so great as this.

> Believe me
> *Yours very sincerely*
> Harold J. Laski

From this time onward I used to send periodical cables to President Lowell, explaining that Sheffer was a man of the highest ability and that Harvard would be eternally disgraced if it dismissed him either because he was a Jew or because it disliked his wife. Fortunately these cables just succeeded in their object.

Harvard University
Cambridge
September 29, 1919

Dear Mr Russell

Thank you heartily for your letter. I am sending you some semi-legal papers and a more general one on administration. The book I ventured to send you earlier. I am very grateful for your kindness in wanting them.

And I am still more grateful for your word on Sheffer. I have given it to Hoernle who will show it to the members of the Philosophy Department and, if necessary, to Lowell. And I have sent copies to two members of the Corporation who will fight if there is need. I don't think there is anything further to be done at the moment. It would do no good to write to Perry. These last years, particularly twelve months in the War Department of the U.S. have made him very conservative and an eager adherent of 'correct form'. He is the head and centre of the enemy forces and I see no good in trying to move him directly. He wants respectable neo-Christians in the Department who will explain the necessity of ecclesiastical sanctions; or, if they are not religious, at least they must be materially successful. I don't think universities are ever destined to be homes of liberalism; and the American system is in the hands of big business and dominated by its grosser ideals. Did you ever read Veblen's *Higher Learning in America*?

You may be interested to know that I have a graduate class at Yale this term reading *Roads to Freedom*. I've never met Yale men before; but it was absorbingly interesting to see their amazement that Marx and Bakunin and the rest could be written of without abuse. Which reminds me that in any new edition of that book I wish you would say a good word for Proudhon! I think his *Du Principe Fédératif* and his *Justice Dans La Révolution* are two very great books.

And may I have a photograph with your name on it to hang in my study. That would be an act of genuine nobility on your part.

Yours very sincerely
Harold J. Laski

Harvard University
Cambridge
November 2 1919

Dear Mr Russell

Many thanks for the photograph. Even if it is bad, it gives a basis to the imagination and that's what I wanted.

The matter with Perry is the war. He got converted to conscription, was at Washington with the educational(!) section of the War Office and became officialised. The result is that he looks aslant at all outside the 'correct' things much as a staff major who saw life from Whitehall and the Army and Navy Club. He still means well—all New Englanders do; but he has lost hold of Plato's distinction between willing what is right and knowing what it is right to will. I think he might be turned on Sheffer's side if Sheffer would get his paper out amid the applause of you and Whitehead and Lewis; but Sheffer is a finnicky little fellow and publication halts on his whims and fancies. I haven't given up hope, but I don't dare to hope greatly.

Yale is really interesting, or perhaps all youth, when one is twenty-six, is interesting. I find that when one presents the student-mind with syndicalism or socialism namelessly they take it as reasonable and obvious; attach the name and they whisper to the parents that nameless abominations are being perpetrated. I spoke for the striking police here the other day—one of those strikes which makes one equally wonder at the endurance of the men and the unimaginative stupidity of the officials. Within a week two papers and two hundred alumni demanded my dismissal—teaching sovietism was what urging that men who get $1100 and work 73 hours are justified in striking after 13 years agitation was called. As it happens Lowell does believe in freedom of speech, so that I stay; but you get some index to the present American state of mind.

> *Yours very sincerely*
> Harold J. Laski

> Harvard University
> Cambridge
> December 4 1919

Dear Mr Russell

Hoernle tells me that Sheffer's paper is on its way to you. May I tell you how the position stands? Hocking and Hoernle definitely fight for his re-appointment. Perry wavers on account of Huntingdon's emphatic praise of Sheffer's work and says his decision will depend most largely on what you and Moore of Chicago feel. So if you do approve of it, the more emphatic your telegram the more helpful it will be. There is a real fighting chance at the moment.

Things here are in a terrible mess. Injunctions violating specific government promises; arrest of the miners' leaders because the men refused to go back; recommendation of stringent legislation against 'reds'; arrest of men in the West for simple possession of an I.W.W. card; argument by even moderates like Eliot that the issue is a straight fight between labor and constitutional government; all these are in the ordinary course of events. And neither Pound nor I think the crest of the wave has been reached. Some papers have actually demanded that the Yale University Press withdraw my books from circulation because they preach 'anarchy'. On the other hand Holmes and Brandeis wrote (through Holmes) a magnificent dissent in defence of freedom of speech in an espionage act case. I've sent the two opinions to Massingham and suggested that he show them to you.

This sounds very gloomy; but since America exported Lady Astor to England there's an entire absence of political comedy.

> *Yours very sincerely*
> Harold J. Laski

[*Plus ça change.*]

> Harvard University
> Cambridge
> January 5, 1919 [1920]

Dear Mr Russell

It was splendid to have your telegram about Sheffer's paper. I am afraid we are fighting a lost battle as it looks as if Hoernle will go to Yale, which means the withdrawal of our main support. Harvard is determined to be socially respectable at all costs. I have recently been interviewed by the Board of Overseers to know (a) whether I believe in a revolution with blood (b) whether I believe in the Soviet form of government (c) whether I do not believe that the American form of government is superior to any other (d) whether I believe in the right of revolution.

In the last three days they have arrested five thousand socialists with a view to deportation. I feel glad that Graham Wallas is going to try and get me home!

Yours very sincerely
Harold J. Laski

Harvard University
Cambridge
February 18th, 1920

Dear Mr Russell

Above all, warm congratulations on your return to Cambridge. That sounds like a real return of general sanity. I hope you will not confine your lectures to mathematical logic. . . .

I sent you the other day a volume of Duguit's my wife and I translated last year; I hope you will find time to glance at it. I am very eager to get away from this country, as you guessed, but rather baffled as to how to do it. I see no hope in Oxford and I know no one at all in Cambridge. Wallas is trying to do something for me in London, but I don't know with what success. I am heartily sick of America and I would like to have an atmosphere again where an ox does not tread upon the tongue.

Yours very sincerely
Harold Laski

16, Warwick Gardens
[London] W.14
2.1.22

Dear Russell

This enclosure formally. Informally let me quote from Rivers: We asked him to stand as the labour candidate for London. This is part of his reply. 'I think that a distinct factor in my decision has been *The Analysis of Mind* which I have now read really carefully. It is a great book, and makes me marvel at his intellect. It has raised all kinds of problems with which I should like to deal, and I certainly should not be able to do so if I entered on a political life. κτλ.'

What about Rivers, Joad, Delisle Burns, Clifford Allen as the nucleus of our new utilitarians?

Yours
H. J. Laski

115

From Ludwig Wittgenstein
[a postcard]

Cassino
Provincia Caserta
Italy
9.2.19

Dear Russell

I don't know your precise address but hope these lines will reach you somehow. I am prisoner in Italy since November and hope I may communicate with you after a three years interruption. I have done lots of logikal work which I am dying to let you know before publishing it.

Ever yours
Ludwig Wittgenstein

[Postcard]

Cassino
10.3.19

You cann't immagine how glad I was to get your cards! I am affraid though there is no hope that we may meet before long. Unless you came to see me here, but this would be too much joy for me. I cann't write on Logic as I'm not allowed to write more than 2 Cards (15 lines each) a week. I've written a book which will be published as soon as I get home. I think I have solved our problems finaly. Write to me often. It will shorten my prison. God bless you.

Ever yours
Wittgenstein

13.3.19

Dear Russell

Thanks so much for your postcards dated 2nd and 3rd of March. I've had a *very* bad time, not knowing wether you were dead or alive! I cann't write on Logic as I'm not allowed to write more than two p.cs. a week (15 lines each). This letter is an ecception, it's posted by an Austrian medical student who goes home tomorrow. I've written a book called *Logisch-Philosophische Abhandlung* containing all my work of the last 6 years. I believe I've solved our problems finally. This may sound arrogant but I cann't help believing it. I finished the book in August 1918 and two months after was made Prigioniere. I've got the manuscript here with me. I wish I could copy it out for you; but it's pretty long and I would have no safe way of sending it to you. In fact you would not understand it without a previous explanation as it's written in quite short remarks. (This of cours means that *nobody* will understand it; allthough I believe it's all as clear as crystall. But it upsets all our theory of truth, of classes, of numbers and all the rest.) I will publish it as soon as I get home. Now I'm affraid this *won't* be 'before long'. And consequently it will be a long time yet till we can meet. I can hardly immagine

116

seeing you again! It will be too much! I supose it would be impossible for you to come and see me here? Or perhaps you think it's collossal cheek of me even to think of such a thing. But if you were on the other end of the world and I *could* come to you I would do it.

Please write to me how you are, remember me to Dr Whitehead. Is old Johnson still alive? Think of me often!

Ever yours
Ludwig Wittgenstein

[Cassino
12.6.19]

Lieber Russell!

Vor einigen Tagen schickte ich Dir mein Manuskript durch Keynes's Vermittelung. Ich schrieb damals nur ein paar Zeilen fuer Dich hinein. Seither ist nun Dein Buch ganz in meine Haende gelangt und nun haette ich ein grosses Beduerfnis Dir einiges zu schreiben.—Ich haette nicht geglaubt, dass das, was ich vor 6 Jahren in Norwegen dem Moore diktierte an Dir so spurlos voruebergehen wuerde. Kurz ich fuerchte jetzt, es moechte sehr schwer fuer mich sein mich mit Dir zu verstaendigen. Und der geringe Rest von Hoffnung mein Manuskript koenne Dir etwas sagen, ist ganz verschwunden. Einen Komentar zu meinem Buch zu schreiben, bin ich wie Du Dir denken kannst, nicht im Stande. Nur muendlich koennte ich Dir einen geben. Ist Dir irgend an dem Verstaendnis der Sache etwas gelegen und kannst Du ein Zusammentreffen mit mir bewerkstelligen, so, bitte, tue es.—Ist dies nicht moeglich, so sei so gut und schicke das Manuskript so bald Du es gelesen hast auf sicherem Wege nach Wien zurueck. Es ist das einzige korrigierte Exemplar, welches ich besitze und die Arbeit meines Lebens! Mehr als je brenne ich jetzt darauf es gedruckt zu sehen. Es ist bitter, das vollendete Werk in der Gefangenschaft herumschleppen zu muessen und zu sehen, wir der Unsinn draussen sein Spiel treibt! Und ebenso bitter ist es zu denken dass niemand es verstehen wird, auch wenn es gedruckt sein wird!—Hast Du mir jemals seit Deinen zwei ersten Karten geschrieben? Ich habe nichts erhalten.

Sei herzlichst gegruesst und glaube nicht, dass alles Dummheit ist was Du nicht verstehen wirst.

Dein treuer
Ludwig Wittgenstein

[This and the following translations of Wittgenstein's letters in German are by B. F. McGuinness.]

[Cassino
12.6.19]

Dear Russell

Some days ago I sent you my manuscript, through Keynes's good offices. I enclosed only a couple of lines for you at the time. Since then your book has arrived here safely and I now feel a great need to write you a number of things.—I should never have believed that what I dictated to Moore in Norway six years ago would pass over you so completely without trace. In short, I am afraid it might be very difficult for me to reach an understanding with you. And my small remaining hope that my manuscript would convey something to you has now quite vanished. Writing a commentary on my book is out of the question for me, as you can imagine. I could only give you an oral one. If you attach any importance whatsoever to understanding the thing, and if you can arrange a meeting with me, please do so.—If that is impossible, then be so good as to send the manuscript back to Vienna by a safe route as soon as you have read it. It is the only corrected copy I possess and it is my life's work! I long to see it in print, *now* more than ever. It is bitter to have to lug the completed work around with me in captivity and to see nonsense rampant in the world outside. And it is just as bitter to think that no one will understand it even if it is printed!—Have you written to me at all since your first two cards? I have received nothing. Kindest regards, and *don't suppose that everything that you won't be able to understand is a piece of stupidity!*

Yours ever
Ludwig Wittgenstein

Cassino
19.8.1919

Dear Russell

Thanks so much for your letter dated 13 August. As to your queries, I cann't answer them *now*. For firstly I don't know allways what the numbers refer to, having no copy of the M.S. here. Secondly some of your questions want a very lengthy answer and you know how difficult it is for me to write on logic. That's also the reason why my book is so short, and consequently so obscure. But that I cann't help.—Now I'm affraid you haven't realy got hold of my main contention, to which the whole business of logical props is only a corolary. The main point is the theory of what can be expressed (*gesagt*) by props—i.e. by linguage—(and, which comes to the same, what can be *thought*) and what can not be expressed by props, but only shown (*gezeigt*); which, I believe, is the cardinal problem of philosophy.—

I also sent my M.S. to Frege. He wrote to me a week ago and I gather that he doesn't understand a word of it all. So my only hope is to see *you* soon and explain all to you, for it is *very* hard not to be understood by a single sole!

Now the day after tomorrow we shall probably leave the campo concentramento and go home. Thank God!—But how can we meet as soon as possible. I should like to come to England, but you can imagine that it's rather awkward for a German to travel to England now. (By far more so, than for an Englishman to travel to Germany) But in fact I didn't think of asking you to come to Vienna now, but it would seem to me the best thing to meet in Holland or Svitserland. Of cors, if you cann't come abroad I will do my best to get to England. Please write to me as soon as possible about this point, letting me know when you are likely to get the permission of coming abroad. Please write to Vienna IV Alleegasse 16. As to my M.S., please send it to the same address; but only if there is an absolutely safe way of sending it. Otherwise please keep it. I should be very glad though, to get it soon, as it's the only corrected coppy I've got.—My mother wrote to me, she was very sorry not to have got your letter, but glad that you tried to write to her at all.

Now write soon. Best wishes.

Ever *yours*
Ludwig Wittgenstein

118

P.S. After having finished my letter I feel tempted after all to answer some of your simpler points. . . .[1]

20.9.20

Lieber Russell!

Dank' Dir fuer Deinen lieben Brief! Ich habe jetzt eine Anstellung bekommen; und zwar als Volksschullehrer in einem der kleinsten Doerfer; es heisst Trattenbach ung liegt 4 Stunden suedlich von Wien im Gebirge. Es duerfte wohl das erste mal sein, dass der Volksschullehrer von Trattenbach mit einem Universitaetsprofessor in Peking korrespondiert. Wie geht es Dir und was traegst Du vor? Philosophie? Dann wollte ich, ich koennte zuhoeren und dann mit Dir streiten. Ich war bis vor kurzem schrecklich bedrueckt und lebensmuede, jetzt aber bin ich etwas hoffnungsvoller und jetzt hoffe ich auch, dass wir uns wiedersehen werden.

Gott mit Dir! Und sei herzlichst gegruesst

von Deinem treuen
Ludwig Wittgenstein

20.9.20

Dear Russell

Thank you for your kind letter. I have now obtained a position: I am to be an elementary-school teacher in a tiny village called Trattenbach. It's in the mountains, about four hours' journey south of Vienna. It must be the first time that the schoolmaster at Trattenbach has ever corresponded with a professor in Peking. How are you? And what are you lecturing on? Philosophy? If so, I wish I could be there and could argue with you afterwards. A short while ago I was *terribly depressed* and tired of living, but now I am slightly more hopeful, and one of the things I hope is that we'll meet again.

God be with you! Kindest regards.

Yours ever
Ludwig Wittgenstein

[Trattenbach]
23.10.21

Lieber Russell!

Verzeih, dass ich Dir erst jetzt auf Deinen Brief aus China antworte. Ich habe ihn sehr verspaetet erhalten. Er traf mich nicht in Trattenbach und wurde mir an verschiedene Orte nachgeschickt, ohne mich zu erreichen.—Es tut mir sehr leid, dass Du krank warst; und gar schwer! Wie geht es denn jetzt?! Bei mir hat sich nichts veraendert. Ich bin noch immer in Trattenbach und bin nach wie vor von Gehaessigkeit und Gemeinheit umgeben. Es ist wahr, dass die Menschen im Durchschnitt nirgends sehr viel wert sind; aber hier sind sie viel mehr als anderswo nichtsnutzig und unverantwortlich. Ich werde vielleicht noch dieses Jahr in Trattenbach bleiben, aber laenger wohl nicht, da ich mich hier auch mit den uebrigen Lehrern nicht gut vertrage. (Vielleicht wird das wo anders auch nicht besser sein.) Ja,

---

[1]The postcript to this letter has been omitted because of its technical nature. It can be found in Wittgenstein's *Notebooks 1914–1916*, pp. 129–130.

das waere schoen, wenn Du mich einmal besuchen wolltest! Ich bin froh zu hoeren, dass mein Manuskript in Sicherheit ist. Wenn es gedruckt wird, wird's mir auch recht sein.—

Schreib mir bald ein paar Zeilen, wie es Dir geht, etc. etc.

Sei herzlich gegruesst

von Deinem treuen
Ludwig Wittgenstein

Empfiehl mich der Miss Black.

[Trattenbach]
23.10.21

Dear Russell

Forgive me for only now answering your letter from China. I got it after a very long delay. I wasn't in Trattenbach when it arrived and it was forwarded to several places before it reached me.—I am very sorry that you have been ill—and seriously ill! *How are you now, then?* As regards me, nothing has changed. I am still at Trattenbach, surrounded, as ever, by odiousness and baseness. I know that human beings on the average are not worth much anywhere, but here they are much more good-for-nothing and irresponsible than elsewhere. I will perhaps stay on in Trattenbach for the present year but probably not any longer, because I don't get on well here even with the other teachers (perhaps that won't be any better in another place). Yes, it would be nice indeed, if you would visit me sometime. I am glad to hear that my manuscript is in safety. And if it's printed, that will suit me too.—

Write me a few lines soon, to say how you are, etc. etc.

Kindest regards
Yours ever
Ludwig Wittgenstein

Remember me to Miss Black.

[Trattenbach]
28.11.21

Lieber Russell!

Dank Dir vielmals fuer Deinen lieben Brief. Ehrlich gestanden: es freut mich, dass mein Zeug gedruckt wird. Wenn auch der Ostwald ein Erzscharlatan ist! Wenn er es nur nicht verstuemmelt! Liest Du die Korrekturen? Dann bitte sei so lieb und gib acht, dass er es genau so druckt, wie es bei mir steht. Ich traue dem Ostwald zu, dass er die Arbeit nach seinem Geschmack, etwa nach seiner bloed-sinnigen Orthographie, veraendert. Am liebsten ist es mir, dass die Sache in England erscheint. Moege sie der vielen Muehe die Du und andere mit ihr hatten wuerdig sein!—

Du hast recht: nicht die Trattenbacher allein sind schlechter, als alle uebrigen Menschen; wohl aber ist Trattenbach ein besonders minderwertiger Ort in Oester-reich und die Oesterreicher sind—seit dem Kreig—bodenlos tief gesunken, dass es zu traurig ist, davon zu reden! So ist es.—Wenn Du diese Zeilen kriegst, ist vielleicht schon Dein Kind auf dieser merkwuerdigen Welt. Also: ich gratuliere Dir und Deiner Frau herzlichst. Verzeih, dass ich so lange nicht geschrieben habe; auch ich bin etwas kraenklich und riesig beschaeftigt. Bitte schreibe wieder einmal wenn Du Zeit hast. Von Ostwald habe ich keinen Brief erhalten. Wenn alles gut geht werde ich Dich mit tausend Freuden besuchen!

> *Herzlichste Gruesse*
> *Dein*
> *Ludwig Wittgenstein*

> [Trattenbach]
> 28.11.21

Dear Russell

Many thanks for you kind letter! I must admit I am pleased that my stuff is going to be printed. Even though Ostwald[1] is an utter charlatan. As long as he doesn't tamper with it! Are you going to read the proofs? If so, please take care that he prints it exactly as I have it. He is quite capable of altering the work to suit his own tastes—putting it into his idiotic spelling, for example. What pleases me most is that the whole thing is going to appear in England. I hope it may be worth all the trouble that you and others have taken with it.

You are right: the Trattenbachers are not uniquely worse than the rest of the human race. But Trattenbach is a particularly insignificant place in Austria and the *Austrians* have sunk so miserably low since the war that it's too dismal to talk about. That's what it is.

By the time you get this letter your child will perhaps already have come into this remarkable world. So: warmest congratulations to you and your wife! Forgive me for not having written to you for so long. I too haven't been very well and I've been tremendously busy. Please write again when you have time. I have not had a letter from Ostwald. If all goes well, I will come and visit you with the greatest of pleasure.

> *Kindest regards*
> *Yours*
> *Ludwig Wittgenstein*

From C. K. Ogden

> The International Library of
> Psychology
> Nov. 5, 1921

Dear Russell

Kegan Paul ask me to give them some formal note for their files with regard to the Wittgenstein rights.

I enclose, with envelope for your convenience, the sort of thing I should like. As they can't drop less than £50 on doing it I think it very satisfactory to have got it accepted—though of course if they did a second edition soon and the price of printing went suddenly down they might get their costs back. I am still a little uneasy about the title and don't want to feel that we decided in a hurry on *Philosophical Logic*. If on second thoughts you are satisfied with it, we can go ahead with that. But you might be able to excogitate alternatives that I could submit.

Moore's Spinoza title which he thought obvious and ideal is no use if you feel Wittgenstein wouldn't like it. I suppose his *sub specie aeterni* in the last sentences of the book made Moore think the contrary, and several Latin quotes. But as a selling title *Philosophical Logic* is better, if it conveys the right impression.

[1]Wilhelm Ostwald, editor of *Annalen der Naturphilosophie*, where the *Tractatus* with my Introduction first appeared in 1921.

Looking rapidly over the off print in the train last night, I was amazed that Nicod and Miss Wrinch had both seemed to make so very little of it. The main lines seem so reasonable and intelligible—apart from the Types puzzles. I know you are frightfully busy just as present, but I should very much like to know why all this account of signs and symbols cannot best be understood in relation to a thoroughgoing causal theory. I mean the sort of thing in the enclosed:—on 'Sign Situations' (= Chapter II of the early Synopsis attached). The whole book which the publishers want to call *The Meaning of Meaning* is now passing through the press; and before it is too late we should like to have discussed it with someone who has seriously considered Watson. Folk here still don't think there is a problem of *Meaning* at all, and though your *Analysis of Mind* has disturbed them, everything still remains rather astrological.

With best wishes for, and love to the family,

Yours sincerely
C. K. Ogden

P.S. On second thoughts, I think that as you would prefer Wittgenstein's German to appear as well as the English, it might help if you added the P.S. I have stuck in, and I will press them further if I can.[1]

To Ottoline Morrell

Hotel Continental
Stockholm
25th June 1920

Dearest O

I have got thus far on my return, but boats are very full and it may be a week before I reach England. I left Allen in a nursing home in Reval, no longer in danger, tho' twice he had been given up by the Doctors. Partly owing to his illness, but more because I loathed the Bolsheviks, the time in Russia was infinitely painful to me, in spite of being one of the most interesting things I have ever done. Bolshevism is a close tyrannical bureaucracy, with a spy system more elaborate and terrible than the Tsar's, and an aristocracy as insolent and unfeeling, composed of Americanised Jews. No vestige of liberty remains, in thought or speech or action. I was stifled and oppressed by the weight of the machine as by a cope of lead. Yet I think it the right government for Russia at this moment. If you ask yourself how Dostoevsky's characters should be governed, you will understand. Yet it is terrible. They are a nation of artists, down to the simplest peasant; the aim of the Bolsheviks is to make them industrial and as Yankee as possible. Imagine yourself governed in every detail by a mixture of Sidney Webb and Rufus Isaacs, and you will have a picture of modern Russia. I went hoping to find the promised land.

All love—I hope I shall see you soon.

Your B.

[1]This note now appears at the beginning of the *Tractatus*.

From Emma Goldman

Mrs E. G. Kerschner
Bei Von Futtkamer
Rudesheimerstr. 3
Wilmersdorf, Berlin
July 8th [1922]

My dear Mr Russell

My niece forwarded your kind letter to her of June 17th. I should have replied earlier, but I was waiting for her arrival, as I wanted to talk the matter over with her.

Thank you very much for your willingness to assist me. I daresay you will meet with very great difficulties. I understand that the British Foreign Office refused vises to such people as Max Eastman of the *Liberator*, and Lincoln Steffens, the journalist. It is not likely that the Government will be more gracious to me.

I was rather amused at your phrase 'that she will not engage in the more violent forms of Anarchism?' I know, of course, that it has been my reputation that I indulged in such forms, but it has never been borne out by the facts. However, I should not want to gain my right of asylum in England or any country by pledging to abstain from the expression of my ideas, or the right to protest against injustice. The Austrian Government offered me asylum if I would sign such a pledge. Naturally, I refused. Life as we live it today is not worth much. I would not feel it was worth anything if I had to forswear what I believe and stand for.

Under these conditions, if it is not too great a burden, I would appreciate any efforts made in my behalf which would give me the right to come to England. For the present I will probably get an extension of my vise in Germany because I have had an offer to write a book on Russia from Harper Bros. of New York.

No, the Bolsheviki did not compel me to leave Russia. Much to my surprise they gave me passports. They have however made it difficult for me to obtain vises from other countries. Naturally they can not endure the criticism contained in the ten articles I wrote for the *New York World*, in April last, after leaving Russia.

Very sincerely yours
Emma Goldman

Emma Goldman did at last acquire permission to come to England. A dinner was given in her honour at which I was present. When she rose to speak, she was welcomed enthusiastically; but when she sat down, there was dead silence. This was because almost the whole of her speech was against the Bolsheviks.

CHAPTER III

CHINA

WE TRAVELLED to China from Marseilles in a French boat called *Portos*. Just before we left London, we learned that, owing to a case of plague on board, the sailing would be delayed for three weeks. We did not feel, however, that we could go through all the business of saying goodbye a second time, so we went to Paris and spent the three weeks there. During this time I finished my book on Russia, and decided, after much hesitation, that I would publish it. To say anything against Bolshevism was, of course, to play into the hands of reaction, and most of my friends took the view that one ought not to say what one thought about Russia unless what one thought was favourable. I had, however, been impervious to similar arguments from patriots during the War, and it seemed to me that in the long run no good purpose would be served by holding one's tongue. The matter was, of course, much complicated for me by the question of my personal relations with Dora. One hot summer night, after she had gone to sleep, I got up and sat on the balcony of our room and contemplated the stars. I tried to see the question without the heat of party passion and imagined myself holding a conversation with Cassiopeia. It seemed to me that I should be more in harmony with the stars if I published what I thought about Bolshevism than if I did not. So I went on with the work and finished the book on the night before we started for Marseilles.

The bulk of our time in Paris, however, was spent in a more frivolous manner, buying frocks suitable for the Red Sea, and the rest of the trousseau required for unofficial marriage. After a few days in Paris, all the appearance of estrangement which had existed between us ceased, and we became gay and light-hearted. There were, however, moments on the boat when things were difficult. I was sensitive because of the contempt that Dora had poured on my head for not liking Russia. I suggested to her that we had made a mistake in coming away together, and that the best way out would be to jump into the sea. This mood, however, which was largely induced by the heat, soon passed.

The voyage lasted five or six weeks, so that one got to know one's fellow-passengers pretty well. The French people mostly belonged to the official classes. They were much superior to the English, who were rubber planters and business men. There were rows between the English and the French, in which we had to act as mediators. On one occasion the English asked me to give an address about Soviet Russia. In view of the sort of people that they were, I said only favourable things about the Soviet Government, so there was nearly a riot, and when we reached Shanghai our English fellow-passengers sent a telegram to the Consulate General in Peking, urging that we should not be allowed to land. We consoled ourselves with the thought of what had befallen the ring-leader among our enemies at Saigon. There was at Saigon an elephant whose keeper sold bananas which the visitors gave to the elephant. We each gave him a banana, and he made us a very elegant bow, but our enemy refused, whereupon the elephant squirted dirty water all over his immaculate clothes, which also the keeper had taught him to do. Perhaps our amusement at this incident did not increase his love of us.

When we arrived at Shanghai there was at first no-one to meet us. I had had from the first a dark suspicion that the invitation might be a practical joke, and in order to test its genuineness I had got the Chinese to pay my passage money before I started. I thought that few people would spend £125 on a joke, but when nobody appeared at Shanghai our fears revived, and we began to think we might have to creep home with our tails between our legs. It turned out, however, that our friends had only made a little mistake as to the time of the boat's arrival. They soon appeared on board and took us to a Chinese hotel, where we passed three of the most bewildering days that I have ever experienced. There was at first some difficulty in explaining about Dora. They got the impression that she was my wife, and when we said that this was not the case, they were afraid that I should be annoyed about their previous misconception. I told them that I wished her treated as my wife, and they published a statement to that effect in the Chinese papers. From the first moment to the last of our stay in China, every Chinese with whom we came in contact treated her with the most complete and perfect courtesy, and with exactly the same deference as would have been paid to her if she had been in fact my wife. They did this in spite of the fact that we insisted upon her always being called 'Miss Black'.

Our time in Shanghai was spent in seeing endless people, Europeans, Americans, Japanese, and Koreans, as well as Chinese. In general the various people who came to see us were not on speaking terms with each other; for instance, there could be no social relations between the Japanese and the Korean Christians who had been exiled for bomb-throwing. (In Korea at that time a Christian was practically synonymous with a bomb-thrower.) So we had to put our guests at separate tables in the public room, and move round from table to table throughout the day. We had also to attend an enormous banquet, at which various Chinese made after-dinner speeches in the best English style, with exactly the type of joke which is demanded of such an occasion. It was our first experience of the Chinese, and we were somewhat surprised by their wit and fluency. I had not realized until then that a civilized Chinese is the most civilized person in the world. Sun Yat-sen invited me to dinner, but to my lasting regret the evening he suggested was after my departure, and I had to refuse. Shortly after this he went to Canton to inaugurate the nationalist movement which afterwards conquered the whole country, and as I was unable to go to Canton, I never met him.

Our Chinese friends took us for two days to Hangchow to see the Western Lake. The first day we went round it by boat, and the second day in chairs. It was marvellously beautiful, with the beauty of ancient civilization, surpassing even that of Italy. From there we went to Nanking, and from Nanking by boat to Hankow. The days on the Yangtse were as delightful as the days on the Volga had been horrible. From Hankow we went to Changsha, where an educational conference was in progress. They wished us to stay there for a week, and give addresses every day, but we were both exhausted and anxious for a chance to rest, which made us eager to reach Peking. So we refused to stay more than twenty-four hours, in spite of the fact that the Governor of Hunan in person held out every imaginable inducement, including a special train all the way to Wuchang.

However, in order to do my best to conciliate the people of Changsha, I gave four lectures, two after-dinner speeches, and an after-lunch speech, during the twenty-four hours. Changsha was a place without modern hotels, and the missionaries very kindly offered to put us up, but they made it clear that Dora was to stay with one set of missionaries, and I with another. We therefore thought it best to decline their invitation, and stayed at a Chinese hotel. The experience was not altogether pleasant. Armies of bugs walked across the bed all through the night.

The Tuchun[1] gave a magnificent banquet, at which we first met the Deweys, who behaved with great kindness, and later, when I became ill, John Dewey treated us both with singular helpfulness. I was told that when he came to see me in the hospital, he was much touched by my saying, 'We must make a plan for peace' at a time when everything else that I said was delirium. There were about a hundred guests at the Tuchun's banquet. We assembled in one vast hall and then moved into another for the feast, which was sumptuous beyond belief. In the middle of it the Tuchun apologized for the extreme simplicity of the fare, saying that he thought we should like to see how they lived in everyday life

[1] The military Governor of the Province.

rather than to be treated with any pomp. To my intense chagrin, I was unable to think of a retort in kind, but I hope the interpreter made up for my lack of wit. We left Changsha in the middle of a lunar eclipse, and saw bonfires being lit and heard gongs beaten to frighten off the Heavenly Dog, according to the traditional ritual of China on such occasions. From Changsha, we travelled straight through to Peking, where we enjoyed our first wash for ten days.

Our first months in Peking were a time of absolute and complete happiness. All the difficulties and disagreements that we had had were completely forgotten. Our Chinese friends were delightful. The work was interesting, and Peking itself inconceivably beautiful.

We had a house boy, a male cook and a rickshaw boy. The house boy spoke some English and it was through him that we made ourselves intelligible to the others. This process succeeded better than it would have done in England. We engaged the cook sometime before we came to live in our house and told him that the first meal we should want would be dinner some days hence. Sure enough, when the time came, dinner was ready. The house boy knew everything. One day we were in need of change and we had hidden what we believed to be a dollar in an old table. We described its whereabouts to the house boy and asked him to fetch it. He replied imperturbably, 'No, Madam. He bad.' We also had the occasional services of a sewing woman. We engaged her in the winter and dispensed with her services in the summer. We were amused to observe that while, in winter, she had been very fat, as the weather grew warm, she became gradually very thin, having replaced the thick garments of winter gradually by the elegant garments of summer. We had to furnish our house which we did from the very excellent second-hand furniture shops which abounded in Peking. Our Chinese friends could not understand our preferring old Chinese things to modern furniture from Birmingham. We had an official interpreter assigned to look after us. His English was very good and he was especially proud of his ability to make puns in English. His name was Mr Chao and, when I showed him an article that I had written called 'Causes of the Present Chaos', he remarked, 'Well, I suppose, the causes of the present Chaos are the previous Chaos.' I became a close friend of his in the course of our journeys. He was engaged to a Chinese girl and I was able to remove some difficulties that had impeded his marriage. I still hear from him occasionally and once or twice he and his wife have come to see me in England.

I was very busy lecturing, and I also had a seminar of the more advanced students. All of them were Bolsheviks except one, who was the nephew of the Emperor. They used to slip off to Moscow one by one. They were charming youths, ingenuous and intelligent at the same time, eager to know the world and to escape from the trammels of Chinese tradition. Most of them had been betrothed in infancy to old-fashioned girls, and were troubled by the ethical question whether they would be justified in breaking the betrothal to marry some girl of modern education. The gulf between the old China and the new was vast, and family bonds were extraordinarily irksome for the modern-minded young man. Dora used to go to the Girls' Normal School, where those who were to be teachers were being trained. They would put to her every kind of question about marriage, free love, contraception, etc., and she answered all their questions with complete frankness. Nothing of the sort would have been possible in any similar European institution. In spite of their freedom of thought, traditional habits of behaviour had a great hold upon them. We occasionally gave parties to the young men of my seminar and the girls at the Normal School. The girls at first would take refuge in a room to which they supposed no men would penetrate, and they had to be fetched out and encouraged to associate with males. It must be said that when once the ice was broken, no further encouragement was needed.

The National University of Peking for which I lectured was a very remarkable institution. The Chancellor and the Vice-Chancellor were men passionately devoted to the modernizing of China. The Vice-Chancellor was one of the most whole-hearted idealists that I have ever known. The funds which should have gone to pay salaries were always being appropriated by Tuchuns, so that the teaching was mainly a labour of love. The students deserved what their professors had to give them. They were ardently desirous of knowledge, and there was no limit to the sacrifices that they were prepared to make for their country. The atmosphere was electric with the hope of a great awakening. After centuries of slumber, China was becoming aware of the modern world, and at that time the sordidnesses and compromises that go with governmental responsibility had not yet descended upon the reformers. The English sneered at the reformers, and said that China would always be China. They assured me that it was silly to listen to the frothy talk of half-baked young men; yet within a few years those half-baked young men had conquered China and deprived the English of many of their most cherished privileges.

Since the advent of the Communists to power in China, the policy of the British towards that country has been somewhat more enlightened than that of the United States, but until that time the exact opposite was the case. In 1926, on three several occasions, British troops fired on unarmed crowds of Chinese students, killing and wounding many. I wrote a fierce denunciation of these outrages, which was published first in England and then throughout China. An American missionary in China, with whom I corresponded, came to England shortly after this time, and told me that indignation in China had been such as to endanger the lives of all Englishmen living in that country. He even said—though I found this scarcely credible—that the English in China owed their preservation to me, since I had caused infuriated Chinese to conclude that not all Englishmen are vile. However that may be, I incurred the hostility, not only of the English in China, but of the British Government.

White men in China were ignorant of many things that were common knowledge among the Chinese. On one occasion my bank (which was American) gave me notes issued by a French bank, and I found that Chinese tradesmen refused to accept them. My bank expressed astonishment, and gave me other notes instead. Three months later, the French bank went bankrupt, to the surprise of all other white banks in China.

The Englishman in the East, as far as I was able to judge of him, is a man completely out of touch with his environment. He plays polo and goes to his club. He derives his ideas of native culture from the works of eighteenth century missionaries, and he regards intelligence in the East with the same contempt which he feels for intelligence in his own country. Unfortunately for our political sagacity, he overlooks the fact that in the East intelligence is respected, so that enlightened Radicals have an influence upon affairs which is denied to their English counterparts. MacDonald went to Windsor in knee-breeches, but the Chinese reformers showed no such respect to their Emperor, although our monarchy is a mushroom growth of yesterday compared to that of China.

My views as to what should be done in China I put into my book *The Problem of China* and so shall not repeat them here.

In spite of the fact that China was in a ferment, it appeared to us, as compared with Europe, to be a country filled with philosophic calm. Once a week the mail would arrive from England, and the letters and newspapers that came from there seemed to breathe upon us a hot blast of insanity like the fiery heat that comes from a furnace door suddenly opened. As we had to work on Sundays, we made a practice of taking a holiday on Mondays, and we usually spent the whole day in the Temple of Heaven, the most beautiful building that it has ever been my good fortune to see. We would sit in the winter sunshine saying little, gradually absorbing peace, and would come away prepared to face the madness and passion of our own distracted continent with poise and calm. At other times, we used to walk on the walls of Peking. I remember with particular vividness a walk one evening starting at sunset and continuing through the rise of the full moon.

The Chinese have (or had) a sense of humour which I found very congenial. Perhaps communism has killed it, but when I was there they constantly reminded me of the people in their ancient books. One hot day two fat middle-aged business men invited me to motor into the country to see a certain very famous half-ruined pagoda. When we reached it, I climbed the spiral staircase, expecting them to follow, but on arriving at the top I saw them still on the ground. I asked why they had not come up, and with portentous gravity they replied:

'We thought of coming up, and debated whether we should do so. Many weighty arguments were advanced on both sides, but at last there was one which decided us. The pagoda might crumble at any moment, and we felt that, if it did, it would be well there should be those who could bear witness as to how the philosopher died.'

What they meant was that it was hot and they were fat.

Many Chinese have that refinement of humour which consists in enjoying a joke more when the other person cannot see it. As I was leaving Peking a Chinese friend gave me a long classical passage microscopically engraved by hand on a very small surface; he also gave me the same passage written out in exquisite calligraphy. When I asked what it said, he replied: 'Ask Professor Giles when you get home.' I took his advice, and found that it was 'The Consultation of the Wizard', in which the wizard merely advises his clients to do whatever they like. He was poking fun at me because I always refused to give advice to the Chinese as to their immediate political difficulties.

The climate of Peking in winter is very cold. The wind blows almost always from the north, bringing an icy breath from the Mongolian mountains. I got bronchitis, but paid no attention to it. It seemed to get better, and one day, at the invitation of some Chinese friends, we went to a place about two hours by motorcar from Peking, where there were hot springs. The hotel provided a very good tea, and someone suggested that it was unwise to eat too much tea as it would spoil one's dinner. I objected to such prudence on the ground that the Day of Judgment might intervene. I was right, as it was three months before I ate another square meal. After tea, I suddenly began to shiver, and after I had been shivering for an hour or so, we decided that we had better get back to Peking at once. On the way home, our car had a puncture, and by the time the puncture was mended, the engine was cold. By this time, I was nearly delirious, but the Chinese servants and Dora pushed the car to the top of a hill, and on the descent the engine gradually began to work. Owing to the delay, the gates of Peking were shut when we reached them, and it took an hour of telephoning to get them open. By the time we finally got home, I was very ill indeed. Before I had time to realize what was happening, I was delirious. I was moved into a German hospital, where Dora nursed me by day, and the only English professional nurse in Peking nursed me by night. For a fortnight the doctors thought every evening that I should be dead before morning. I remember nothing of this time except a few dreams. When I came out of delirium, I did not know where I was, and did not recognize the nurse. Dora told me that I had been very ill and nearly died, to which I replied: 'How interesting', but I was so weak that I forgot it in five minutes, and she had to tell me again. I could not even remember my own name. But although for about a month after my delirium had ceased they kept telling me I might die at any moment, I never believed a word of it. The nurse whom they had found was rather distinguished in her profession, and had been the Sister in charge of a hospital in Serbia during the War. The whole hospital had been captured by the Germans, and the nurses removed to Bulgaria. She was never tired of telling me how intimate she had become with the Queen of Bulgaria. She was a deeply religious woman, and told me when I began to get better that she had seriously considered whether it was not her duty to let me die. Fortunately, professional training was too strong for her moral sense.

All through the time of my convalescence, in spite of weakness and great physical discomfort, I was exceedingly happy. Dora was very devoted, and her devotion made me forget everything unpleasant. At an early stage of my convalescence Dora discovered that she was pregnant, and this was a source of immense happiness to us both. Ever since the moment when I walked on Richmond Green with Alys, the desire for children had been growing stronger and stronger within me, until at last it had become a consuming passion. When I discovered that I was not only to survive myself, but to have a child, I became completely indifferent to the circumstances of convalescence, although, during convalescence, I had a whole series of minor diseases. The main trouble had been double pneumonia, but in addition to that I had heart disease, kidney disease, dysentery, and phlebitis. None of these, however, prevented me from feeling perfectly happy, and in spite of all gloomy prognostications, no ill effects whatever remained after my recovery.

Lying in my bed feeling that I was not going to die was surprisingly delightful. I had always imagined until then that I was fundamentally pessimistic and did not greatly value being alive. I discovered that in this I had been completely mistaken, and that life was infinitely sweet to me. Rain in Peking is rare, but during my convalescence there came heavy rains bringing the delicious smell of damp earth through the windows, and I used to think how dreadful it would have been to have never smelt that smell again. I had the same feeling about the light of the sun, and the sound of the wind. Just outside my windows were some very beautiful acacia trees, which came into blossom at the first moment when I was well enough to enjoy them. I have known ever since that at bottom I am glad to be alive. Most people, no doubt, always know this, but I did not.

I was told that the Chinese said that they would bury me by the Western Lake and build a shrine to my memory. I have some slight regret that this did not happen, as I might have become a god, which would have been very *chic* for an atheist.

There was in Peking at that time a Soviet diplomatic mission, whose members showed great kindness. They had the only good champagne in Peking, and supplied it liberally for my use, champagne being apparently the only proper beverage for pneumonia patients. They used to take first Dora, and later Dora and me, for motor drives in the neighbourhood of Peking. This was a pleasure, but a somewhat exciting one, as they were as bold in driving as they were in revolutions.

I probably owe my life to the Rockefeller Institute in Peking which provided a serum that killed the *pneumococci*. I owe them the more gratitude on this point, as both before and after I was strongly opposed to them politically, and they regarded me with as much horror as was felt by my nurse.

The Japanese journalists were continually worrying Dora to give them interviews when she wanted to be nursing me. At last she became a little curt with them, so they caused the Japanese newspapers to say that I was dead. This news was forwarded by mail from Japan to America and from America to England. It appeared in the English newspapers on the same day as the news of my divorce. Fortunately, the Court did not believe it, or the divorce might have been postponed. It provided me with the pleasure of reading my obituary notices, which I had always desired without expecting my wishes to be fulfilled. One missionary paper, I remember, had an obituary notice of one sentence: 'Missionaries may be pardoned for heaving a sigh of relief at the news of Mr Bertrand Russell's death.' I fear they must have heaved a sigh of a different sort when they found that I was not dead after all. The report caused some pain to friends in England. We in Peking knew nothing about it until a telegram came from my brother enquiring whether I was still alive. He had been remarking meanwhile that to die in Peking was not the sort of thing I would do.

The most tedious stage of my convalescence was when I had phlebitis, and had to lie motionless on my back for six weeks. We were very anxious to return home for the confinement, and as time went on it began to seem doubtful whether we should be able to do so. In these circumstances it was difficult not to feel impatience, the more so as the doctors said there was nothing to do but wait. However, the trouble cleared up just in time, and on July 10th we were able to leave Peking, though I was still very weak and could only hobble about with the help of a stick.

Shortly after my return from China, the British Government decided to deal with the question of the Boxer indemnity. When the Boxers had been defeated, the subsequent treaty of peace provided that the Chinese Government should pay an annual sum to all those European Powers which had been injured by it. The Americans very wisely decided to forego any payment on this account. Friends of China in England urged England in vain to do likewise. At last it was decided that, instead of a punitive payment, the Chinese should make some payment which should be profitable to both China and Britain. What form this payment should take was left to be determined by a Committee on which there should be two Chinese members. While MacDonald was Prime Minister he invited Lowes Dickinson and me to be members of the Committee, and consented to our recommendation of V. K. Ting and Hu Shih as the Chinese members. When, shortly afterwards, MacDonald's Government fell, the succeeding Conservative Government informed Lowes Dickinson and myself that our services would not be wanted on the Committee, and they would not accept either V. K. Ting or Hu Shih as Chinese members of it, on the ground that we knew nothing about China. The Chinese Government replied that it desired the two Chinese whom I had recommended and would not have anyone else. This put an end to the very feeble efforts at securing Chinese friendship. The only thing that had been secured during the Labour period of friendship was that Shantung should become a golf course for the British Navy and should no longer be open for Chinese trading.

Before I became ill I had undertaken to do a lecture tour in Japan after leaving China. I had to cut this down to one lecture, and visits to various people. We spent twelve hectic days in Japan, days which were far from pleasant, though very interesting. Unlike the Chinese, the Japanese proved to be destitute of good manners, and incapable of avoiding intrusiveness. Owing to my being still very feeble, we were anxious to avoid all unnecessary fatigues, but the journalists proved a very difficult matter. At the first port at which our boat touched, some thirty journalists were lying in wait, although we had done our best to travel secretly, and they only discovered our movements through the police. As the Japanese papers had refused to contradict the news of my death, Dora gave each of them a type-written slip saying that as I was dead I could not be interviewed. They drew in their breath through their teeth and said: 'Ah! veree funnee!'

We went first to Kobe to visit Robert Young, the editor of the *Japan Chronicle*. As the boat approached the quay, we saw vast processions with banners marching along, and to the surprise of those who knew Japanese, some of the banners were expressing a welcome to me. It turned out that there was a great strike going on in the dock-yards, and that the police would not tolerate processions except in honour of distinguished foreigners, so that this was their only way of making a demonstration. The strikers were being led by a Christian pacifist called Kagawa, who took me to strike meetings, at one of which I made a speech. Robert Young was a delightful man, who, having left England in the 'eighties, had not shared in the subsequent deterioration of ideas. He had in his study a large picture of Bradlaugh, for whom he had a devoted admiration. His was, I think, the best newspaper I have ever known, and he had started it with a capital of £10, saved out of his wages as a compositor. He took me to Nara, a place of exquisite beauty, where Old Japan was still to be seen. We then fell into the hands of the enterprising editors of an up-to-date magazine called *Kaizo*, who conducted us around Kyoto and Tokyo, taking care always to let the journalists know when we were coming, so that we were perpetually pursued by flashlights and photographed even in our sleep. In both places they invited large numbers of professors to visit us. In both places we were treated with the utmost obsequiousness and dogged by police-spies. The room next to ours in the hotel would be occupied by a collection of policemen with a typewriter. The waiters treated us as if we were royalty, and walked backwards out of the room. We would say: 'Damn this waiter', and immediately hear the police typewriter clicking. At the parties of professors which were given in our honour, as soon as I got into at all animated conversation with anyone, a flashlight photograph would be taken, with the result that the conversation was of course interrupted.

The Japanese attitude towards women is somewhat primitive. In Kyoto we both had mosquito nets with holes in them, so that we were kept awake half the night by mosquitoes. I complained of this in the morning. Next evening my mosquito net was mended, but not Dora's. When I complained again the next day, they said: 'But we did not know it mattered about the lady.' Once, when we were in a suburban train with the historian Eileen Power, who was also travelling in Japan, no seats were available, but a Japanese kindly got up and offered his seat to me. I gave it to Dora. Another Japanese then offered me *his* seat. I gave this to Eileen Power. By this time the Japanese were so disgusted by my unmanly conduct that there was nearly a riot.

We met only one Japanese whom we really liked, a Miss Ito. She was young and beautiful, and lived with a well-known anarchist, by whom she had a son. Dora said to her: 'Are you not afraid that the authorities will do something to you?' She drew her hand across her throat, and said: 'I know they will do that sooner or later.' At the time of the earthquake, the police came to the house where she lived with the anarchist, and found him and her and a little nephew whom they believed to be the son, and informed them that they were wanted at the police station. When they arrived at the police station, the three were put in separate rooms and strangled by the police, who boasted that they had not had much trouble with the child, as they had managed to make friends with him on the way to the police station. The police in question became national heroes, and school children were set to write essays in their praise.

We made a ten hours' journey in great heat from Kyoto to Yokohama. We arrived there just after dark, and were received by a series of magnesium explosions, each of which made Dora jump, and increased my fear of a miscarriage. I became blind with rage, the only time I have been so since I tried to strangle FitzGerald.[1] I pursued the boys with the flashlights, but being lame, was unable to catch them, which was fortunate, as I should certainly have committed murder. An enterprising photographer succeeded in photographing me with my eyes blazing. I should not have known that I could have looked so completely insane. This photograph was my introduction to Tokyo. I felt at that moment the same type of passion as must have been felt by Anglo-Indians during the Mutiny, or by white men surrounded by a rebel coloured population. I realized then that the desire to protect one's family from injury at the hands of an alien race is probably the wildest and most passionate feeling of which man is capable. My last experience of Japan was the publication in a patriotic journal of what purported to be my farewell message to the Japanese nation, urging them to be more Chauvinistic. I had not sent either this or any other farewell message to that or any other newspaper.

We sailed from Yokohama by the Canadian Pacific, and were seen off by the anarchist, Ozuki, and Miss Ito. On the *Empress of Asia* we experienced a sudden change in the social atmosphere. Dora's condition was not yet visible to ordinary eyes, but we saw the ship's doctor cast a professional eye upon her, and we learned that he had communicated his observations to the passengers. Consequently, almost nobody would speak to us, though everybody was anxious to photograph us. The only people willing to speak to us were Mischa Elman, the violinist, and his party. As everybody else on the ship wished to speak to him, they were considerably annoyed by the fact that he was always in our company. After an uneventful journey, we arrived in Liverpool at the end of August. It was raining hard, and everybody complained of the drought, so we felt we had reached home. Dora's mother was on the dock, partly to welcome us, but partly to give Dora wise advise, which she was

[1] Cf. Vol. I, p. 44.

almost too shy to do. On September 27th we were married, having succeeded in hurrying up the King's Proctor, though this required that I should swear by Almighty God on Charing Cross platform that Dora was the woman with whom I had committed the official adultery. On November 16th, my son John was born, and from that moment my children were for many years my main interest in life.

LETTERS

From Johnson Yuan

6 Yu Yang Li
Avenue Joffre
Shanghai, China
6th Oct. [? Nov.] 1920

Dear Sir

We are very glad to have the greatest social philosopher of world to arrive here in China, so as to salve the Chronic deseases of the thought of Chinese Students. Since 1919, the student's circle seems to be the greatest hope of the future of China; as they are ready to welcome to have revolutionary era in the society of China. In that year, Dr John Dewey had influenced the intellectual class with great success.

But I dare to represent most of the Chinese Students to say a few words to you:

Although Dr Dewey is successful here, but most of our students are not satisfied with his conservative theory. Because most of us want to acquire the knowledge of Anarchism, Syndicalism, Socialism, etc.; in a word, we are anxious to get the knowledge of the social revolutionary philosophy. We are the followers of Mr Kropotkin, and our aim is to have an anarchical society in China. We hope you, Sir, to give us fundamentally the thorough Social philosophy, base on Anarchism. Moreover, we want you to recorrect the theory of Dr Dewey, the American Philosopher. We hope you have the absolute freedom in China, not the same as in England. So we hope you to have a greater success than Dr Dewey here.

I myself am old member of the Peking Govt. University, and met you in Shanghai many times, the first time is in 'The Great Oriental Hotel', the first time of your reception here, in the evening.

The motto, you often used, of Lao-Tzu ought to be changed in the first word, as 'Creation without Possession . . .' is better than the former translative; and it is more correctly according to what you have said 'the creative impulsive and the possessive impulse'. Do you think it is right?

Your Fraternally Comrade
Johnson Yuan
(Secretary of the Chinese Anar-
chist-Communist Association)

From The General Educational Association of Hunan

Changsha
October 11th, 1920

Dear Sir

We beg to inform you that the educational system of our province is just at infancy and is unfortunately further weekened by the fearful disturbances of the civil war of late years, so that the guidance and assistances must be sought to sagacious scholars.

The extent to which your moral and intellectual power has reached is so high that all the people of this country are paying the greatest regard to you. We, Hunanese, eagerly desire to hear your powerful instructions as a compass.

A few days ago, through Mr Lee-Shuh-Tseng, our representative at Shanghai, we requested you to visit Hunan and are very grateful to have your kind acceptance. A general meeting will therefore be summoned on the 25th instant in order to receive your instructive advices. Now we appoint Mr Kun-Chao-Shuh to represent us all to welcome you sincerely. Please come as soon as possible.

We are, Sir
Your obedient servants
The General Educational
Association of Hunan
(Seal)

I wrote the following account on the Yiangtse:
To Ottoline Morrel[1]

28th October, 1920

Since landing in China we have had a most curious and interesting time, spent, so far, entirely among Chinese students and journalists, who are more or less Europeanised. I have delivered innumerable lectures—on Einstein, education and social questions. The eagerness for knowledge on the part of students is quite extraordinary. When one begins to speak, their eyes have the look of starving men beginning a feast. Everywhere they treat me with a most embarrassing respect. The day after I landed in Shanghai they gave a vast dinner to us, at which they welcomed me as Confucius the Second. All the Chinese newspapers that day in Shanghai had my photograph. Both Miss Black and I had to speak to innumerable schools, teachers' conferences, congresses, etc. It is a country of curious contrasts. Most of Shanghai is quite European, almost American; the names of streets, and notices and advertisements are in English (as well as Chinese). The buildings are magnificent offices and banks; everything looks very opulent. But the side streets are still quite Chinese. It is a vast city about the size of Glasgow. The Europeans almost all look villainous and ill. One of the leading Chinese newspapers invited us to lunch, in a modern building, completed in 1917, with all the latest plant (except linotype, which can't be used for Chinese characters). The editorial staff gave us a Chinese meal at the top of the house with Chinese wine made of rice, and innumerable dishes which we ate with chopsticks. When

[1] Published in *The Nation*, January 8th, 1921.

we had finished eating they remarked that one of their number was fond of old Chinese music, and would like to play to us. So he produced an instrument with seven strings, made by himself on the ancient model, out of black wood two thousand years old, which he had taken from a temple. The instrument is played with the finger, like a guitar, but is laid flat on a table, not held in the hand. They assured us that the music he played was four thousand years old, but that I imagine must be an overstatement. In any case, it was exquisitely beautiful, very delicate, easier for a European ear than more recent music (of which I have heard a good deal). When the music was over they became again a staff of bustling journalists.

From Shanghai our Chinese friends took us for three nights to Hangchow on the Western Lake, said to be the most beautiful scenery in China. This was merely holiday. The Western Lake is not large—about the size of Grasmere—it is surrounded by wooded hills, on which there are innumerable pagodas and temples. It has been beautified by poets and emperors for thousands of years. (Apparently poets in ancient China were as rich as financiers in modern Europe.) We spent one day in the hills—a twelve hour expedition in Sedan chairs—and the next in seeing country houses, monasteries, etc. on islands in the lake.

Chinese religion is curiously cheerful. When one arrives at a temple, they give one a cigarette and a cup of delicately fragrant tea. Then they show one round. Buddhism, which one thinks of as ascetic, is here quite gay. The saints have fat stomachs, and are depicted as people who thoroughly enjoy life. No one seems to believe the religion, not even the priests. Nevertheless, one sees many rich new temples.

The country houses are equally hospitable—one is shewn round and given tea. They are just like Chinese pictures, with many arbours where one can sit, with everything made for beauty and nothing for comfort—except in the grandest rooms, where there will be a little hideous European furniture.

The most delicious place we saw on the Western Lake was a retreat for scholars, built about eight hundred years ago on the lake. Scholars certainly had a pleasant life in the old China.

Apart from the influence of Europeans, China makes the impression of what Europe would have become if the eighteenth century had gone on till now without industrialism or the French Revolution. People seem to be rational hedonists, knowing very well how to obtain happiness, exquisite through intense cultivation of their artistic sensibilities, differing from Europeans through the fact that they prefer enjoyment to power. People laugh a great deal in all classes, even the lowest.

The Chinese cannot pronounce my name, or write it in their characters. They call me 'Luo-Su' which is the nearest they can manage. This, they can both pronounce and print.

From Hangchow we went back to Shanghai, thence by rail to Nanking, an almost deserted city. The wall is twenty-three miles in circumference, but most of what it encloses is country. The city was destroyed at the end of the Taiping rebellion, and again injured in the Revolution of 1911, but it is an active educational centre, eager for news of Einstein and Bolshevism.

From Nanking we went up the Yiangtse to Hangkow, about three days' journey, through very lovely scenery—thence by train to Cheng-Sha, the capital of Hu-Nan, where a great educational conference was taking place. There are about three hundred Europeans in Cheng-Sha, but Europeanisation has not gone at all far. The town is just like a mediaeval town—narrow streets, every house a shop with a gay sign hung out, no traffic possible except Sedan chairs and a few rickshaws. The Europeans have a few factories, a few banks, a few missions and a hospital—the whole gamut of damaging and repairing body and soul by western methods. The Governor of Hu-Nan is the most virtuous of all the Governors of Chinese provinces, and entertained us last night at a magnificent banquet. Professor and Mrs Dewey were present; it was the first time I had met them. The Governor cannot talk any European language, so, though I sat next to him, I could only exchange compliments through an interpreter. But I got a good impression of him; he is certainly very anxious to promote education, which seems the most crying need of China. Without it, it is hard to see how better government can be introduced. It must be said that bad government seems somewhat less disastrous in China than it would be in a European nation, but this is perhaps a superficial impression which time may correct.

We are now on our way to Pekin, which we hope to reach on October 31st.

Bertrand Russell

From S. Yamamoto

Tokyo, Japan
December 25, 1920

Dear Sir

We heartily thank you for your esteemed favour of the latest date and also for the manuscript on 'The Prospects of Bolshevik Russia', which has just arrived.

When a translation of your article on 'Patriotism' appeared in our New Year issue of the *Kaizo* now already on sale, the blood of the young Japanese was boiled with enthusiasm to read it. All the conversations everywhere among gentlemen classes, students and laborers centered upon your article, so great was the attraction of your thoughts to them.

The only regret was that the government has requested us to omit references you made to Japan in your article as much as possible, and we were obliged to cut out some of your valuable sentences. We trust that you will generously sympathize with us in the position in which we are placed and that you will excuse us for complying with the government's request.

Hereafter, however, we shall publish your articles in the original as well as in a translation according the dictate of our principle.

The admiration for you of the millions of our young men here is something extraordinary.

Your principle is identical with that of ourselves, so that as long as we live we wish to be with you. But that our country is still caught in the obstinate conventional mesh of 3,000 years standing, so that reforms cannot be carried out, is a cause of great regret. We have to advance step by step. Your publications have served as one of the most important factors to move our promising young men of Japan in their steadfast advancement.

In the past thirty odd years, physical and medical sciences have especially advanced in Japan. But it is a question how much progress we have made in the way of original inventions. Yet we are confident that in pure science we are by no means behind America in advancement. Only the majority of our country men are still enslaved by the ideas of class distinctions and other backward thoughts, of which we are greatly ashamed. The Japanese military clique and the gentlemen clique have been anxious to lead Japan in the path of aggression, thereby only inviting the antipathy of the nation. The present Japanese world of thought has been subject to an undercurrent of struggle. We will be very much grieved if our country were regarded as an aggressive nation because of that.

One half of our government officials and almost eighty per cent of the army men have been caught in dreams of aggression, it is true. But recently there has been much awakening from that.

We have confidence in our young men who have begun to awaken, so that they may advance in the path of civilization not to disappoint the world. We trust that you will write your articles with the object in view to encourage our young men in their efforts for advancement.

Please give our regards to Miss Black.

> *Yours respectfully*
> S. *Yamamoto*

[*Humbug is international.*]

To Ottoline Morrell

[1921]

The other day Dora and I went to a Chinese feast given by the Chinese Students here. They made speeches full of delicate wit, in the style of 18th century France, with a mastery of English that quite amazed me. The Chinese Chargé d'Affaires said he had been asked to speak on Chinese Politics—he said the urgent questions were the General Election, economy and limitation of armaments—he spoke quite a long time, saying only things that might have been said in a political speech about England, and which yet were quite all right for China—when he sat down he had not committed himself to anything at all, but had suggested (without ever saying) that China's problems were worse than ours. The Chinese constantly remind me of Oscar Wilde in his first trial when he thought wit would pull one through anything, and found himself in the grip of a great machine that cared nothing for human values. I read of a Chinese General the other day, whose troops had ventured to resist a Japanese attack, so the Japanese insisted that he should apologise to their

Consul. He replied that he had no uniform grand enough for such an august occasion, and therefore to his profound sorrow he must forego the pleasure of visiting a man for whom he had so high an esteem. When they nevertheless insisted, he called the same day on all the other Consuls, so that it appeared as if he were paying a mere visit of ceremony. Then all Japan raised a howl that he had insulted the whole Japanese nation.

I would do anything in the world to help the Chinese, but it is difficult. They are like a nation of artists, with all their good and bad points. Imagine Gertler and [Augustus] John and Lytton set to gcvern the British Empire, and you will have some idea how China has been governed for 2,000 years. Lytton is very like an old fashioned Chinaman, not at all like the modern westernized type.

I must stop. All my love.

Your B.

From my brother Frank

Telegraph House
Chichester
27 January 1921

Dear Bertie

The Bank to which I have rashly given a Guarantee is threatening to sell me up, so that by the time you return I shall probably be a pauper walking the streets. It is not an alluring prospect for my old age but I dare say it will afford great joy to Elizabeth.

I have not seen the elusive little Wrinch again although she seems to spend as much time in London as at Girton. I did not know a don had so much freedom of movement in term time.

Did you know that our disagreeable Aunt Gertrude was running the Punch Bowl Inn on Hindhead? I feel tempted to go and stay there for a week end but perhaps she would not take me in. The Aunt Agatha was very bitter about it when I last saw her and said the horrible woman was running all over Hindhead poisoning people's minds against her by saying the most shocking things—we can guess what about. I think when one reflects on the P.L. [Pembroke Lodge] atmosphere it is amusing to think of the Aunt Agatha becoming an object of scandal in her old age. [1] Naturally she feels that something must be seriously wrong with the world for such a thing to be possible. She was quite amusingly and refreshingly bitter about Gertrude and next time I see her I will draw her out a bit.

I am afraid I have no more news to tell you: my mind is entirely occupied with thoughts of what it is like to be a bankrupt—and how—and where—to live on nothing a year. The problem is a novel one and I dislike all its solutions.

Yours affectionately
Russell

[1] She was suspiciously friendly with her chauffeur. The Duke of Bedford gave her a car, which she was too nervous ever to use, but she kept the chauffeur.

From Robert Young
The Japan Chronicle
P.O. Box No. 91 Sannomiya
Kobe, Japan
January 18, 1921

Dear Mr Russell

Your books have always been so helpful to me that when I heard you were coming out here I ventured to send you a copy of the *Chronicle* in the hope that you might find something of interest in it from time to time. Please do not trouble about the subscription; I am very glad if the paper has been of service.

When I was in England a year ago I hoped to have the opportunity of a talk with you, and Francis Hirst tried to arrange it but found you were away from London at the time. Do you intend to visit Japan before you return to England? If so I shall hope to have a chance of meeting you, and if I can do anything here in connection with such a visit please let me know.

I shall be glad to read your new book on Bolshevism. Since you wrote you will perhaps have noticed a review of *Bolshevism in Theory and Practice*. It may perhaps be interesting to you to know that I can remember your father's will being upset in the Courts, and that as a result I have followed your career with interest.

Sincerely Yours
Robert Young

The Japan Chronicle
P.O. Box No. 91 Sannomiya
Kobe, Japan
Kobe, January 2, 1922

Dear Mr Russell

It is a long time since August, when you wrote to me from the *Empress of Asia*, and I ought to have acknowledged your letter earlier, but with my small staff I am always kept very busy, and my correspondence tends to accumulate.

I have just heard from Mrs Russell of the birth of an heir, and I congratulate you in no formal sense, for it has given us great pleasure and much relief to learn that Mrs Russell did not suffer from her experiences in Japan. I published the letter you sent me, and I think some good has been done by the protest. So few people have courage to protest against an evil of this character, lest worse things may befall them in the way of criticism.

What a farce the Washington Conference is. From the first I doubted the sincerity of this enthusiasm for peace on the part of those who made the war. Perhaps it is the head rather than the heart that is at fault. The statesmen do not seem to realise that so long as the old policies are pursued, we shall have the same results, and that a limitation of armaments to the point they have reached during the war puts us in a worse position regarding the burden carried and the danger of explosion than in 1914. Japan has sulkily accepted the ratio proposed by America, but is supporting the French demand for more submarines. France is showing herself a greater danger to Europe than Germany ever was. China has been betrayed at the Washington Conference, as we expected. The Anglo–Japanese Alliance has been scrapped, to be replaced by a Four-Power agreement which is still more dangerous to China. Her salvation, unhappily, lies in the jealousies of the Powers. United, the pressure on her will be increased. But I doubt whether the Senate will endorse the treaty, once its full implications are understood.

You are very busy, I note, and I hope that you will be able to make people think. But it is a wicked and perverse generation, I am afraid. Sometimes I despair. It looks as if all the ideals with which I started life had been overthrown. But I suppose when one is well into the sixties, the resilience of youth has disappeared.

By the way, I have suggested to the Conway Memorial Committee that you be asked to deliver the annual lecture. If you are asked, I hope you will see your way to consent. Moncure Conway was a fine character, always prepared to champion the oppressed and defend free speech. He stood by Bradlaugh and Mrs Besant when they were prosecuted for the publication of the *Fruits of Philosophy*, as he stood by Foote when prosecuted on account of the *Freethinker*, though personally objecting to that style of propaganda.

I have given Mrs Russell some Japan news in a letter I have just written to her, so I will not repeat here. I hope you are receiving the *Japan Weekly Chronicle* regularly, so that you can keep in touch with news in this part of the world. It has been sent to you care of George Allen & Unwin. Now I have your Chelsea address I will have it sent there. For some years our Weekly has been steadily increasing in circulation, going all over the world. But from the 1st of this year the Japanese Post Office has doubled the foreign postage rates, which makes 6 yen for postage alone per annum on a copy of the Weekly, and I am afraid our circulation will suffer accordingly.

It is very good to hear that you are completely restored to health. Mrs Russell says you would scarcely be recognised by those who only saw you in Japan. Your visit was a great pleasure to me. For years I had admired your writings and been encouraged by the stand you had taken in public affairs when even the stoutest seemed to waver. It therefore meant much to me to make your acquaintance and I hope your friendship.

With our united good wishes,

Sincerely yours
Robert Young

From C. P. Sanger

5 New Square
Lincolns Inn, W.C.2
2 June 1921

My dear Bertie

How kind of you to write; and to say such kind things. Until there was a false rumour of your death I never really knew how *very* fond I am of you. I didn't believe the rumour, but the mere idea that I might never see you again had never come into my mind; and it was an intense relief when the Chinese Embassy ascertained that the rumour was false. You will take care of your health now, won't you?

The Political situation is, as always, damnable—millions of unemployed—soldiers camping in the parks—but an excellent day yesterday for the Derby which is all that anyone apparently cares about.

Einstein lectures at King's College in 10 days time, but I can't get a ticket. I've been reading some of Einstein's actual papers and they give me a most tremendous impression of the clearness of his thoughts.

We spent a delightful Whitsuntide at the Shiffolds: Tovey[1] was there and talked endlessly and played Beethoven Sonatas and Bach, so I was very happy.

I enclose a letter for Miss Black—I'm afraid its a little inadequate but it's so difficult to write to a person one has never seen. I hope this experience with her and her devoted nursing of you will form an eternal basis for you both.

Dora sends her love.

> *Yours fraternally and*
> *affectionately*
> C. P. Sanger

From Joseph Conrad

Oswalds
Bishopsbourne, Kent
2. Nov. 1921

My Dear Russell

We were glad to hear that your wife feels none the worse for the exertions and agitations of the move.[2] Please give her our love and assure her that she is frequently in our thoughts.

As to yourself I have been dwelling with you mentally for several days between the covers of your book[3]—an habitation of great charm and most fascinatingly furnished; not to speak of the wonderful quality of light that reigns in there. Also all the windows (I am trying to write in images) are, one feels, standing wide open. Nothing less stuffy—of the Mansions of the mind—could be conceived! I am sorry for the philosophers (p. 212—end) who (like the rest of us) cannot have their cake and eat it. There's no exactitude in the vision or in the words. I have a notion that we are condemned in all things to the *à-peu-près*, which no scientific passion for weighing and measuring will ever do away with.

It is very possible that I haven't understood your pages—but the good try I have had was a delightful experience. I suppose you are enough of a philosopher not to have expected more from a common mortal.

I don't believe that Charles I was executed (pp 245–246 et seq.) but there is not enough paper left here to explain why. Next time perhaps. For I certainly intend to meet you amongst your Chinoiseries at the very earliest fitting time.

> *Always affectly yours*
> J. Conrad

---

[1] The music critic.
[2] The move from one abode to another in London after we returned from China.
[3] *The Analysis of Mind.*

Oswalds
Bishopsbourne, Kent
18th Nov. 1921

My Dear Russell

Jessie must have sent yesterday our congratulations and words of welcome to the 'comparative stranger' who has come to stay with you (and take charge of the household as you will soon discover). Yes! Paternity is a great experience of which the least that can be said is that it is eminently worth having—if only for the deepened sense of fellowship with all men it gives one. It is the only experience perhaps whose universality does not make it common but invests it with a sort of grandeur on that very account. My affection goes out to you both, to him who is without speech and thought as yet and to you who have spoken to men profoundly with effect and authority about the nature of the mind. For your relation to each other will have its poignant moments arising out of the very love and loyalty binding you to each other.

Of all the incredible things that come to pass this—that there should be one day a Russell bearing mine for one of his names is surely the most marvellous. Not even my horoscope could have disclosed that for I verily believe that all the sensible stars would have refused to combine in that extravagant manner over my cradle. However it has come to pass (to the surprise of the Universe) and all I can say is that I am profoundly touched—more than I can express—that I should have been present to your mind in that way and at such a time.

Please kiss your wife's hand for me and tell her that in the obscure bewildered masculine way (which is not quite unintelligent however) I take part in her gladness. Since your delightful visit here she was much in our thoughts—and I will confess we felt very optimistic. She has justified it fully and it is a great joy to think of her with two men in the house. She will have her hands full presently. I can only hope that John Conrad has been born with a disposition towards indulgence which he will consistently exercise towards his parents. I don't think that I can wish you anything better and so with my dear love to all three of you, I am

always yours
Joseph Conrad

P.S. I am dreadfully offended at your associating me with some undesirable acquaintance of yours[1] who obviously should not have been allowed inside the B. Museum reading-room. I wish you to understand that my attitude towards [the] King Charles question is not phantastic but philosophical and I shall try to make it clear to you later when you will be more in a state to follow my reasoning closely. Knowing from my own experience I imagine that it's no use talking to you seriously just now.

[1] Who did not agree that Julius Caesar is dead, and when I asked why, replied: 'Because I am Julius Caesar.'

From Eileen Power   184 Ebury Street
                                                            S.W.1
                                                            Saturday, [December, 1921]

Dear Bertie

The book is *The Invention of a New Religion* by Professor Chamberlain. If you want to consult it, here it is and perhaps you would let me have it back anon.

I am so glad that you and Dora can come to luncheon to meet Dr Wise on Wednesday and tell Dora that 1.30 will do beautifully. I am also asking B. K. Martin, a very intelligent young man who is now teaching history at Magdalene, having got his B.A. last year. He wrote to me three days ago and said 'if you would introduce me to Bertrand Russell I should be forever in your debt. I'd rather meet him than any other living (or dead) creature.' I felt that in view of this pre-eminence over the shades of Plato, Julius Caesar, Cleopatra, Descartes, Ninon de l'Enclos and Napoleon the Great, you would consent to shine upon him! Also he is extremely clever and a nice boy.

                                                            Yours ever
                                                            Eileen Power

I was asked to dine with the Webbs the other day, but I don't think I ever shall be again for we nearly came to blows over the relative merits of China and Japan!

From Claud Russell   Sept. 22. 1923
                                                            British Legation
                                                            Adis Ababa

Dear Bertie

I have just read with great pleasure your *Problem of China*, where I spent some years. It is a fact that the Treaty of Versailles (article 131) provided for the restoration of the astronomical instruments to China, but I am under the impression that the obligation has not been carried out. If so, I fear you cannot count it among the 'important benefits' secured to the world by that treaty. Perhaps you might suggest to your friends in China the occupation of Swabia or Oldenburg to secure its enforcement. I must say, however, in fairness to the Treaty of Versailles, that you do it less than justice. You have overlooked article 246, under which 'Germany will hand over to H.B.M.'s Government the skull of the Sultan Mkwawa. . . .'

I think, if I may say so, that on page 24 (top) 'animal' should be 'annual'. I feel sure the Temple of Heaven was never the scene of the sort of sacrifice that pleased the God of Abel.

                                                            Your affec cousin
                                                            Claud Russell

From J. Ramsay MacDonald   Foreign Office
                                             S.W.1
                                             31st May, 1924

My dear Russell

For some time past, His Majesty's Government have been considering the best means of allocating and administering the British share of the China Boxer Indemnity, which, it has been decided, should be devoted to purposes mutually beneficial to British and Chinese interests.

In order to obtain the best results from the policy thus indicated, it has been decided to appoint a committee to advise His Majesty's Government; and I am approaching you in the hope that you may be able to serve on this Committee, feeling confident that your experience would be of the greatest assistance in this matter, which will so deeply and permanently affect our relations with China.

The terms of reference will probably be as follows:—

'In view of the decision of His Majesty's Government to devote future payments of the British share of the Boxer Indemnity to purposes mutually beneficial to British and Chinese interests.

'To investigate the different objects to which these payments should be allocated, and the best means of securing the satisfactory administration of the funds, to hear witnesses and to make such recommendations as may seem desirable.'

For the sake of efficiency, the Committee will be kept as small as possible, especially at the outset of its proceedings. But it will of course be possible to appoint 'ad hoc' additional members for special subjects, if such a course should recommend itself later on. The following are now being approached, as representing the essential elements which should go to the composition of the Committee:

Chairman: Lord Phillimore.
Foreign Office: Sir John Jordan and Mr S. P. Waterlow.
Department of Overseas Trade: Sir William Clark.
House of Commons: Mr H. A. L. Fisher, M.P.
Finance: Sir Charles Addis.
Education: Mr Lowes Dickinson and The Honourable Bertrand Russell.
Women: Dame Adelaide Anderson.
China: A suitable Chinese.

It will be understood that the above list is of a tentative character and should be regarded as confidential.

I enclose a brief memorandum which shows the present position with regard to the Indemnity, and to the legislation which has now been introduced into the House. I trust that you will be able to see your way to undertake this work, to which I attach the highest importance.

                                             Yours very sincerely
                                             J. Ramsay MacDonald

Note on a scrap of paper:

'It is desired that the Committee should consist wholly of men with an extensive knowledge of China and its affairs.'

MEMORANDUM ON THE BOXER INDEMNITY

by

Bertrand Russell

The Boxer Indemnity Bill, now in Committee, provides that what remains unpaid of the Boxer Indemnity shall be spent on purposes to the mutual advantage of Great Britain & China. It does not state that these purposes are to be educational. In the opinion of all who know China (except solely as a field for capitalist exploitation), it is of the utmost importance that an Amendment should be adopted specifying Chinese education as the sole purpose to which the money should be devoted. The following are the chief grounds in favour of such an Amendment:

(1) That this would be the expenditure most useful to China.

(2) That no other course would produce a good effect on influential Chinese opinion.

(3) That the interests of Great Britain, which are to be considered, can only be secured by winning the good will of the Chinese.

(4) That any other course would contrast altogether too unfavourably with the action of America, which long ago devoted all that remained of the American share of the Boxer indemnity to Chinese education.

(5) That the arguments alleged in favour of other courses all have a corrupt motive, i.e. are designed for the purpose of securing private profit through Government action.

For these reasons, it is profoundly desirable that Labour Members of Parliament should take action to secure the necessary Amendment before it is too late.

The China Indemnity Bill, in its present form, provides that the remainder of the Boxer Indemnity shall be applied to 'purposes, educational or other', which are mutually beneficial to Great Britain and China.

Sir Walter de Frece proposed in Committee that the words 'connected with education' should be substituted for 'educational or other'.

It is much to be hoped that the House of Commons will carry this Amendment on the Report stage. Certain interests are opposed to the Amendment for reasons with which Labour can have no sympathy. The Government thinks it necessary to placate these interests, but maintains that the Committee to be appointed will be free to decide in favour of education only. The Committee, however, is appointed by Parliament, and one third of its members are to retire every two years; there is therefore no guarantee against its domination by private interests in the future.

The Bill in its present form opens the door to corruption, is not calculated to please Chinese public opinion, displays Great Britain as less enlightened than America and Japan, and therefore fails altogether to achieve its nominal objects. The Labour Party ought to make at least an attempt to prevent the possibility of the misapplication of public money to purposes of private enrichment. This will be secured by the insertion of the words 'connected with education' in Clause 1, after the word 'purposes'.

Bertrand Russell

From Y. R. Chao   Berlin August 22 '24

Dear Russell

Here is an abbreviated translation of C. L. Lo's letter to me (Lo & S. N. Fu being S. Hu [Hu Shih]'s chief disciples, both in Berlin).

'Heard from China that Wu pei fu advised Ch. Governm. to use funds for railways. *Morning Post* said (4 weeks ago) that Brit. Gov't cabled Ch. Gov't to send a delegate. If so, it would be terrible. Already wrote to London Ch. stud. Club to inquire Chu. If report true, try to cancel action by asking Tsai to mount horse with his prestige. In any case, Brit. Gov't still has full power. We have written trying to influence Chu, but on the other hand you please write to Lo Su [Russell] to influence Brit. For. Office, asking him to recommend Tsai if nothing else is possible. There is already a panic in Peking educ'l world. There was a cable to Brit. Gov't, and another to Tsai asking him to go to London. . . .'

Another letter, from Chu, came to me last night:

'I did give my consent (?) to the nomination (?) of Mr Ting. I quite agree (?) with you Ting is the most desirable man for the post, but recently I learnt that Peking (For. Office?) is in favor of (?) Dr C. H. Wang, who is not in Europe. I doubt whether the latter would accept the appt'm't. . . . I will talk over this question with Mr Russell when he ret ırns to town.'

I know Wang (brother of C. T. Wang of Kuo Ming Tang (National People Party) fame), C. H. Wang is a fine gentle fellow, recently worked in business and a Christian. One should emphasize the personal attractiveness and goodness but do the opposite to his suitability to this in-its-nature roughneck tussle of a job.

My noodles are getting cold and my Kleines helles bier is getting warm 200 meters away where my wife is waiting.

Excuse me 1000 times for not reading this letter over again.

Yrs ever
Y. R. Chao

CHAPTER IV

SECOND MARRIAGE

WITH MY RETURN from China in September 1921, my life entered upon a less dramatic phase, with a new emotional centre. From adolescence until the completion of *Principia Mathematica*, my fundamental pre-occupation had been intellectual. I wanted to understand and to make others understand; also I wished to raise a monument by which I might be remembered, and on account of which I might feel that I had not lived in vain. From the outbreak of the First World War until my return from China, social questions occupied the centre of my emotions: the War and Soviet Russia alike gave me a sense of tragedy, and I had hopes that mankind might learn to live in some less painful way. I tried to discover some secret of wisdom, and to proclaim it with such persuasiveness that the world should listen and agree. But, gradually, the ardour cooled and the hope grew less; I did not change my views as to how men should live, but I held them with less of prophetic ardour and with less expectation of success in my campaigns.

Ever since the day, in the summer of 1894, when I walked with Alys on Richmond Green after hearing the medical verdict, I had tried to suppress my desire for children. It had, however, grown continually stronger, until it had become almost insupportable. When my first child was born, in November 1921, I felt an immense release of pent-up emotion, and during the next ten years my main purposes were parental. Parental feeling, as I have experienced it, is very complex. There is, first and foremost, sheer animal affection, and delight in watching what is charming in the ways of the young. Next, there is the sense of inescapable responsibility, providing a purpose for daily activities which scepticism does not easily question. Then there is an egoistic element, which is very dangerous: the hope that one's children may succeed where one has failed, that they may carry on one's work when death or senility puts an end to one's own efforts, and, in any case, that they will supply a biological escape from death, making one's own life part of the whole stream, and not a mere stagnant puddle without any overflow into the future. All this I experienced, and for some years it filled my life with happiness and peace.

The first thing was to find somewhere to live. I tried to rent a flat, but I was both politically and morally undesirable, and landlords refused to have me as a tenant. So I bought a freehold house in Chelsea, No. 31 Sydney Street, where my two older children were born. But it did not seem good for children to live all the year in London, so in the spring of 1922 we acquired a house in Cornwall, at Porthcurno, about four miles from Land's End. From then until 1927 we divided our time about equally between London and Cornwall; after that year, we spent no time in London and less in Cornwall.

The beauty of the Cornish coast is inextricably mixed in my memories with the ecstasy of watching two healthy happy children learning the joys of sea and rocks and sun and storm. I spent a great deal more time with them than is possible for most fathers. During the six months of the year we spent in Cornwall we had a fixed and leisurely routine. During the morning my wife and I worked while the children were in the care of a nurse, and later a governess. After lunch we all went to one or other of the many beaches that were within a walk of our house. The children played naked, bathing or climbing or making sand castles as the spirit moved them, and we, of course, shared in these activities. We came home very hungry to a very late and a very large tea; then the children were put to bed and the adults reverted to their grown-up pursuits. In my memory, which is of course fallacious, it was always sunny, and always warm after April. But in April the winds were cold. One April day, when Kate's age was two years three and a half months, I heard her talking to herself and wrote down what she said:

> The North wind blows over the North Pole.
> The daisies hit the grass.
> The wind blows the bluebells down.
> The North wind blows to the wind in the South.

She did not know that any one was listening, and she certainly did not know what 'North Pole' means.

In the circumstances it was natural that I should become interested in education. I had already written briefly on the subject in *Principles of Social Reconstruction*, but now it occupied a large part of my mind. I wrote a book, *On Education, especially in early childhood*, which was published in 1926 and had a very large sale. It seems to me now somewhat unduly optimistic in its psychology, but as regards values I find nothing in it to recant, although I think now that the methods I proposed with very young children were unduly harsh.

It must not be supposed that life during these six years from the autumn of 1921 to the autumn of 1927 was all one long summer idyll. Parenthood had made it imperative to earn money. The purchase of two houses had exhausted almost all the capital that remained to me. When I returned from China I had no obvious means of making money, and at first I suffered considerable anxiety. I took whatever odd journalistic jobs were offered me: while my son John was being born, I wrote an article on Chinese pleasure in fireworks, although concentration on so remote a topic was difficult in the circumstances. In 1922 I published a book on China, and in 1923 (with my wife Dora) a book on *The Prospects of Industrial Civilization*, but neither of these brought much money. I did better with two small books, *The A.B.C. of Atoms* (1923) and *The A.B.C. of Relativity* (1925), and with two other small books, *Icarus or The Future of Science* (1924) and *What I Believe* (1925). In 1924 I earned a good deal by a lecture tour in America. But I remained rather poor until the book on education in 1926. After that, until 1933, I prospered financially, especially with *Marriage and Morals* (1929) and *The Conquest of Happiness* (1930). Most of my work during these years was popular, and was done in order to make money, but I did also some more technical work. There was a new edition of *Principia Mathematica* in 1925, to which I made various additions; and in 1927 I published *The Analysis of Matter*, which is in some sense a companion volume to *The Analysis of Mind*, begun in prison and published in 1921. I also stood for Parliament in Chelsea in 1922 and 1923, and Dora stood in 1924.

In 1927, Dora and I came to a decision, for which we were equally responsible, to found a school of our own in order that our children might be educated as we thought best. We believed, perhaps mistakenly, that children need the companionship of a group of other children, and that, therefore, we ought no longer to be content to bring up our children without others. But we did not know of any existing school that seemed to us in any way satisfactory. We wanted an unusual combination: on the one hand, we disliked prudery and religious instruction and a great many restraints on freedom which are taken for granted in conventional schools; on the other hand, we could not agree with most 'modern' educationists in thinking scholastic instruction unimportant, or in advocating a *complete* absence of discipline. We therefore endeavoured to collect a group of about twenty children, of roughly the same ages as John and Kate, with a view to keeping these same children throughout their school years.

For the purposes of the school we rented my brother's house, Telegraph House, on the South Downs, between Chichester and Petersfield. This owed its name to having been a semaphore station in the time of George III, one of a string of such stations by which messages were flashed between Portsmouth and London. Probably the news of Trafalgar reached London in this way.

The original house was quite small, but my brother gradually added to it. He was passionately devoted to the place, and wrote about it at length in his autobiography, which he called *My Life and Adventures*. The house was ugly and rather absurd, but the situation was superb. There were enormous views to East and South and West; in one direction one saw over the Sussex Weald to Leith Hill, in another one saw the Isle of Wight and the liners approaching Southampton. There was a tower with large windows on all four sides. Here I made my study, and I have never known one with a more beautiful outlook.

With the house went two hundred and thirty acres of wild downland, partly heather and bracken, but mostly virgin forest—magnificent beech trees, and yews of vast age and unusual size. The woods were full of every kind of wild life, including deer. The nearest houses were a few scattered farms about a mile away. For fifty miles, going eastward, one could walk on footpaths over unenclosed bare downs.

It is no wonder that my brother loved the place. But he had speculated unwisely, and lost every penny that he possessed. I offered him a much higher rent than he could have obtained from anyone else, and he was compelled by poverty to accept my offer. But he hated it, and ever after bore me a grudge for inhabiting his paradise.

The house must, however, have had for him some associations not wholly pleasant. He had acquired it originally as a discreet retreat where he could enjoy the society of Miss Morris, whom, for many years, he hoped to marry if he could ever get free from his first wife. Miss Morris, however, was ousted from his affections by Molly, the lady who became his second wife, for whose sake he suffered imprisonment after being condemned by his Peers for bigamy. For Molly's sake he had been divorced from his first wife. He became divorced in Reno and immediately thereupon married Molly, again at Reno. He returned to England and found that British law considered his marriage to Molly bigamous on the ground that British law acknowledges the validity of Reno marriages, but not of Reno divorces. His second wife, who was very fat, used to wear green corduroy knickerbockers; the view of her from behind when she was bending over a flower-bed at Telegraph House used to make one wonder that he had thought her worth what he had gone through for her sake.

Her day, like Miss Morris's, came to an end, and he fell in love with Elizabeth. Molly, from whom he wished to be divorced, demanded £400 a year for life as her price; after his death, I had to pay this. She died at about the age of ninety.

Elizabeth, in her turn, left him and wrote an intolerably cruel novel about him, called *Vera*. In this novel, Vera is already dead; she had been his wife, and he is supposed to be heartbroken at the loss of her.

She died by falling out of one of the windows of the tower of Telegraph House. As the novel proceeds, the reader gradually gathers that her death was not an accident, but suicide brought on by my brother's cruelty. It was this that caused me to give my children an emphatic piece of advice: 'Do not marry a novelist.'

In this house of many memories we established the school. In managing the school we experienced a number of difficulties which we ought to have foreseen. There was, first, the problem of finance. It became obvious that there must be an enormous pecuniary loss. We could only have prevented this by making the school large and the food inadequate, and we could not make the school large except by altering its character so as to appeal to conventional parents. Fortunately I was at this time making a great deal of money from books and from lecture tours in America. I made four such tours altogether—during 1924 (already mentioned), 1927, 1929, and 1931. The one in 1927 was during the first term of the school, so that I had no part in its beginnings. During the second term, Dora went on a lecture tour in America. Thus throughout the first two terms there was never more than one of us in charge. When I was not in America, I had to write books to make the necessary money. Consequently, I was never able to give my whole time to the school.

A second difficulty was that some of the staff, however often and however meticulously our principles were explained to them, could never be brought to act in accordance with them unless one of us was present.

A third trouble, and that perhaps the most serious, was that we got an undue proportion of problem children. We ought to have been on the look-out for this pit-fall, but at first we were glad to take almost any child. The parents who were most inclined to try new methods were those who had difficulties with their children. As a rule, these difficulties were the fault of the parents, and the ill effects of their unwisdom were renewed in each holiday. Whatever may have been the cause, many of the children were cruel and destructive. To let the children go free was to establish a reign of terror, in which the strong kept the weak trembling and miserable. A school is like the world: only government can prevent brutal violence. And so I found myself, when the children were not at lessons, obliged to supervise them continually to stop cruelty. We divided them into three groups, bigs, middles, and smalls. One of the middles was perpetually ill-treating the smalls, so I asked him why he did it. His answer was: 'The bigs hit me, so I hit the smalls; that's fair.' And he really thought it was.

Sometimes really sinister impulses came to light. There were among the pupils a brother and sister who had a very sentimental mother, and had been taught by her to profess a completely fantastic degree of affection for each other. One day the teacher who was superintending the midday meal found part of a hatpin in the soup that was about to be ladled out. On inquiry, it turned out that the supposedly affectionate sister had put it in. 'Didn't you know it might kill you if you swallowed it?' we said. 'Oh yes,' she replied, 'but I don't take soup.' Further investigation made it fairly evident that she had hoped her brother would be the victim. On another occasion, when a pair of rabbits had been given to a child that was unpopular, two other children made an attempt to burn them to death, and in the attempt, made a vast fire which blackened several acres, and, but for a change of wind, might have burnt the house down.

For us personally, and for our two children, there were special worries. The other boys naturally thought that our boy was unduly favoured, whereas we, in order not to favour him or his sister, had to keep an unnatural distance between them and us except during the holidays. They, in turn, suffered from a divided loyalty: they had either to be sneaks or to practise deceit towards their parents. The complete happiness that had existed in our relations to John and Kate was thus destroyed, and was replaced by awkwardness and embarrassment. I think that something of the sort is bound to happen whenever parents and children are at the same school.

In retrospect, I feel that several things were mistaken in the principles upon which the school was conducted. Young children in a group cannot be happy without a certain amount of order and routine. Left to amuse themselves, they are bored, and turn to bullying or destruction. In their free time, there should always be an adult to suggest some agreeable game or amusement, and to supply an initiative which is hardly to be expected of young children.

Another thing that was wrong was that there was a pretence of more freedom than in fact existed. There was very little freedom where health and cleanliness were concerned. The children had to wash, to clean their teeth, and to go to bed at the right time. True, we had never professed that there should be freedom in such matters, but foolish people, and especially journalists in search of a sensation, had said or believed that we advocated a complete absence of all restraints and compulsions. The older children, when told to brush their teeth, would sometimes say sarcastically: 'Call this a free school!' Those who had heard their parents talking about the freedom to be expected in the school would test it by seeing how far they could go in naughtiness without being stopped. As we only forbade things that were obviously harmful, such experiments were apt to be very inconvenient.

In 1929, I published *Marriage and Morals*, which I dictated while recovering from whooping-cough. (Owing to my age, my trouble was not diagnosed until I had infected most of the children in the school.) It was this book chiefly which, in 1940, supplied material for the attack on me in New York. In it, I developed the view that complete fidelity was not to be expected in most marriages, but that a husband and wife ought to be able to remain good friends in spite of affairs. I did not maintain, however, that a marriage could with advantage be prolonged if the wife had a child or children of whom the husband was not the father; in that case, I thought, divorce was desirable. I do not know what I think now about the subject of marriage. There seem to be insuperable objections to every general theory about it. Perhaps easy divorce causes less unhappiness than any other system, but I am no longer capable of being dogmatic on the subject of marriage.

In the following year, 1930, I published *The Conquest of Happiness*, a book consisting of common-sense advice as to what an individual can do to overcome temperamental causes of unhappiness, as opposed to what can be done by changes in social and economic systems. This book was differently estimated by readers of three different levels. Unsophisticated readers, for whom it was intended, liked it, with the result that it had a very large sale. Highbrows, on the contrary, regarded it as a contemptible pot-boiler, an escapist book, bolstering up the pretence that there were useful things to be done and said outside politics. But at yet another level, that of professional psychiatrists, the book won very high praise. I do not know which estimate was right; what I do know is that the book was written at a time when I needed much self-command and much that I had learned by painful experience if I was to maintain any endurable level of happiness.

I was profoundly unhappy during the next few years and some things which I wrote at the time give a more exact picture of my mood than anything I can now write in somewhat pale reminiscence.

At that time I used to write an article once a week for the Hearst Press. I spent Christmas Day, 1931, on the Atlantic, returning from one of my American lecture tours. So I chose for that week's article the subject of 'Christmas at Sea'. This is the article I wrote:

CHRISTMAS AT SEA

For the second time in my life, I am spending Christmas Day on the Atlantic. The previous occasion when I had this experience was thirty-five years ago, and by contrasting what I feel now with what I remember of my feelings then, I am learning much about growing old.

Thirty-five years ago I was lately married, childless, very happy, and beginning to taste the joys of success. Family appeared to me as an external power hampering to freedom: the world, to me, was a world of individual adventure. I wanted to think my own thoughts, find my own friends, and choose my own abode, without regard to tradition or elders or anything but my own tastes. I felt strong enough to stand alone, without the need of buttresses.

Now, I realize, what I did not know then, that this attitude was dependent upon a superabundant vitality. I found Christmas at sea a pleasant amusement, and enjoyed the efforts of the ship's officers to make the occasion as festive as possible. The ship rolled prodigiously, and with each roll all the steamer trunks slid from side to side of all the state-rooms with a noise like thunder. The louder the noise became, the more it made me laugh: everything was great fun.

Time, they say, makes a man mellow. I do not believe it. Time makes a man afraid, and fear makes him conciliatory, and being conciliatory he endeavours to appear to others what they will think mellow. And with fear comes the need of affection, of some human warmth to keep away the chill of the cold universe. When I speak of fear, I do not mean merely or mainly personal fear: the fear of death or decrepitude or penury or any such merely mundane misfortune. I am thinking of a more metaphysical fear. I am thinking of the fear that enters the soul through experience of the major evils to which life is subject: the treachery of friends, the death of those whom we love, the discovery of the cruelty that lurks in average human nature.

During the thirty-five years since my last Christmas on the Atlantic, experience of these major evils has changed the character of my unconscious attitude to life. To stand alone may still be possible as a moral effort, but is no longer pleasant as an adventure. I want the companionship of my children, the warmth of the family fire-side, the support of historic continuity and of membership of a great nation. These are very ordinary human joys, which most middle-aged persons enjoy at Christmas. There is nothing about them to distinguish the philosopher from other men; on the contrary, their very ordinariness makes them the more effective in mitigating the sense of sombre solitude.

And so Christmas at sea, which was once a pleasant adventure, has become painful. It seems to symbolize the loneliness of the man who chooses to stand alone, using his own judgment rather than the judgment of the herd. A mood of melancholy is, in these circumstances, inevitable, and should not be shirked.

But there is something also to be said on the other side. Domestic joys, like all the softer pleasures, may sap the will and destroy courage. The indoor warmth of the traditional Christmas is good, but so is the South wind, and the sun rising out of the sea, and the freedom of the watery horizon. The beauty of these things is undiminished by human folly and wickedness, and remains to give strength to the faltering idealism of middle age.

December 25, 1931.

As is natural when one is trying to ignore a profound cause of unhappiness, I found impersonal reasons for gloom. I had been very full of personal misery in the early years of the century, but at that time I had a more or less Platonic philosophy which enabled me to see beauty in the extra-human universe. Mathematics and the stars consoled me when the human world seemed empty of comfort. But changes in my philosophy have robbed me of such consolations. Solipsism oppressed me, particularly after studying such interpretations of physics as that of Eddington. It seemed that what we had thought of as laws of nature were only linguistic conventions, and that physics was not really concerned with an external world. I do not mean that I quite believed this, but that it became a haunting nightmare, increasingly invading my imagination. One foggy night, sitting in my tower at Telegraph House after everyone else was asleep, I expressed this mood in a pessimistic meditation:

MODERN PHYSICS

Alone in my tower at midnight, I remember the woods and downs, the sea and sky, that daylight showed. Now, as I look through each of the four windows, north, south, east and west, I see only myself dimly reflected, or shadowed in monstrous opacity upon the fog. What matter? To-morrow's sunrise will give me back the beauty of the outer world as I wake from sleep.

But the mental night that has descended upon me is less brief, and promises no awakening after sleep. Formerly, the cruelty, the meanness, the dusty fretful passion of human life seemed to me a little thing, set, like some resolved discord in music, amid the splendour of the stars and the stately procession of geological ages. What if the universe was to end in universal death? It was none the less unruffled and magnificent. But now all this has shrunk to be no more than my own reflection in the windows of the soul through which I look out upon the night of nothingness. The revolutions of nebulae, the birth and death of stars, are no more than convenient fictions in the trivial work of linking together my own sensations, and perhaps those of other men not much better than myself. No dungeon was ever constructed so dark and narrow as that in which the shadow physics of our time imprisons us, for every prisoner has believed that outside his walls a free world existed; but now the prison has become the whole universe. There is darkness without, and when I die there will be darkness within. There is no splendour, no vastness, anywhere; only triviality for a moment, and then nothing. Why live in such a world? Why even die?

In May and June, 1931, I dictated to my then secretary, Peg Adams, who had formerly been secretary to a Rajah and Ranee, a short auto-biography, which has formed the basis of the present book down to 1921. I ended it with an epilogue, in which, as will be seen, I did not admit private unhappiness, but only political and metaphysical dis-illusionment. I insert it here, not because it expressed what I now feel, but because it shows the great difficulty I experienced in adjusting myself to a changing world and a very sober philosophy.

EPILOGUE

My personal life since I returned from China has been happy and peace-ful. I have derived from my children at least as much instinctive satis-faction as I anticipated, and have in the main regulated my life with reference to them. But while my personal life has been satisfying, my impersonal outlook has become increasingly sombre, and I have found it more and more difficult to believe that the hopes which I formerly cherished will be realized in any measurable future. I have endeavoured, by concerning myself with the education of my children and with making money for their benefit, to shut out from my thoughts the impersonal despairs which tend to settle upon me. Ever since puberty I have believed in the value of two things: kindness and clear thinking. At first these two remained more or less distinct; when I felt triumphant I believed most in clear thinking, and in the opposite mood I believed most in kindness. Gradually, the two have come more and more together in my feelings. I find that much unclear thought exists as an excuse for cruelty, and that much cruelty is prompted by superstitious beliefs. The War made me vividly aware of the cruelty in human nature, but I hoped for a reaction when the War was over. Russia made me feel that little was to be hoped from revolt against existing govern-ments in the way of an increase of kindness in the world, except possibly in regard to children. The cruelty to children involved in conventional methods of education is appalling, and I have been amazed at the horror which is felt against those who propose a kinder system.

As a patriot I am depressed by the downfall of England, as yet only partial, but likely to be far more complete before long. The history of England for the last four hundred years is in my blood, and I should have wished to hand on to my son the tradition of public spirit which has in the past been valuable. In the world that I foresee there will be no place for this tradition, and he will be lucky if he escapes with his life. The feeling of impending doom gives a kind of futility to all activities whose field is in England.

In the world at large, if civilization survives, I foresee the domination of either America or Russia, and in either case of a system where a tight organization subjects the individual to the State so completely that splendid individuals will be no longer possible.

And what of philosophy? The best years of my life were given to the Principles of Mathematics, in the hope of finding somewhere some certain knowledge. The whole of this effort, in spite of three big volumes, ended inwardly in doubt and bewilderment. As regards metaphysics, when, under the influence of Moore, I first threw off the belief in German idealism, I experienced the delight of believing that the sensible world is real. Bit by bit, chiefly under the influence of physics, this delight has faded, and I have been driven to a position not unlike that of Berkeley, without his God and his Anglican complacency.

When I survey my life, it seems to me to be a useless one, devoted to impossible ideals. I have not found in the post-war world any attainable ideals to replace those which I have come to think unattainable. So far as the things I have cared for are concerned, the world seems to me to be entering upon a period of darkness. When Rome fell, St Augustine, a Bolshevik of the period, could console himself with a new hope, but my outlook upon my own time is less like his than like that of the unfortunate Pagan philosophers of the time of Justinian, whom Gibbon describes as seeking asylum in Persia, but so disgusted by what they saw there that they returned to Athens, in spite of the Christian bigotry which forbade them to teach. Even they were more fortunate than I am in one respect, for they had an intellectual faith which remained firm. They entertained no doubt as to the greatness of Plato. For my part, I find in the most modern thought a corrosive solvent of the great systems of even the recent past, and I do not believe that the constructive efforts of present-day philosophers and men of science have anything approaching the validity that attaches to their destructive criticism.

My activities continue from force of habit, and in the company of others I forget the despair which underlies my daily pursuits and pleasures. But when I am alone and idle, I cannot conceal for myself that my life had no purpose, and that I know of no new purpose to which to devote my remaining years. I find myself involved in a vast mist of solitude both emotional and metaphysical, from which I can find no issue.

[June 11, 1931.]

LETTERS

From Joseph Conrad   Oswalds
                                            Bishopsbourne, Kent
                                            Oct. 23rd. 1922

My Dear Russell

When your book[1] arrived we were away for a few days. Perhaps *les convenances* demanded that I should have acknowledged the receipt at once. But I preferred to read it before I wrote. Unluckily a very unpleasant affair was sprung on me and absorbed all my thinking energies for a fortnight. I simply did not attempt to open the book till all the worry and flurry was over, and I could give it two clear days.

I have always liked the Chinese, even those that tried to kill me (and some other people) in the yard of a private house in Chantabun, even (but not so much) the fellow who stole all my money one night in Bankok, but brushed and folded my clothes neatly for me to dress in the morning, before vanishing into the depths of Siam. I also received many kindnesses at the hands of various Chinese. This with the addition of an evening's conversation with the secretary of His Excellency Tseng on the verandah of an hotel and a perfunctory study of a poem, *The Heathen Chinee*, is all I know about Chinese. But after reading your extremely interesting view of the Chinese Problem I take a gloomy view of the future of their country.

He who does not see the truth of your deductions can only be he who does not want to see. They strike a chill into one's soul especially when you deal with the American element. That would indeed be a dreadful fate for China or any other country. I feel your book the more because the only ray of hope you allow is the advent of international socialism, the sort of thing to which I cannot attach any sort of definite meaning. I have never been able to find in any man's book or any man's talk anything convincing enough to stand up for a moment against my deep-seated sense of fatality governing this man-inhabited world. After all it is but a system, not very recondite and not very plausible. As a mere reverie it is not of a very high order and wears a strange resemblance to a hungry man's dream of a gorgeous feast guarded by a lot of beadles in cocked hats. But I know you wouldn't expect me to put faith in *any* system. The only remedy for Chinamen and for the rest of us is the change of hearts, but looking at the history of the last 2000 years there is not much reason to expect that thing, even if man has taken to flying—a great 'uplift', no doubt, but no great change. He doesn't fly like an eagle; he flies like a beetle. And you must have noticed how ugly, ridiculous and fatuous is the flight of a beetle.

Your chapter on Chinese character is the sort of marvellous achievement that one would expect from you. It may not be complete. That I don't know. But as it stands, in its light touch and profound insight, it seems to me flawless. I have no difficulty in accepting it, because I do believe in amenity allied to barbarism, in compassion co-existing with complete brutality, and in essential

---

[1] *The Problem of China.*

rectitude underlying the most obvious corruption. And on this last point I would offer for your reflection that we ought not to attach too much importance to that trait of character—just because it is *not* a trait of character! At any rate no more than in other races of mankind. Chinese corruption is, I suspect, institutional: a mere method of paying salaries. Of course it was very dangerous. And in that respect the Imperial Edicts recommending honesty failed to affect the agents of the Government. But Chinese, essentially, are creatures of Edicts and in every other sphere their characteristic is, I should say, scrupulous honesty.

There is another suggestion of yours which terrifies me, and arouses my compassion for the Chinese, even more than the prospect of an Americanised China. It is your idea of some sort of selected council, the strongly disciplined society arriving at decisions etc. etc. (p. 244). If a constitution proclaimed in the light of day, with at least a chance of being understood by the people, is not to be relied on, then what trust could one put in a self-appointed and probably secret association (which from the nature of things must be above the law) to commend or condemn individuals or institutions? As it is unthinkable that you should be a slave to formulas or a victim of self-delusion, it is with the greatest diffidence that I raise my protest against your contrivance which must *par la force des choses* and by the very manner of its inception become but an association of mere swelled-heads of the most dangerous kind. There is not enough honour, virtue and selflessness *in the world* to make any such council other than the greatest danger to every kind of moral, mental and political independence. It would become a centre of delation, intrigue and jealousy of the most debased kind. No freedom of thought, no peace of heart, no genius, no virtue, no individuality trying to raise its head above the subservient mass, would be safe before the domination of such a council, and the unavoidable demoralization of the instruments of its power. For, I must suppose that you mean it to have power and to have agents to exercise that power—or else it would become as little substantial as if composed of angels of whom ten thousand can sit on the point of a needle. But I wouldn't trust a society of that kind even if composed of angels. . . . More! I would not, my dear friend, (to address you in Salvation Army style) trust that society if Bertrand Russell himself were, after 40 days of meditation and fasting, to undertake the selection of the members. After saying this I may just as well resume my wonted calm; for, indeed, I could not think of any stronger way of expressing my utter dislike and mistrust of such an expedient for working out the salvation of China.

I see in this morning's *Times* (this letter was begun yesterday) a leader on your *Problem of China* which I hope will comfort and sustain you in the face of my savage attack. I meant it to be deadly; but I perceive that on account of my age and infirmities there was never any need for you to fly the country or ask for police protection. You will no doubt be glad to hear that my body is disabled by a racking cough and my enterprising spirit irretrievably tamed by an unaccountable depression. Thus are the impious stricken, and things of the order that 'passeth understanding' brought home to one! . . . But I will not treat you to a meditation on my depression. That way madness lies.

Your—truly Christian in its mansuetude—note has just reached me. I admire your capacity for forgiving sinners, and I am warmed by the glow of your friendliness. But I protest against your credulity in the matter of newspaper pars. I did not know I was to stay in town to attend rehearsals. Which is the rag that decreed it I wonder? The fact is I came up for just 4 hours and 20 min. last Wednesday; and that I may have to pay another visit to the theatre (the whole thing is like an absurd dream) one day this week. You can not doubt *mon Compère* that I *do* want to see the child whose advent has brought about this intimate relation between us. But I shrink from staying the night in town. In fact I am afraid of it. This is no joke. Neither is it a fact that I would shout on housetops. I am confiding it to you as a sad truth. However—this cannot last; and before long I'll make a special trip to see you all on an agreed day. Meantime my love to him—special and exclusive. Please give my duty to your wife as politeness dictates and—as my true feelings demand—remember me most affectionately to *ma très honorée Commère*. And pray go on cultivating forgiveness towards this insignificant and unworthy person who dares to subscribe himself

Always yours
Joseph Conrad

From Wm. F. Philpott   Chelsea, S.W.
                                       14.11.22

Dear Sir

Herewith I return some of the literature you have sent for my perusal.

One of the papers says 'Why do thinking people vote Labor'.

Thinking people don't vote Labor at all, it is only those who cannot see beyond their nose who vote Labor.

According to your Photo it does not look as though it is very long since you left your cradle so I think you would be wise to go home and suck your titty. The Electors of Chelsea want a man of experience to represent them. Take my advice and leave Politics to men of riper years. If you cannot remember the Franco Prussian War of 1870 or the Russo Turkish War of 1876/7 then you are not old enough to be a Politician.

I can remember both those Wars and also the War of –/66 when the Battle of Sadowa was fought.

England had men of experience to represent them then.

I am afraid we shall never get anyone like Lord Derby (The Rupert of Debate) and Dizzy to lead us again.

Yours obedy
Wm. F. Philpott

Parliamentary General Election, 15th November, 1922.

To the Electors of Chelsea

Dear Sir or Madam

At the invitation of the Executive Committee of the Chelsea Labour Party, I come before you as Labour candidate at the forthcoming General Election.

I have been for many years a member of the Independent Labour Party, and I am in complete agreement with the programme of the Labour Party as published on October 26.

The Government which has been in power ever since the Armistice has done nothing during the past four years to restore normal life to Europe. Our trade suffers because our customers are ruined. This is the chief cause of the unemployment and destitution, unparalleled in our previous history, from which our country has suffered during the past two years. If we are to regain any measure of prosperity, the first necessity is a wise and firm foreign policy, leading to the revival of Eastern and Central Europe, and avoiding such ignorant and ill-considered adventures as nearly plunged us into war with the Turks. The Labour Party is the only one whose foreign policy is sane and reasonable, the only one which is likely to save Britain from even worse disasters than those already suffered. The new Government, according to the statement of its own supporters, does not differ from the old one on any point of policy. The country had become aware of the incompetence of the Coalition Government, and the major part of its supporters hope to avert the wrath of the electors by pretending to be quite a different firm. It is an old device—a little too old to be practised with success at this time of day. Those who see the need of new policies must support new men, not the same men under a new label.

There is need of drastic economy, but not at the expense of the least fortunate members of the community, and above all not at the expense of education and the care of children, upon which depends the nation's future. What has been thrown away in Irak and Chanak and such places has been wasted utterly, and it is in these directions that we must look for a reduction in our expenditure.

I am a strong supporter of the capital levy, and of the nationalization of mines and railways, with a great measure of control by the workers in those industries. I hope to see similar measures adopted, in the course of time, in other industries.

The housing problem is one which must be dealt with at the earliest possible moment. Something would be done to alleviate the situation by the taxation of land values, which would hinder the holding up of vacant land while the owner waits for a good price. Much could be done if public bodies were to eliminate capitalists' profits by employing the Building Guild. By these methods, or by whatever methods prove available, houses must be provided to meet the imperative need.

The main cure for unemployment must be the improvement of our trade by the restoration of normal conditions on the Continent. In the meantime, it is unjust that those who are out of work through no fault of their own should suffer destitution; for the present, therefore, I am in favour of the continuation of unemployed benefit.

I am in favour of the removal of all inequalities in the law as between men and women. In particular, I hold that every adult citizen, male or female, ought to be entitled to a vote.

As a result of mismanagement since the armistice, our country and the world are faced with terrible dangers. The Labour Party has a clear and sane policy for dealing with these dangers. I am strongly opposed to all suggestions of violent revolution, and I am persuaded that only by constitutional methods can a better state of affairs be brought about. But I see no hope of improvement from parties which advocate a continuation of the muddled vindictiveness which has brought Europe to the brink of ruin. For the world at large, for our own country, and for every man, woman and child in our country, the victory of Labour is essential. On these grounds I appeal for your votes.

Bertrand Russell

From G. B. Shaw

10 Adelphi Terrace, W.C.2
[1922]

Dear Russell

I should say yes with pleasure if the matter were in my hands; but, as you may imagine, I have so many calls that I must leave it to the Labor Party, acting through the Fabian Society as far as I am concerned, to settle where I shall go. You had better therefore send in a request at once to the Fabian Society, 25 Tothill Street, Westminster, S.W.1. for a speech from me.

I must warn you, however, that though, when I speak, the hall is generally full, and the meeting is apparently very successful, the people who run after and applaud me are just as likely to vote for the enemy, or not vote at all, on polling day. I addressed 13 gorgeous meetings at the last election; but not one of my candidates got in.

Faithfully
G. Bernard Shaw

P.S. As you will see, this is a circular letter, which I send only because it explains the situation. Nothing is settled yet except that I am positively engaged on the 2nd, 3rd and 10th.

I suppose it is too late to urge you not to waste any of your own money on Chelsea, where no Progressive has a dog's chance. In Dilke's day it was Radical; but Lord Cadogan rebuilt it fashionably and drove all the Radicals across the bridges to Battersea. It is exasperating that a reasonably winnable seat has not been found for you. I would not spend a farthing on it myself, even if I could finance the 400 or so Labor candidates who would like to touch me for at least a fiver apiece.

From and to Jean Nicod

France
15 June [1919]

Dear Mr Russell

We shall come with joy. We are both so happy to see you. How nice of you to ask us!

I have not written to you all this time because I was doing nothing good, and was in consequence a little ashamed.

Your *Justice in War Time* is slowly appearing in *La Forge*, and is intended to be published in book-form afterwards. I ought to have done better, I think.

And I have done no work, only studied some physics. I have been thinking a tremendous time on the External World, with no really clear results. Also, I have been yearning in vain to help it *à faire peau neuve*.

So you will see us coming at the beginning of September at Lulworth. We feel quite elated at the thought of being some time with you.

Yours very sincerely
Jean Nicod

53 rue Gazan
Paris XIV*e*
28th September 1919

Dear Mr Russell

I could not see Romain Rolland, who is not in Paris now. I shall write to him and send him your letter with mine.

We are not going to Rumania. I am going to Cahors to-morrow, and Thérèse is staying here. There is now a prospect of our going to Brazil in eighteen months. Of course I am ceasing to believe in any of these things; but we are learning a great deal of geography.

I have definitely arranged to write a thesis on the external world. Part of it will be ready at Christmas, as I am being assured that I shall find very little work at Cahors.

We hope to hear that you are back in Cambridge now.

You know how glad we both are to have seen you again.

Yours
Jean Nicod

1, rue Pot Trinquat, Cahors
20 April [1920]

Dear Mr Russell

Here is the geometry of the fish, as you said you liked it. It will appear in the *Revue de Métaphysique*, but I cannot refrain from sending it to you now as a prolongation of our talk. I hope you will look through it, but please do not feel bound to write to me about it. I know you are very busy.

It was so nice of you to stop. When I heard that you were to come, it seemed like the realisation of a dream. This day with you has been a great joy to me.

Yours very sincerely
Jean

I do not want the MS. back

Campagne Saunex
Prégny, Genève
22 Sept. 1921

Dear Mr Russell

Do you know that your death was announced in a Japanese paper? I sent a telegram to the University of Peking, who answered 'Recovered'—but we were terribly anxious. We hope you are quite well again now.

I shall leave this office in February or March, with some money, and do nothing till next October at the very least. I do hope that I shall see you.

Yours affectionately
Jean Nicod

70, Overstrand Mansions
Prince of Wales Road
Battersea, S.W.11
2.10.21

Dear Nicod

I have sent your query to Whitehead, as I have forgotten his theory and never knew it very thoroughly. I will let you know his answer as soon as I get it. I *am* glad your book is so nearly done. *Please* let me see it when it is.—I know about the announcement of my death—it was a fearful nuisance. It was in the English and American papers too. I am practically well now but I came as near dying as one can without going over the edge—Pneumonia it was. I was delirious for three weeks, and I have no recollection of the time whatever, except a few dreams of negroes singing in deserts, and of learned bodies that I thought I had to address. The Doctor said to me afterwards: 'When you were ill you behaved like a true philosopher; every time that you came to yourself you made a joke.' I never had a compliment that pleased me more.

Dora and I are now married, but just as happy as we were before. We both send our love to you both. It *will* be delightful to see you when you leave Geneva. We shall be in London.

Yours aff.
Bertrand Russell

31 Sydney Street
London, S.W.3
13.9.23

Dear Nicod

I have been meaning to write to you for the last eight months, but have somehow never done so. Did Keynes ever answer your letter? He is now so busy with politics and money-making that I doubt if he ever thinks about probability. He has become enormously rich, and has acquired *The Nation*. He is Liberal, not Labour.

Principia Mathematica is being reprinted, and I am writing a new introduction, abolishing axiom of reducibility, and assuming that functions of props are always truth-functions, and functions of functions only occur through values of the functions and are always extensional. I don't know if these assumptions are true, but it seems worth while to work out their consequences.

What do you think of the enclosed proposal? I have undertaken to try to get articles. I asked if they would admit Frenchmen, and they say yes, if they write in German or English. Will you send me an article for them? I want to help them as much as I can. *Do.*

All goes well with us. Dora expects another child about Xmas time, and unfortunately I have to go to America to lecture for three months at the New Year.

The world gets more and more dreadful. What a misfortune not to have lived fifty years sooner. And now God has taken a hand at Tokyo. As yet, he beats human war-mongers, but they will equal him before long.

> *Yours ever*
> *Bertrand Russell*

From Moritz Schlick, founder of the Vienna Circle

> Philosophisches
> Institut der Universität
> in Wien
> Vienna, Sep. 9th 1923

Dear Mr Russell

Thank you most heartily for your kind letter. I was overjoyed to receive your affirmative answer. I feel convinced that the future of the magazine is safe since you have consented to lend your help by being one of the editors. It is a pity, of course, that you cannot send an article of your own immediately and that you have not much hope of getting contributions from your English and American friends during the next months, but we must be patient and shall be glad to wait till you have more time. I am sure that the scheme will work very well later on. It already means a great deal to know that we have your support, that your name will in some way be identified with the spirit of the magazine.

Thank you for your further suggestions. In my opinion contributions by M. Nicod would be most welcome, and I have no doubt that none of the editors would object to French articles, but unfortunately the publisher (who of course takes the business standpoint) has declared that at present he cannot possibly print anything in French, but I hope he will have nothing against publishing articles by French authors in the German or English language.

I have written to Reichenbach about your suggestion concerning the Polish logicians at Warsaw; I do not think there will be any political difficulties in approaching them. I believe we must be careful not to have too many articles dealing with mathematical logic or written in symbolic form in the first issues, as they might frighten away many readers, they must get used to the new forms gradually.

I have asked Reichenbach to send you some offprints of his chief papers; I hope you have received them by the time these lines reach you.

I should like to ask you some philosophical questions, but I am extremely busy just now. Our 'Internationale Hochschulkurse' are beginning this week, with lecturers and students from many countries. It would be splendid if you would be willing to come to Vienna on a similar occasion next year.

Thanking you again I remain

> *yours very sincerely*
> *M. Schlick*

From Jean Nicod.

Chemin des Coudriers
Petit Saconnex, Genève
17 September, 1923

Dear Mr Russell

I should like very much to dedicate my book *La Géométrie dans le Monde sensible* to you. It is not very good; but I still hope that bits of it may be worth something. Will you accept it, such as it is? I have thought of the following inscription:

*A mon maître
L'Honorable Bertrand Russell
Membre de la Société Royale d'Angleterre
en témoignage de reconnaissante affection*

Can I let it go like that? The book is the chief one of my theses. The other one is *Le Problème logique de l'Induction*, which is a criticism of Keynes. I think I prove there that two instances differing only numerically (or in respects assumed to be immaterial) *do* count for more than one only; also, that Keynes' Limitation of Variety does *not* do what he thinks it does. Both books will be printed in three weeks or so (although they cannot be published till after their discussion en Sorbonne some time next winter).

I've sent my ms. to Keynes, offering to print his answer along with it. But he says he is too absorbed by other things; and altogether, I fear that he does not take me seriously—which is sad, because I am sure my objections well deserve to be considered.

Physically, I am settling down to a state which is not health, but which allows some measure of life, and may improve with time.

We hope you three are flourishing, and send you our love.

Jean Nicod

Chemin des Coudriers
Petit Saconnex, Genève
19 Sept. 1923

Dear Mr Russell

I got your letter the very morning I had posted mine to you.

I should love to write an article for this new review. But I have just sent one to the *Revue de Métaphysique* (on relations of values (i.e. truth values) and relations of meanings in Logic) and have nothing even half ready. I have been thinking of a sequel to my book, dealing with a universe of perspectives where objects are in motion (uniform) and Restricted Relativity applies, everything being as simple as possible. I would set forth what the observer (more like an angel than a man) would observe, and the order of his sensible world. What attracts me to that sort of thing is its quality of freshness of vision—to take stock of a world as of something entirely new. But it may well be rather childish, and I don't propose to go on with it until you have seen the book itself and tell me it is worth while.

Since you are re-publishing *Principia*, I may remind you that I have proved *both* Permutation *and* Association by help of the other three primitive props (Tautology, Addition, and the syllogistic prop.), where I only changed the order of some letters. It is in a Memoir I wrote for the B.A. degree. I have entirely forgotten how it is done, but I daresay I could find it again for you, if you wished to reduce your 5 prim. props to those three (observe there is one with one letter, one with two letters, and one with three letters).

Keynes did answer the letter I sent you. His answer convinced me I was right on both points; so I went on with my small book. It is a pity he will not do anything more for the theory of Induction.

Your son does look pleased with the stones he holds. His appearance is splendid.

We send our love.

Yours ever
Jean Nicod

From and to Thérèse Nicod

le 18 février [1924]

Dear Mr Russell

Jean has died on Saturday last after a short illness.

Je veux vous l'écrire pendant qu'il repose encore près de moi dans cette maison où il a tant travaillé, tant espéré guérir—et où nous avons été si heureux.

Vous savez combien il vous aimait—quelle lumière vous avez été pour lui—vous savez aussi l'être délicieux et noble qu'il était. C'est absolument déchirant.

Je voudrais avoir des nouvelles de Dora.

Affectueusement à vous deux.

Thérèse Nicod

Genève 22 Juillet 1924

Dear Mr Russell

Please pardon me for not having thanked you sooner for the Preface (or introduction, we shall call it what you think best). I do not tell you how grateful I am to you because I know you did it for Jean.

I shall translate it as soon as I get some free time. We are absolutely loaded with things to do.

Of course your preface is everything and more that we could want it to be. I mean to say that it is very beautiful—How could I suggest a single alteration to it.

I remember that last winter I wrote to Jean that he was the most beautiful type of humanity I knew. (I do not recollect what about—We had outbreaks like that from time to time) and he answered immediately: '*Moi le plus beau type d'humanity que je connais c'est Russell.*'

Thank you again most deeply.

Yours very sincerely
Thérèse Nicod

12 *Chemin Thury*
Genève
le 19 *octobre* 1960

Cher Lord Russell

Permettez-moi de m'adresser à vous à travers toutes ces années. J'ai toujours eu l'intention de faire une réédition des thèses de Jean Nicod et je sais qu'aujourd'hui encore, sa pensée n'est pas oubliée. J'ai eu l'occasion de rencontrer dernièrement M. Jean Hyppolite, Directeur de l'Ecole normale supérieure qui m'a vivement conseillée de rééditer en premier Le problème logique de l'induction *dont il avait gardé un souvenir tout à fait précis et qu'il recommande aux jeunes philosophes.*

Parmi ceux qui m'ont donné le même conseil je citerai le Professeur Gonseth de Zurich, M. Gaston Bachelard, Jean Lacroix, etc. J'ai même trouvé, l'autre jour, par hasard, dans un manuel paru en 1959 un passage intitulé: 'Axiome de Nicod'.

L'ouvrage réédité paraîtrait à Paris, aux Presses universitaires de France, qui en assureront la diffusion.

Je viens vous demander, si vous jugez cette réédition opportune, de bien vouloir accepter d'écrire quelques lignes qui s'ajouteraient à la première préface de M. Lalande. Qui mieux que vous pourrait donner à ce tardif hommage le poids et l'envol?

Veuillez, cher Lord Russell, recevoir l'assurance de ma profonde admiration et de mes sentiments respectueux.

Thérèse Nicod

Je vous écris à une adresse que j'ai trouvée par hasard dans un magazine et dont je suis si peu sûre que je me permets de recommander le pli.

Plas Penrhyn
1 November, 1960

Dear Thérèse Nicod

Thank you for your letter of October 19. I was very glad to have news of you. I entirely agree with you that it is very desirable to bring out a new edition of Nicod's work on induction which I think is very important and which has not received adequate recognition. I am quite willing to make a short addition to the preface by Monsieur Lalande. I suppose that you are in communication with Sir Roy Harrod (Christ Church, Oxford) who has been for some time concerned in obtaining a better English translation of Nicod's work than the one made long ago.

I was very sorry to hear of the death of your son.

If ever you are in England it would be a very great pleasure to see you.

Yours very sincerely
Bertrand Russell

From G. B. Shaw[1]

Hotel Metropole
Minehead, Somerset
11 April 1923

My dear Russell

The other day I read your laudably unapologetic *Apologia* from cover to cover with unflagging interest. I gather from your *Au Revoir* that it is to be continued in your next.

I was brought up—or left to bring myself up—on your father's plan all through. I can imagine nothing more damnable than the position of a boy started that way, and then, when he had acquired an adult freethinking habit of mind and character, being thrust back into the P.L. sort of tutelage. You say you have a bad temper; but the fact that you neither burnt the lodge nor murdered Uncle Rollo is your eternal testimonial to the contrary.

No doubt Winchester saved Rollo and his shrine. Your description of the school is the only really descriptive description of one of the great boy farms I have ever read.

ever
G. *Bernard Shaw*

Extract from *Unity*, Chicago   19 Jun. 1924

Bertrand Russell has returned to England, and one of the most impressive tours ever made in this country by a distinguished foreigner has thus come to an end. Everywhere Professor Russell spoke, he was greeted by great audiences with rapturous enthusiasm, and listened to with a touching interest and reverence. At most of his meetings, admission was charged, frequently at regular theater rates, but this seemed to make no difference in the attendance. Throngs of eager men and women crowded the auditoriums where he appeared, and vied with one another in paying homage to the distinguished man whom they so honored. From this point of view, Bertrand Russell's visit was a triumph. From another and quite different point of view, it was a failure and disgrace! What was the great public at large allowed to know about this famous Englishman and the message which he brought across the seas to us Americans? Nothing! The silence of our newspapers was wellnigh complete. Only when Mr Russell got into a controversy with President Lowell, of Harvard, which gave opportunity to make the eagle scream, did his name or words appear in any conspicuous fashion in our public prints. The same journals which publish columns of stuff about millionaires, actors, singers, prizefighters and soldiers from abroad, and blazen forth their most casual comments about anything from women to the weather, reported almost nothing about this one of the most eminent Europeans of the day. But this is not the worst. Turn from the newspapers to the colleges and universities! Here is Mr Russell, the ablest and most famous mathematical philosopher of modern times—for long an honored

[1] This letter was addressed to my brother and is about his *My Life and Adventures*, published 1923.

Fellow of Cambridge, England—author of learned essays and treatises which are the standard authorities in their field—at the least, a great scholar, at the most, one of the greatest of scholars! But how many colleges in America officially invited him to their halls? How many gave him degrees of honor? So far as we know, Smith College was the only institution which officially received him as a lecturer, though we understand that he appeared also at the Harvard Union. Practically speaking, Professor Russell was ignored. A better measure of the ignorance, cowardice and Pharisaism of American academic life we have never seen!

From T. S. Eliot

9, Clarence Gate Gardens
N.W.1
15.X.23

Dear Bertie

I was delighted to get your letter. It gives me very great pleasure to know that you like the *Waste Land,* and especially Part V which in my opinion is not only the best part, but the only part that justifies the whole, at all. It means a great deal to me that you like it.

I must tell you that 18 months ago, before it was published anywhere, Vivien wanted me to send you the MS. to read, because she was sure that you were one of the very few persons who might possibly see anything in it. But we felt that *you* might prefer to have nothing to do with *us*: It is absurd to say that we wished to drop you.

Vivien has had a frightful illness, and nearly died, in the spring—as Ottoline has probably told you. And that she has been in the country ever since. She has not yet come back.

Dinner is rather difficult for me at present. But might I come to tea with you on Saturday? I should like to see you very much—there have been *many times* when I have thought that.

Yours ever
T. S. E.

9, Clarence Gate Gardens
N.W.1
21 April. [1925]

Dear Bertie

If you are still in London I should very much like to see you.

My times and places are very restricted, but it is unnecessary to mention them unless I hear from you.

I want words from you which only you can give. But if you have now ceased to care at all about either of us, just write on a slip 'I do not care to see you' or 'I do not care to see either of you'—and I will understand.

In case of that, I will tell you now that everything has turned out as you predicted 10 years ago. You are a great psychologist.

Yours
T.S.E.

The Criterion
17, Thavies Inn
London, E.C.1
7 May [1925]

My dear Bertie

Thank you very much indeed for your letter. As you say, it is very difficult for you to make suggestions until I can see you. For instance, I don't know to what extent the changes which have taken place, since we were in touch with you, would seem to you material. What you suggest seems to me of course what should have been done years ago. Since then her[1] health is a thousand times worse. Her only alternative would be to live quite alone—if she could. And the fact that living with me has done her so much damage does not help me to come to any decision. I need the help of someone who understands her—I find her still perpetually baffling and deceptive. She seems to me like a child of 6 with an immensely clever and precocious mind. She writes *extremely* well (stories, etc.) and great originality. And I can never escape from the spell of her persuasive (even coercive) gift of argument.

Well, thank you very much, Bertie—I feel quite desperate. I hope to see you in the Autumn.

Yours ever
T.S.E.

From my brother Frank

50 Cleveland Square
London, W.2
8 June, 1925

Dear Bertie

I lunched with the Aunt Agatha on Friday, and she was even more tedious than usual. In fact, she gave me the treatment that I think she generally reserves for you. She began by being very sighful and P.L.y about Alys, and said how she still loved you and how determined you had been to marry her. She infuriated me so that I reminded her at last that at the time the P.L. view, which she had fully shared, was that you were an innocent young man pursued by a designing woman, and that the one view was not any truer than the other. Then she went on to Birth Control, with a sniff at Dora, and aggravated me to such an extent that I was bound to tell her that I did not think old women of seventy-three were entitled to legislate for young ones of twenty-five. Thereupon she assured me that she had been twenty-five herself once, but I unfortunately lacked the courage to say Never! You can gather how provoking she must have been from the fact that I was driven to reply, which I don't generally do. She then went on to try and make mischief about you and Elizabeth, by telling me how much you were in love with Elizabeth and how regularly you saw her.[2] She really is a villainous old cat.

In order to take the taste of her out of my mouth when I got home I read, or at any rate looked through, three books I had not seen before: *Daedalus*,

---

[1] This refers to his first wife.
[2] This, of course, was quite untrue.

Icarus and *Hypatia*. Haldane's 'Test Tube Mothers' gave me the shivers: I prefer the way of the music-hall song! I liked what I read of Dora's book, and intend to read it more carefully.

Will you tell Dora that I am not the least anxious to go to the Fabian people, as it would bore me to tears, and would only have done it to back her up, so I hope she won't put anyone else on to me. Dora says you are fat, and something that at first I thought was 'beneath consideration', which gave me a faint hope that you had ceased to be a philosopher, but on looking at it again I see that it is 'writing about education'.

Dorothy Wrinch said that she was coming down to see you early in August, and I suggested driving her down, but I suppose that means taking old Heavyweight too. The time she suggested, shortly after the August Bank Holiday, would suit me if you could have me then. You will no doubt be surprised to hear that I am going to the British Ass. this year, as it is held at Southampton, quite convenient.

Damn that acid old spinster!

> *Yours affectionately*
> *Russell*

> 50 Cleveland Square
> London, W.2
> 15 June, 1925

Dear Bertie

Thanks for your amusing letter. I was going to write to you anyhow, because I have been reading your delightful *What I believe*. My word! You have compressed it, and succeeded in saying a good many things calculated to be thoroughly annoying and disconcerting to the virtuous in the space. I am so delighted with it that I am going to get half-a-dozen copies and give them away where I think they will be appreciated. I like your conclusive proof that bishops are much more brutal than Aztecs who go in for human sacrifices. I don't think I shall try a copy on my tame bishop because, although I am very fond of him, intellect is not his strong point.

I am going to write to Dorothy and make your suggestion.

> *Yours affectionately*
> *Russell*

From Gertrude Beasly

> 8 Woburn Place, W.C.1
> Gresham Hotel, London
> June 21. 1925

Dear Mr Russell

Shortly after you left in March I found a publisher for my book, a semi-private company in Paris. Several weeks ago a few of the proofs reached me. Yesterday morning I found myself before the Magistrate at Bow Street after a night in prison.

In the afternoon of June 19 an officer from Scotland Yard called to see me bringing with him a bundle of the proofs of my book which he described as 'grossly obscene'. He said I would have to appear before the Magistrate on the charge of sending improper matter through the post. He examined my passport and found it had not been registered. I was arrested and escorted to Bow Street to register my passport, and detained over night. The Alien Officer brought a charge of failure to register my passport to which I pleaded guilty before the Magistrate and offered explanation of my negligence. The Scotland Yard agent brought a charge of sending obscene literature by post and asked the Magistrate to punish (I believe he said) and make arrangement for my deportation. The punishment, I believe, refers to a heavy fine or imprisonment.

I am on bail, 10 pounds, and the case is to be tried on Saturday June 27 at about 11 o'clock, I shall find out definitely tomorrow as to the hour.

Mr Ewer thinks he can find an attorney to take my case. I shall go to the American Consul tomorrow and talk with others here who know me. Shall probably see Dr Ellis tomorrow.

If you can offer any advice I shall be glad.

> *Sincerely yours*
> *Gertrude Beasly*

Miss Beasly was a schoolteacher from Texas, who wrote an autobiography. It was truthful, which is illegal.

To Max Newman, the distinguished mathematician

24th April 1928

Dear Newman

Many thanks for sending me the off-print of your article about me in *Mind*. I read it with great interest and some dismay. You make it entirely obvious that my statements to the effect that nothing is known about the physical world except its structure are either false or trivial, and I am somewhat ashamed at not having noticed the point for myself.

It is of course obvious, as you point out, that the only effective assertion about the physical world involved in saying that it is susceptible to such and such a structure is an assertion about its cardinal number. (This by the way is not quite so trivial an assertion as it would seem to be, if, as is not improbable, the cardinal number involved is finite. This, however, is not a point upon which I wish to lay stress.) It was quite clear to me, as I read your article, that I had not really intended to say what in fact I did say, that *nothing* is known about the physical world except its structure. I had always assumed spacio-temporal continuity with the world of percepts, that is to say, I had assumed that there might be co-punctuality between percepts and non-percepts, and even that one could pass by a finite number of steps from one event to another compresent with it, from one end of the universe to the other. And co-punctuality I regarded as a relation which might exist among percepts and is itself perceptible.

I have not yet had time to think out how far the admission of co-punctuality alone in addition to structure would protect me from your criticisms, nor yet how far it would weaken the plausibility of my metaphysic. What I did realise was that spacio-temporal continuity of percepts and non-percepts was so axiomatic in my thought that I failed to notice that my statements appeared to deny it.

I am at the moment much too busy to give the matter proper thought, but I should be grateful if you could find time to let me know whether you have any ideas on the matter which are not merely negative, since it does not appear from your article what your own position is. I gathered in talking with you that you favoured phenomenalism, but I do not quite know how definitely you do so.

Yours sincerely
Bertrand Russell

To Harold Laski

12th May 1928

My dear Laski

I am afraid it is quite impossible for me to speak to the Socratic Society this term, much as I should like to do so. But the fact is I am too busy to have any ideas worth having, like Mrs Eddy who told a friend of mine that she was too busy to become the second incarnation.

I am not at all surprised that Bentham suggests companionate marriage; in fact one could almost have inferred it. I discovered accidentally from an old envelope used as a bookmark that at the moment of my birth my father was reading Bentham's *Table of the Springs of Action*. Evidently this caused me to be Benthamitically 'conditioned', as he has always seemed to me a most sensible fellow. But as a schoolmaster, I am gradually being driven to more radical proposals, such as those of Plato. If there were an international government I should seriously be in favour of the root and branch abolition of the family, but as things are, I am afraid it would make people more patriotic.

Yours ever
Bertrand Russell

To Mr Gardner Jackson

28th May 1929

Dear Mr Jackson

I am sorry I shall not be in America at the time of your meeting on August 23rd, the more so as I shall be there not so very long after that. I think you are quite right to do everything possible to keep alive the memory of Sacco and Vanzetti. It must, I think, be clear to any unprejudiced person that there was not such evidence against them as to warrant a conviction, and I have no doubt in my own mind that they were wholly innocent. I am forced to conclude that they were condemned on account of their political opinions and that men who ought to have known better allowed themselves to express misleading views as to the evidence because they held that men with such opinions have no right to live. A view of this sort is one which is very dangerous, since it transfers from the theological to the political sphere a form of persecution which it was thought that civilized countries had outgrown. One is not so surprised at occurrences of this sort in Hungary or Lithuania, but in America they must be matters of grave concern to all who care for freedom of opinion.

Yours sincerely
Bertrand Russell

P.S. I hope that out of the above you can make a message for the meeting; if you do not think it suitable, please let me know, and I will concoct another.

From and to Mr C. L. Aiken

8, Plympton St.
Cambridge, Mass.
March 2, 1930

My Dear Mr Russell

I am preparing a free-lance article on the subject of parasitic nuisances who bedevil authors: autograph and photograph hunters, those thoughtless myriads who expect free criticism, poems, speeches, lectures, jobs, and who in general impose on the literary professional. (I suppose you will place me in the same category, but hope you can feel that the end justifies the means in this case.)

Would you be so good as to send me an account of your grievances, the length and nature of which of course I leave to you?

Very truly yours
Clarice Lorenz Aiken

19th March 1930

Dear Mr Aiken

In common with other authors, I suffer a good deal from persons who think that an author ought to do their work for them. Apart from autograph hunters, I get large numbers of letters from persons who wish me to copy out for them the appropriate entry in *Who's Who*, or ask me my opinion on points which I have fully discussed in print.

I get many letters from Hindus, beseeching me to adopt some form of mysticism, from young Americans, asking me where I think the line should be drawn in petting, and from Poles, urging me to admit that while all other nationalism may be bad that of Poland is wholly noble.

I get letters from engineers who cannot understand Einstein, and from parsons who think that I cannot understand Genesis, from husbands whose wives have deserted them—not (they say) that that would matter, but the wives have taken the furniture with them, and what in these circumstances should an enlightened male do?

I get letters from Jews to say that Solomon was not a polygamist, and from Catholics to say that Torquemada was not a persecutor. I get letters (concerning whose genuineness I am suspicious) trying to get me to advocate abortion, and I get letters from young mothers asking my opinion of bottle-feeding.

178

I am sorry to say that most of the subjects dealt with by my correspondents have escaped my memory at the moment, but the few that I have mentioned may serve as a sample.

Yours very truly
Bertrand Russell

To Miss Brooks[1]

5th May 1930

Dear Miss Brooks

I am not sure whether you are right in saying that the problem of America is greater than that of China. It is likely that America will be more important during the next century or two, but after that it may well be the turn of China. I think America is very worrying. There is something incredibly wrong with human relations in your country. We have a number of American children at our school, and I am amazed at their mothers' instinctive incompetence. The fount of affection seems to have dried up. I suppose all Western civilization is going to go the same way, and I expect all our Western races to die out, with the possible exception of the Spaniards and Portuguese. Alternatively the State may take to breeding the necessary citizens and educating them as Janissaries without family ties. Read John B. Watson on mothers. I used to think him mad; now I only think him American; that is to say, the mothers that he has known have been American mothers. The result of this physical aloofness is that the child grows up filled with hatred against the world and anxious to distinguish himself as a criminal, like Leopold and Loeb.

Yours sincerely
Bertrand Russell

Here is part of the preface I wrote:

In view of the aggression of Western nations, the Chinese who were in many respects more civilized than ourselves and at a higher ethical level, were faced with the necessity of developing a policy with more military efficacy than could be derived from the Confucian teaching. Social life in Old China was based upon the family. Sun Yat Sen justly perceived that if China was to resist successfully the onslaughts of military nations, it would be necessary to substitute the state for the family; and patriotism for filial piety—in a word, the Chinese had to choose whether they would die as saints or live as sinners. Under Christian influence they chose the latter alternative.

Assuming the nationalist (Chiang Kai Shek) government to be successful, the outcome must be to add another and very important member to the ruthless militaristic governments which compete in everything except the destruction of civilization on which task alone they are prepared to cooperate. All the intellect, all the heroism, all the martyrdoms, and agonizing disillusionments of Chinese history since 1911, will have led up only to this: to create a new force

[1] Who became the Rev. Rachel Gleason Brooks, for whose still unpublished book on China I in 1931 wrote a preface.

179

for evil and a new obstacle to the peace of the world. The history of Japan should have taught the West caution. But Western civilization with all its intelligence is as blind in its operation as an avalanche, and must take its course to what dire conclusion, I dare not guess.

In her book This is Your Inheritance: A History of the Chemung County, N.Y. Branch of the Brooks Family (*p. 167, published by Century House, Watkins Glen, New York, U.S.A., 1963) she wrote: 'Bertrand Russell's preface (omitting the laudatory remarks about the author) sums up what happened during our lifetime in China. . . . This preface was taken down by me in the parlor of the Mayflower hotel in Akron, Ohio on the morning of Dec. 1st, 1931 as Mr Russell paced the floor, smoking his pipe. Then he signed it and we went to the railroad station; he to go to another lecturing appointment and I to return to Oberlin.'*

To H. G. Wells

24th May '28

My dear H.G.

Thank you very much for sending me your book on *The Open Conspiracy*. I have read it with the most complete sympathy, and I do not know of anything with which I agree more entirely. I enjoyed immensely your fable about Provinder Island. I am, I think, somewhat less optimistic than you are, probably owing to the fact that I was in opposition to the mass of mankind during the war, and thus acquired the habit of feeling helpless.

You speak for example, of getting men of science to join the Open Conspiracy, but I should think there is hardly a single one who would do so, with the exception of Einstein—a not unimportant exception I admit. The rest in this country would desire knighthoods, in France to become *membres de l'institut*, and so on. Even among younger men, I believe your support would be very meagre. Julian Huxley would not be willing to give up his flirtations with the episcopate; Haldane would not forego the pleasure to be derived from the next war.

I was interested to read what you say about schools and education generally, and that you advocate 'a certain sectarianism of domestic and social life in the interests of its children' and 'grouping of its families and the establishment of its own schools'. It was the feeling of this necessity which led us to found Beacon Hill School, and I am every day more convinced that people who have the sort of ideas that we have ought not to expose their children to obscurantist influence, more especially during their early years when these influences can operate upon what will be their unconscious in adult life.

This brings me to a matter which I approach with some hesitation, but which I had decided to write to you about before I read your book. This school is costing me about £2000 a year, that is to say very nearly the whole of my income. I do not think that this is due to any incompetence in management; in fact all experimental schools that I have ever heard of have been expensive propositions. My income is precarious since it depends upon the tastes of American readers who are notoriously fickle, and I am therefore very uncertain as to whether I shall be able to keep the school going. In order to be able to do so I should need donations amounting to about £1000 a year. I have been wondering whether you would be willing to help in any way towards the obtaining of this sum, either directly or by writing an appeal which might influence progressive Americans. I should be very grateful if you would let me know whether you would consider anything of the sort. You will see of course that an appeal written by Dora and me is less effective than one from an impartial pen, especially if that pen were yours.

I believe profoundly in the importance of what we are doing here. If I were to put into one single phrase our educational objects, I should say that we aim at training initiative without diminishing its strength. I have long held that stupidity is very largely the result of fear leading to mental inhibitions, and the experience that we are having with our children confirms me in this view. Their interest in science is at once passionate and intelligent, and their desire to understand the world in which they live exceeds enormously that of children brought up with the usual taboos upon curiosity. What we are doing is of course only an experiment on a small scale, but I confidently expect its results to be very important indeed. You will realise that hardly any other educational reformers lay much stress upon intelligence. A. S. Neill, for example, who is in many ways an admirable man, allows such complete liberty that his children fail to get the necessary training and are always going to the cinema, when they might otherwise be interested in things of more value. Absence of opportunity for exciting pleasures at this place is, I think, an important factor in the development of the children's intellectual interests. I note what you say in your book on the subject of amusements, and I agree with it very strongly.

I hope that if you are back in England you will pay a visit to this school and see what we are doing.

> *Yours very sincerely*
> *Bertrand Russell*

From and to A. S. Neill, the progressive schoolmaster

> Summerhill,
> Lyme Regis, Dorset
> 23.3.26

Dear Mr Russell

I marvel that two men, working from different angles, should arrive at essentially the same conclusions. Your book and mine are complementary. It may be that the only difference between us comes from our respective complexes. I observe that you say little or nothing about handwork in education. My hobby has always been handwork, and where your child asks you about stars my pupils ask me about steels and screw threads. Possibly also I attach more importance to emotion in education than you do.

I read your book with great interest and with very little disagreement. Your method of overcoming your boy's fear of the sea I disagreed with heartily! An introverted boy might react with the thought: 'Daddy wants to drown me.' My complex again . . . arising from my dealing with neurotics mostly.

I have no first-hand knowledge of early childhood, for I am so far unmarried, but your advices about early childhood seem to me to be excellent. Your attitude to sex instruction and masturbation is splendid and you put it in a way that will not shock and offend. (I have not that art!)

I do not share your enthusiasm for Montessori. I cannot agree with a system set up by a strong churchwoman with a strict moral aim. Her orderliness to me is a counterblast against original sin. Besides I see no virtue in orderliness at all. My workshop is always in a mess but my handwork isn't. My pupils have no interest in orderliness until they come to puberty or thereabouts. You may find that at the age of five your children will have no use for Montessori apparatus. Why *not* use the apparatus to make a train with? I argued this out with Madame Macaroni, Montessori's chief lieutenant a few years ago. Is it not our awful attitude to learning that warps our outlook? After all a train is a reality, while an inset frame is purely artificial. I never use artificial apparatus. My apparatus in the school is books, tools, test tubes, compasses. Montessori wants to direct a child. I don't.

By the way, to go back to the sea fear, I have two boys who never enter the water. My nephew age nine (the watch-breaker of the book) and an introverted boy of eleven who is full of fears. I have advised the other children to make no mention of the sea, never to sneer at the two, never to try and persuade them to bathe. If they do not come to bathing from their own inner *Drang* . . . well, it does not much matter. One of my best friends, old Dauvit in my native village, is 89 and he never had a bath in his life.

You will be interested to know Homer Lane's theory about time-table sucking. He used to advocate giving a child the breast whenever it demanded it. He held that in sucking there are two components . . . pleasure and nutrition. The timetable child accumulates both components, and when the sucking begins the pleasure component goes away with a rush and is satisfied in a sort of orgasm. But the nutrition element is unsatisfied, and he held that many cases of mal-nutrition were due to this factor, that the child stopped sucking before the nutrition urge was satisfied.

To me the most interesting thing about your book is that it is scholarly (nasty word) in the sense that it is written by a man who knows history and science. I am ignorant of both and I think that my own conclusions come partly from a blind intuition. I say again that it is marvelous that we should reach very much the same philosophy of education. It is the only possible philosophy today, but we cannot hope to do much in the attack against schools from Eton to the L.C.C. Our only hope is the individual parent.

My chief difficulty is the parent, for my pupils are products of ignorant and savage parents. I have much fear that one or two of them, shocked by my book, may withdraw their children. That would be tragedy.

Well, thank you ever so much for the book. It is the only book on education that I have read that does not make me swear. All the others are morals disguised as education.

One warning however . . . there is always the chance that your son may want to join the Primrose League one day! One in ten million chance, but we must face the fact that human nature has not yet fitted into any cause and effect scheme; and never will fit in.

If you ever motor to your Cornwall home do stop and see us here.

Yours very truly
A. S. Neill

Summerhill School
Leiston, Suffolk
18.12.30

Dear Russell

Have you any political influence? The Labour Ministry are refusing to let me employ a Frenchman to teach French. The chap I want is with me now, has been analysed and is a tiptop man to deal with my bunch of problem kids. Other schools have natives to teach their languages . . . and I naturally ask why the hell a damned department should dictate to me about my educational ways. I have given the dept a full account of the man and why he is necessary to me and the fools reply: 'But the Dept is not satisfied that a British subject could not be trained in the special methods of teaching in operation in your school.'

Have you any political bigbug friend who would or could get behind the bloody idiots who control our departments? I am wild as hell.

Cheerio, help me if you can. I know George Lansbury but hesitate to approach him as he will have enough to do in his own dept.

Yours
A. S. Neill

20th Dec. 30

Dear Neill

What you tell me is quite outrageous. I have written to Charles Trevelyan and Miss Bondfield, and I enclose copies of my letters to them.

I wonder whether you made the mistake of mentioning psycho-analysis in your application. You know, of course, from Homer Lane's case that policemen regard psycho-analysis as merely a cloak for crime. The only ground to put before the department is that Frenchmen are apt to know French better than Englishmen do. The more the department enquires into your methods, the more it will wish to hamper you. Nobody is allowed to do any good in this country except by means of trickery and deceit.

Yours ever
Bertrand Russell

To Charles Trevelyan

20th Dec. 30

Dear Trevelyan

A. S. Neill, of Summerhill School, Leiston, Suffolk, who is, as you probably know, very distinguished in the educational world, having developed from a conventional school dominie into one of the most original and successful

183

innovators of our time, writes to me to say that the Ministry of Labour is refusing to allow him to continue to employ Frenchmen to teach French. He has at present a French master whose services he wishes to retain, but the Ministry of Labour has officially informed him that Englishmen speak French just as well as Frenchmen do, and that his present master is not to be allowed to stay.

I think you will agree with me that this sort of thing is intolerable. I know that many of the most important questions in education do not come under your department but are decided by policemen whose judgment is taken on the question whether a foreigner is needed in an educational post. If the principles upon which the Alien Act is administered had been applied in Italy in the 15th century, the Western world would never have acquired a knowledge of Greek and the Renaissance could not have taken place.

Although the matter is outside your department, I cannot doubt that the slightest word from you would cause the Ministry of Labour to alter its decision. A. S. Neill is a man of international reputation, and I hate the thought of what he may do to hold up British Bumbledom to ridicule throughout the civilised world. If you could do anything to set the matter right, you will greatly relieve my anxiety on this score.

Yours very sincerely
Bertrand Russell

P.S. I have also written to Miss Bondfield on this matter.

From and to A. S. Neill

Summerhill School
Leiston, Suffolk
22.12.30

Dear Russell

Good man! That's the stuff to give the troops. Whatever the result accept my thanks. I didn't mention psychoanalysis to them. I applied on the usual form and they wrote asking me what precise steps I had taken 'to find a teacher of French who was British or an alien already resident in this country'. Then I told them that I wanted a Frenchman but that any blinking Frenchie wouldn't do . . . that mine was a psychological school and any teacher had to be not only an expert in his subject but also in handling neurotic kids.

Apart from this display of what you call Bumbledom I guess that there will be some battle when Trevelyan's Committee on Private Schools issues its report. You and I will have to fight like hell against having a few stupid inspectors mucking about demanding why Tommy can't read. Any inspector coming to me now would certainly be greeted by Colin (aged 6) with the friendly words, 'Who the fucking hell are you?' So that we must fight to keep Whitehall out of our schools.

I'll let you know what happens.

Many thanks,

Yours
A. S. Neill

About time that you and I met again and compared notes.

Leiston. 31.12.30
Dear Russell

You have done the deed. The letter [from the Ministry of Labour] is a nasty one but I guess that the bloke as wrote it was in a nasty position. Sounds to me like a good prose Hymn of Hate.

I have agreed to his conditions . . . feeling like slapping the blighter in the eye at the same time. It is my first experience with the bureaucracy and I am apt to forget that I am dealing with a machine.

Many thanks for your ready help. My next approach to you may be when that Committee on Private Schools gets busy. They will call in all the respectable old deadheads of education as expert witnesses (Badley and Co) and unless men of moment like you make a fight for it we (the out and outer Bolshies of education) will be ignored. Then we'll have to put up with the nice rules advocated by the diehards. Can't we get up a league of heretical dominies called the 'Anal'-ists?

Yours with much gratitude
A. S. Neill

5th Jan. 31
Dear Neill

Thank you for your letter and for the information about your French teacher. I am sorry you accepted the Ministry of Labour's terms, as they were on the run and could, I think, have been induced to grant unconditional permission.

I suppose you do not mind if I express to Miss Bondfield my low opinion of her officials, and to Trevelyan my ditto of Miss Bondfield? It is quite possible that the Ministry may still decide to let you keep your present master indefinitely. I am going away for a short holiday, and I am therefore dictating these letters now to my secretary who will not send them until she hears from you that you are willing they should go. Will you therefore be so kind as to send a line to her (Mrs O. Harrington), and not to me, as to whether you are willing the letters should go.

Yours ever
Bertrand Russell

Neill agreed to my sending the following letters:

To Miss Bondfield

12th Jan. 31
Dear Miss Bondfield

I am much obliged to you for looking into the matter of Mr A. S. Neill's French teacher. I doubt whether you are aware that in granting him permission to retain his present teacher for one year your office made it a condition that he should not even ask to retain his present teacher after the end of that year.

I do not believe that you have at any time been in charge of a school, but if you had, you would know that to change one's teachers once a year is to increase enormously the difficulty of achieving any kind of success. What would the headmaster of one of our great public schools say to your office if it were to insist that he should change his teachers once a year? Mr Neill is attempting an experiment which everybody interested in modern education considers very important, and it seems a pity that the activities of the Government in regard to him should be confined to making a fair trial of the experiment impossible. I have no doubt whatever that you will agree with me in this, and that some subordinate has failed to carry out your wishes in this matter.

With apologies for troubling you,

> *I remain*
> *Yours sincerely*
> *Bertrand Russell*

To Charles Trevelyan

12th Jan. 31

Dear Charles

Thank you very much for the trouble you have taken in regard to the French teacher at A. S. Neill's school. The Ministry of Labour have granted him permission to stay for one year, but on condition that Neill does not ask to have his leave extended beyond that time. You will, I think, agree with me that this is an extraordinary condition to have made. Neill has accepted it, as he has to yield to *force majeure*, but there cannot be any conceivable justification for it. Anybody who has ever run a school knows that perpetual change of masters is intolerable. What would the Headmaster of Harrow think if the Ministry of Labour obliged him to change his masters once a year?

Neill is trying an experiment which everybody interested in education considers most important, and Whitehall is doing what it can to make it a failure. I do not myself feel bound by Neill's undertaking, and I see no reason why intelligent people who are doing important work should submit tamely to the dictation of ignorant busybodies, such as the officials in the Ministry of Labour appear to be. I am quite sure that you agree with me in this.

Thanking you again,

> *Yours very sincerely*
> *Bertrand Russell*

To and from A. S. Neill

27th Jan. 31

Dear Neill

As you will see from the enclosed, there is nothing to be got out of the Ministry of Labour.

I have written a reply which I enclose, but I have not sent it. If you think it will further your case, you are at liberty to send it; but remember Miss Bondfield is celibate.

> *Yours ever*
> *Bertrand Russell*

The enclosed reply to the Ministry of Labour:

27th Jan. 31

Dear Sir

Thank you very much for your letter of January 26th. I quite understand the principle of confining employment as far as possible to the British without regard for efficiency. I think, however, that the Ministry is not applying the principle sufficiently widely. I know many Englishmen who have married foreigners, and many English potential wives who are out of a job. Would not a year be long enough to train an English wife to replace the existing foreign one in such cases?

Yours faithfully
Bertrand Russell

Summerhill School
Leiston, Suffolk
28.1.31

Dear Russell

No, there is no point in replying to the people. Very likely the chief aim in govt offices is to save the face of the officials. If my man wants to stay on later I may wangle it by getting him to invest some cash in the school and teach on AS AN EMPLOYER of labour. Anyway you accomplished a lot as it is. Many thanks. I think I'll vote Tory next time!

Today I have a letter from the widow of Norman MacMunn. She seems to be penniless and asks me for a job as matron. I can't give her one and don't suppose you can either. I have advised her to apply to our millionaire friends in Dartington Hall. I am always sending on the needy to them . . . hating them all the time for their affluence. When Elmhirst needs a new wing he writes out a cheque to Heals . . . Heals! And here am I absolutely gravelled to raise cash for a pottery shed. Pioneering is a wash out, man. I am getting weary of cleaning up the mess that parents make. At present I have a lad of six who shits his pants six times daily . . . his dear mamma 'cured' him by making him eat the shit. I get no gratitude at all . . . when after years of labour I cure this lad the mother will then send him to a 'nice' school. It aint good enough . . . official indifference or potential enmity, parental jealousy . . . the only joy is in the kids themselves. One day I'll chuck it all and start a nice hotel round about Salzburg.

You'll gather that I am rather fed this morning. I'd like to meet you again and have a yarn. Today my *Stimmung* is partly due to news of another bad debt . . . £150 this last year all told. All parents whose problems I bettered.

Yours
A. S. Neill

I wonder what Margaret Bondfield's views would be on my views on Onanie!

187

31st Jan. 31

Dear Neill

I am sorry you are feeling so fed up. It is a normal mood with me so far as the school is concerned. Parents owe me altogether about £500 which I shall certainly never see. I have my doubts as to whether you would find hotel keeping much better. You would find penniless pregnant unmarried women left on your hands, and would undertake the care of them and their children for the rest of their natural lives. You might find this scarcely more lucrative than a modern school. Nobody can make a living, except by dishonesty or cruelty, at no matter what trade.

It is all very sad about Elmhirst. However, I always think that a man who marries money has to work for his living. I have no room for a Matron at the moment, having at last obtained one who is completely satisfactory.

I have sometimes attempted in a mild way to get a little financial support from people who think they believe in modern education, but I have found the thing that stood most in my way was the fact which leaked out, that I do not absolutely insist upon strict sexual virtue on the part of the staff. I found that even people who think themselves quite advanced believe that only the sexually starved can exert a wholesome moral influence.

Your story about the boy who shits in his pants is horrible. I have not had any cases as bad as that to deal with.

I should very much like to see you again. Perhaps we could meet in London at some time or other. . . .

Yours
Bertrand Russell

From Mrs Bernard Shaw
Ayot St Lawrence
Welwyn, Herts.
28 Oct. 1928

Dear Bertrand Russell

I was grateful and *honoured* by your splendidness in sending me your MS of your lecture and saying I may keep it. It's wonderful of you. I have read it once, and shall keep it as you permit until I have time for another good, quiet go at it.

You know you have a humble, but convinced admirer in me. I have a very strong mystical turn in me, which does not appear in public, and I find your stuff the best corrective and *steadier* I ever came across!

My best remembrances to you both. I hope the school is flourishing.

Yours gratefully
C. F. Shaw

To C. P. Sanger
Telegraph House
Harting, Petersfield
23 Dec. 1929

My dear Charlie

I am very sorry indeed to hear that you are so ill. I do hope you will soon be better. Whenever the Doctors will let me I will come and see you. It is a year today since Kate's operation, when you were so kind—I remember how Kate loved your visits. Dear Charlie, I don't think I have ever expressed the deep affection I have for you, but I suppose you have known of it.

I got home three days ago and found everything here satisfactory. The children are flourishing, and it is delicious to be at home. One feels very far off in California and such places. I went to Salt Lake City and the Mormons tried to convert me, but when I found they forbade tea and tobacco I thought it was no religion for me.

My warmest good wishes for a speedy recovery,

Yours very affectionately
Bertrand Russell

From Lord Rutherford

Newnham Cottage
Queen's Road
Cambridge
March 9, 1931

Dear Bertrand Russell

I have just been reading with much interest and profit your book *The Conquest of Happiness* & I would like to thank you for a most stimulating and I think valuable analysis of the factors concerned. The chief point where I could not altogether agree was in your treatment of the factors of envy & jealousy. Even in the simple—and I agree with you—fundamentally happy life of the scientific man, one has naturally sometimes encountered examples of this failing but either I have been unusually fortunate or it may be too obtuse to notice it in the great majority of my friends. I have known a number of men leading simple lives whether on the land or in the laboratory who seemed to me singularly free from this failing. I quite agree with you that it is most obtrusive in those who are unduly class-conscious. These remarks are not in criticism but a mere personal statement of my own observations in these directions.

I was very sorry to hear of the sudden death of your brother whom I knew only slightly, and I sympathize with you in your loss. I hope, however, you will be interested enough to take some part in debates in the House of Lords in the future.

Yours sincerely
Rutherford

CHAPTER V

LATER YEARS OF TELEGRAPH HOUSE

WHEN I LEFT Dora, she continued the school until after the beginning of the Second War, though after 1934 it was no longer at Telegraph House. John and Kate were made wards in Chancery and were sent to Dartington school where they were very happy.

I spent a summer at Hendaye and for part of another summer took the Gerald Brenans' house near Malaga. I had not known either of the Brenans before this and I found them interesting and delightful. Gamel Brenan surprised me by turning out to be a scholar of great erudition and wide interests, full of all sorts of scraps of out-of-the-way knowledge and a poet of haunting and learned rhythms. We have kept up our friendship and she visits us sometimes—a lovely autumnal person.

I spent the summer of 1932 at Carn Voel, which I later gave to Dora. While there, I wrote *Education and the Social Order*. After this, having no longer the financial burden of the school, I gave up writing potboilers. And having failed as a parent, I found that my ambition to write books that might be important revived.

During my lecture tour in America in 1931, I had contracted with W. W. Norton, the publisher, to write the book which was published in 1934 under the title *Freedom and Organization, 1814–1914*. I worked at this book in collaboration with Patricia Spence, commonly known as Peter Spence, first at a flat in Emperor's Gate (where John and Kate were disappointed to find neither an Emperor nor a gate), and then at Deudraeth Castle in North Wales, which was at that time an annex of Portmeirion Hotel. I very much enjoyed this work, and I found the life at Portmeirion pleasant. The hotel was owned by my friends Clough Williams-Ellis, the architect, and his wife, Amabel, tne writer, whose company was delightful.

When the writing of *Freedom and Organization* was finished, I decided to return to Telegraph House and tell Dora she must live elsewhere. My reasons were financial. I was under a legal obligation to pay a rent of £400 a year for Telegraph House, the proceeds being due to my brother's second wife as alimony. I was also obliged to pay alimony to Dora, as well as all the expenses of John and Kate. Meanwhile my income had diminished catastrophically. This was due partly to the depression, which caused people to buy much fewer books, partly to the fact that I was no longer writing popular books, and partly to my having refused to stay with Hearst in 1931 at his castle in California. My weekly articles in the Hearst newspapers had brought me £1000 a year, but after my refusal the pay was halved, and very soon I was told the articles were no longer required. Telegraph House was large, and was only approachable by two private drives, each about a mile long. I wished to sell it, but could not put it on the market while the school was there. The only hope was to live there, and try to make it attractive to possible purchasers.

After settling again at Telegraph House, without the school, I went for a holiday to the Canary Islands. On returning, I found myself, though sane, quite devoid of creative impulse, and at a loss to know what work to do. For about two months, purely to afford myself distraction, I worked on the problem of the twenty-seven straight lines on a cubic surface. But this would never do, as it was totally useless and I was living on capital saved during the successful years that ended in 1932. I decided to write a book on the daily increasing menace of war. I called this book *Which Way to Peace?* and maintained in it the pacifist position that I had taken up during the First War. I did, it is true, make an exception: I held that, if ever a world government were established, it would be desirable to support it by force against rebels. But as regards the war to be feared in the immediate future, I urged conscientious objection.

This attitude, however, had become unconsciously insincere. I had been able to view with reluctant acquiescence the possibility of the supremacy of the Kaiser's Germany; I thought that, although this would be an evil, it would not be so great an evil as a world war and its aftermath. But Hitler's Germany was a different matter. I found the Nazis utterly revolting—cruel, bigoted, and stupid. Morally and intellectually they were alike odious to me. Although I clung to my pacifist convictions, I did so with increasing difficulty. When, in 1940, England was threatened with invasion, I realised that, throughout the First War, I had never seriously envisaged the possibility of utter defeat. I found this possibility unbearable, and at last consciously and definitely decided that I must support what was necessary for victory in the Second War, however difficult victory might be to achieve, and however painful in its consequences.

This was the last stage in the slow abandonment of many of the beliefs that had come to me in the moment of 'conversion' in 1901. I had never been a complete adherent of the doctrine of non-resistance;

191

I had always recognised the necessity of the police and the criminal law, and even during the First War I had maintained publicly that some wars are justifiable. But I had allowed a larger sphere to the method of non-resistance—or, rather, non-violent resistance—than later experience seemed to warrant. It certainly has an important sphere; as against the British in India, Gandhi led it to triumph. But it depends upon the existence of certain virtues in those against whom it is employed. When Indians lay down on railways, and challenged the authorities to crush them under trains, the British found such cruelty intolerable. But the Nazis had no scruples in analogous situations. The doctrine which Tolstoy preached with great persuasive force, that the holders of power could be morally regenerated if met by non-resistance, was obviously untrue in Germany after 1933. Clearly Tolstoy was right only when the holders of power were not ruthless beyond a point, and clearly the Nazis went beyond this point.

But private experience had almost as much to do with changing my beliefs as had the state of the world. In the school, I found a very definite and forceful exercise of authority necessary if the weak were not to be oppressed. Such instances as the hatpin in the soup could not be left to the slow operation of a good environment, since the need for action was immediate and imperative. In my second marriage, I had tried to preserve that respect for my wife's liberty which I thought that my creed enjoined. I found, however, that my capacity for forgiveness and what may be called Christian love was not equal to the demands that I was making on it, and that persistence in a hopeless endeavour would do much harm to me, while not achieving the intended good to others. Anybody else could have told me this in advance, but I was blinded by theory.

I do not wish to exaggerate. The gradual change in my views, from 1932 to 1940, was not a revolution; it was only a quantitative change and a shift of emphasis. I had never held the non-resistance creed absolutely, and I did not now reject it absolutely. But the practical difference, between opposing the First War and supporting the Second, was so great as to mask the considerable degree of theoretical consistency that in fact existed.

Although my reason was wholly convinced, my emotions followed with reluctance. My whole nature had been involved in my opposition to the First War, whereas it was a divided self that favoured the Second. I have never since 1940 recovered the same degree of unity between opinion and emotion as I had possessed from 1914 to 1918. I think that, in permitting myself that unity, I had allowed myself more of a creed than scientific intelligence can justify. To follow scientific intelligence wherever it may lead me had always seemed to me the most imperative of moral precepts for me, and I have followed this precept even when it has involved a loss of what I myself had taken for deep spiritual insight.

About a year and a half was spent by Peter Spence, with whom for some time I had been in love, and me on *The Amberley Papers*, a record of the brief life of my parents. There was something of the ivory tower in this work. My parents had not been faced with our modern problems; their radicalism was confident, and throughout their lives the world was moving in directions that to them seemed good. And although they opposed aristocratic privilege, it survived intact, and they, however involuntarily, profited by it. They lived in a comfortable, spacious, hopeful world, yet in spite of this I could wholly approve of them. This was restful, and in raising a monument to them my feelings of filial piety were assuaged. But I could not pretend that the work was really important. I had had a period of uncreative barrenness, but it had ended, and it was time to turn to something less remote.

My next piece of work was *Power, a new social analysis*. In this book I maintained that a sphere for freedom is still desirable even in a socialist state, but this sphere has to be defined afresh and not in liberal terms. This doctrine I still hold. The thesis of this book seems to me important, and I hoped that it would attract more attention than it has done. It was intended as a refutation both of Marx and of the classical economists, not on a point of detail, but on the fundamental assumptions that they shared. I argued that power, rather than wealth, should be the basic concept in social theory, and that social justice should consist in equalization of power to the greatest practicable degree. It followed that State ownership of land and capital was no advance unless the State was democratic, and even then only if methods were devised for curbing the power of officials. A part of my thesis was taken up and popularized in Burnham's *Managerial Revolution*, but otherwise the book fell rather flat. I still hold, however, that what it has to say is of very great importance if the evils of totalitarianism are to be avoided, particularly under a Socialist régime.

In 1936, I married Peter Spence and my youngest child, Conrad, was born in 1937. This was a great happiness. A few months after his birth, I at last succeeded in selling Telegraph House. For years I had had no offers, but suddenly I had two: one from a Polish Prince, the other from an English business man. In twenty-four hours, owing to their competition, I succeeded in increasing the price they offered by £1000. At last the business man won, and I was rid of the incubus, which had been threatening me with ruin since I had to spend capital so long as it was not disposed of, and very little capital remained.

Although, for financial reasons, I had to be glad to be rid of Telegraph House, the parting was painful. I loved the downs and the woods and my tower room with its views in all four directions. I had known the place for forty years or more, and had watched it grow in my brother's day. It represented continuity, of which, apart from work, my life has had far less than I could have wished. When I sold it, I could say, like the apothecary, 'my poverty but not my will consents'. For a long time after this I did not have a fixed abode, and thought it not likely that I should ever have one. I regretted this profoundly.

After I had finished *Power*, I found my thoughts turning again to theoretical philosophy. During my time in prison in 1918, I had become interested in the problems connected with meaning, which in earlier days I had completely ignored. I wrote something on these problems in *The Analysis of Mind* and in various articles written at about the same time. But there was a great deal more to say. The logical positivists, with whose general outlook I had a large measure of agreement, seemed to me on some points to be falling into errors which would lead away from empiricism into a new scholasticism. They seemed inclined to treat the realm of language as if it were self-subsistent, and not in need of any relation to non-linguistic occurrences. Being invited to give a course of lectures at Oxford, I chose as my subject 'Words and Facts'. The lectures were the first draft of the book published in 1940 under the title *An Inquiry into Meaning and Truth*.

We bought a house at Kidlington, near Oxford, and lived there for about a year, but only one Oxford lady called. We were not respectable. We had later a similar experience in Cambridge. In this respect I have found these ancient seats of learning unique.

LETTERS

To Maurice Amos

16th June 1930

Dear Maurice

You wrote me a very nice letter last October and I have not answered it yet. When you wrote it I was touring America, which leaves one no leisure for anything beyond the day's work. I meant to answer your letter, but as the right moment went by, the impulse died.

I like Jeans's book. It is amusing how the physicists have come round to poor old Bishop Berkeley. You remember how when we were young we were taught that although idealism was, of course, quite the thing, Bishop Berkeley's form of it was rather silly; now it is the only form that survives. I do not see how to refute it, though temperamentally I find it repulsive. It ought, of course, in any case to be solipsism. I lectured on this subject at Harvard, with Whitehead in the Chair, and I said it seemed to me improbable that I had composed the parts of his books which I could not understand, as I should be compelled to believe if I were a solipsist. Nevertheless I have never succeeded in finding any real evidence that I did not do so.

I am very much interested in what you say about your book on the British Constitution, and especially amused that you had written 46,000 out of the 50,000 requisite words before you reached Parliament. Parliament has become a somewhat unimportant body. In the 19th century the Prime Ministers resigned when defeated in Parliament until Gladstone altered the practice; now by the threat of dissolution they terrorise Parliament. The Constitution would not be appreciably changed if the Prime Minister were directly elected, selected the Government, and had to seek re-election either after five years or when a leader appeared against him in his own Party Press.

I think you are entirely right in what you say about the Labour Party. I do not like them, but an Englishman has to have a Party just as he has to have trousers, and of the three Parties I find them the least painful. My objection to the Tories is temperamental, and my objection to the Liberals is Lloyd George. I do not think that in joining a Party one necessarily abrogates the use of one's reason. I know that my trousers might be better than they are; nevertheless they seem to me better than none.

It is true that I had never heard of Holdsworth's *History of English Law*, but in fact I have never read any books at all about law except one or two of Maitland's.

Since I returned from America I have been very much tied here, but I expect to be in London occasionally during the autumn and I should very much like to see you then.

Sanger's death was a great grief to me.

Ever yours affectionately
Bertrand Russell

From and to Bronislaw Malinowski, the anthropologist

The London School of Economics
13th November 1930

Dear Russell

On the occasion of my visit to your School I left my only presentable brown hat in your anteroom. I wonder whether since then it has had the privilege of enclosing the only brains in England which I ungrudgingly regard as better than mine; or whether it has been utilized in some of the juvenile experimentations in physics, technology, dramatic art, or prehistoric symbolism; or whether it naturally lapsed out of the anteroom.

If none of these events, or shall we rather call them hypotheses, holds good or took place, could you be so good as to bring it in a brown paper parcel or by some other concealed mode of transport to London and advise me on a post card where I could reclaim it? I am very sorry that my absentmindedness, which is a characteristic of high intelligence, has exposed you to all the inconvenience incidental to the event.

I do hope to see you some time soon.

Yours sincerely
B. Malinowski

15th Nov. 1930

Dear Malinowski

My secretary has found a presentable brown hat in my lobby which I presume is yours, indeed the mere sight of it reminds me of you.

I am going to the School of Economics to give a lecture to the Students' Union on Monday (17th), and unless my memory is as bad and my intelligence as good as yours, I will leave your hat with the porter at the School of Economics, telling him to give it to you on demand.

I too hope that we may meet some time soon. I made the acquaintance of Briffault[1] the other day, and was amazed by his pugnacity.

> *Yours sincerely*
> *Bertrand Russell*

From and to G. E. Moore

86, Chesterton Road
Cambridge
Mar. 9/30

Dear Russell

The Council of Trinity made a grant to Wittgenstein last June to enable him to carry on his researches on the foundations of Mathematics. There is now a question of making him a further grant; & they wish, before they decide, to have expert reports on the work he has done since the last grant was made. They have authorised me to ask you to make such a report for them. I'm afraid it will involve a good deal of trouble. Wittgenstein has written a great deal; but he says it would be absolutely necessary for him to explain it to you in conversation, if you are to understand it. I think he would be very glad to have an opportunity of doing this, but it would no doubt take up a good deal of your time. I hope very much that you will nevertheless be willing to do it; for there seems to be no other way of ensuring him a sufficient income to continue his work, unless the Council do make him a grant; and I am afraid there is very little chance that they will do so, unless they can get favourable reports from experts in the subject: and you are, of course, by far the most competent person to make one. They would, of course, pay a fee for the report.

There would be no need for you to come here to see Wittgenstein. He would arrange to go to see you, when & where it suited you best.

> *Yours fraternally*
> *G. E. Moore*

Beacon Hill School
Harting, Petersfield
11th March 1930

Dear Moore

I do not see how I can refuse to read Wittgenstein's work and make a report on it. At the same time, since it involves arguing with him, you are

[1] Briffault was a general practitioner from New Zealand who ventured into sociology, and for whose book *Sin and Sex* I did an introduction in 1931.

right that it will require a great deal of work. I do not know anything more fatiguing than disagreeing with him in an argument.

Obviously the best plan for me would be to read the manuscript carefully first, and see him afterwards. How soon could you let me have his stuff? I should like if possible to see him here before the 5th of April: on that date I shall be going to Cornwall for Easter, and I do not want to have any work to do while there, as I have been continuously very busy since the end of last summer. I do not know how long it will be necessary to argue with him. I could spare three days, say the Friday, Saturday and Sunday preceding April 5th, but it would be difficult for me to spare more. Do you think this would be enough?

> *Yours fraternally*
> *Bertrand Russell*

> 86, Chesterton Road
> Cambridge
> March 13/30

Dear Russell

Wittgenstein says that he has nothing written which it would be worth while to let you see: all that he has written is at present in too confused a state. I am sorry that I had not clearly understood this when I wrote to you before. What he wants is merely to have a chance of explaining to you some of the results which he has arrived at, so that you might be able to report to the Council whether, even if you thought them mistaken, you thought them important & such that he ought to be given a chance of going on working on the same lines; and I hope that a report of this kind would be sufficient for the Council. And I should think 3 days would be ample for this, & that it wouldn't be necessary for you to argue with him much. He is wiring to you now to ask if he could see you on Saturday either at Harting or in London (if you should be there), so as to try to make some arrangement with you. I think he will be in Austria on April 5th.

> *Yours fraternally*
> *G. E. Moore*

> 17th March 1930

Dear Moore

Wittgenstein has been here for the weekend, and we have talked as much as there was time for.

I should be glad to know what is the latest date for reporting to the Council, since my impressions at the moment are rather vague, and he intends while in Austria to make a synopsis of his work which would make it much easier for me to report adequately. If it is impossible to wait another month or so, I will do my best to draw up a report on the basis of our conversations, but I hope this is not necessary. He intends to visit me again in Cornwall just before the beginning of the May term, with his synopsis.

> *Yours fraternally*
> *Bertrand Russell*

5th May 1930

Dear Moore

I had a second visit from Wittgenstein, but it only lasted thirty-six hours, and it did not by any means suffice for him to give me a synopsis of all that he has done. He left me a large quantity of typescript, which I am to forward to Littlewood as soon as I have read it. Unfortunately I have been ill and have therefore been unable to get on with it as fast as I hoped. I think, however, that in the course of conversation with him I got a fairly good idea of what he is at. He uses the words 'space' and 'grammar' in peculiar senses, which are more or less connected with each other. He holds that if it is significant to say 'This is red', it cannot be significant to say 'This is loud'. There is one 'space' of colours and another 'space' of sounds. These 'spaces' are apparently given a priori in the Kantian sense, or at least not perhaps exactly that, but something not so very different. Mistakes of grammar result from confusing 'spaces'. Then he has a lot of stuff about infinity, which is always in danger of becoming what Brouwer has said, and has to be pulled up short whenever this danger becomes apparent. His theories are certainly important and certainly very original. Whether they are true, I do not know; I devoutly hope they are not, as they make mathematics and logic almost incredibly difficult. One might define a 'space', as he uses the word, as a complete set of possibilities of a given kind. If you can say 'This is blue', there are a number of other things you can say significantly, namely, all the other colours.

I am quite sure that Wittgenstein ought to be given an opportunity to pursue his work. Would you mind telling me whether this letter could possibly suffice for the Council? The reason I ask is that I have at the moment so much to do that the effort involved in reading Wittgenstein's stuff thoroughly is almost more than I can face. I will, however, push on with it if you think it is really necessary.

> *Yours fraternally*
> *Bertrand Russell*

> 86, Chesterton Road
> Cambridge
> May 7/30

Dear Russell

I don't think your letter to me, as it stands, will quite do as a report to the Council; but I don't think it is necessary that you should spend any more time in reading Wittgenstein's synopsis. What I think is important is that you should write a formal report (which they might, perhaps, want to keep in their Report-Book), not necessarily any longer than your letter, but stating quite clearly & expressly some things which are only implicit in your letter. I think the report should state quite clearly just how much you have been able to do by way of discovering what work W. has been doing since last June, i.e. partly reading of the Synopsis & partly W.'s verbal explanations; and should emphasize that your opinion of its importance, & that W. ought certainly to be given an opportunity of continuing it, is based upon what you have been able to learn of the nature of this new work itself, & not merely on your previous knowledge of W. You see the Council already know that you have a very high opinion of W.'s work in general, and what they want is your opinion as to the importance of this particular new work, not merely based on a presumption that anything W. does is likely to be important. I think you should try to state, very briefly, what its nature is & what its originality & importance consists in.

I'm afraid that to write such a report will be troublesome; but I hope it wouldn't take you very long; and I do think it's important that it should be done.

Yours fraternally
G. E. Moore

Beacon Hill School
Harting, Petersfield
8th May 1930

Dear Moore

I have just sent Wittgenstein's typescript to Littlewood with a formal report which he can pass on to the Council. It says just the same things as my letter to you, but it says them in grander language, which the Council will be able to understand. I enclose a copy.

I find I can only understand Wittgenstein when I am in good health, which I am not at the present moment.

Yours fraternally
Bertrand Russell

My report to the Council of Trinity on Wittgenstein's work:

Beacon Hill School
Harting, Petersfield
8th May 1930

Owing to illness I have been prevented from studying Wittgenstein's recent work as thoroughly as I had intended to do. I spent five days in discussion with him, while he explained his ideas, and he left with me a bulky typescript, *Philosophische Bemerkungen*, of which I have read about a third. The typescript, which consists merely of rough notes, would have been very difficult to understand without the help of the conversations. As it is, however, I believe that the following represents at least a part of the ideas which are new since the time of his *Tractatus*:

According to Wittgenstein, when anything is the case there are certain other things that might have been the case in regard, so to speak, to that particular region of fact. Suppose, for example, a certain patch of wall is blue; it might have been red, or green, or &c. To say that it is any of these colours is false, but not meaningless. On the other hand, to say that it is loud, or shrill, or to apply to it any other adjective appropriate to a sound, would be to talk nonsense. There is thus a collection of possibilities of a certain kind which is concerned in any fact. Such a collection of possibilities Wittgenstein calls a 'space'. Thus there is a 'space' of colours, and a 'space' of sounds. There are various relations among colours which constitute the geometry of that 'space'.

All this is, in one sense, independent of experience: that is to say, we need the kind of experience through which we know what 'green' is, but not the kind through which we know that a certain patch of wall is green. Wittgenstein uses the word 'grammar' to cover what corresponds in language to the existence of these various 'spaces'. Wherever a word denoting a region in a certain 'space' occurs, the word denoting another region in that 'space' can be substituted without producing nonsense, but a word denoting any region belonging to any other 'space' cannot be substituted without bad grammar, i.e. nonsense.

A considerable part of Wittgenstein's work is concerned with the interpretation of mathematics. He considers it false to say that mathematics is logic or consists of tautologies. He discusses 'infinity' at considerable length and links it with the conception of possibility that he has developed in connection with his various 'spaces'. He believes in 'infinite possibility', as he calls it, but not in actual 'infinite classes' or 'infinite series'. What he says about infinity tends, obviously against his will, to have a certain resemblance to what has been said by Brouwer. I think perhaps the resemblance is not so close as it appears at first sight. There is much discussion of mathematical induction.

The theories contained in this new work of Wittgenstein's are novel, very original, and indubitably important. Whether they are true, I do not know. As a logician who likes simplicity, I should wish to think that they are not, but from what I have read of them I am quite sure that he ought to have an opportunity to work them out, since when completed they may easily prove to constitute a whole new philosophy.

Bertrand Russell

To W. W. Norton, publisher

27th Jan. 1931

Dear Norton

Thank you for your letter of January 14th. . . .

With regard to *The Meaning of Science*, I have an abstract of it and have done some 10,000 words. I am afraid I could not do the sort of conclusion that you suggest. I do not believe that science *per se* is an adequate source of happiness, nor do I think that my own scientific outlook has contributed very greatly to my own happiness, which I attribute to defecating twice a day with unfailing regularity. Science in itself appears to me neutral, that is to say, it increases men's power whether for good or for evil. An appreciation of the ends of life is something that must be superadded to science if it is to bring happiness. I do not wish, in any case, to discuss individual happiness, but only the kind of society to which science is apt to give rise. I am afraid you may be disappointed that I am not more of an apostle of science, but as I grow older, and no doubt as a result of the decay of my tissues, I begin to see the good life more and more as a matter of balance and to dread all over-emphasis upon any one ingredient. This has always been the view of elderly men and must therefore have a physiological source, but one cannot escape from one's physiology by being aware of it.

I am not surprised at what people thought of *The Conquest of Happiness* on your side of the Atlantic. What surprised me much more was that English highbrows thought well of it. I think people who are unhappy are always proud of being so, and therefore do not like to be told that there is nothing grand about their unhappiness. A man who is melancholy because lack of exercise has upset his liver always believes that it is the loss of God, or the menace of Bolshevism, or some such dignified cause that makes him sad. When you tell people that happiness is a simple matter, they get annoyed with you.

All best wishes,

Yours sincerely
Bertrand Russell

17th Feb. 1931

Dear Norton

Thank you for your letter of February 9th. My method of achieving happiness was discovered by one of the despised race of philosophers, namely, John Locke. You will find it set forth in great detail in his book on education. This is his most important contribution to human happiness; other minor contributions were the English, American, and French revolutions.

The abstract [of *The Scientific Outlook*] that I sent you is not to be taken as covering all the ground that I shall, in fact, cover. Certainly education must be included in technique in society, though I had regarded it as a branch of advertising. As for behaviourism, I have included it under Pavlov. Pavlov did the work which Watson has advertised.

I have now done 36,000 words of the book, but after I have finished it, I shall keep it by me until the end of May for purposes of revision, and of adding malicious foot-notes.

I have already done a chapter on 'Science and Religion', which is explicitly atheistical. Do you object to this? It would, of course, be possible to give the whole thing an ironical twist, and possibly this might make it better literature. One could go through the arguments of the scientists, Eddington, Jeans, and their accomplices, pointing out how bad they are, and concluding that fortunately our faith need not depend upon them, since it is based upon the impregnable rock of Holy Scripture. If you prefer this as a literary form, I am prepared to re-cast the chapter in that sense. At present it is straightforward, sincere, and full of moral earnestness.

Unless I hear from you to suggest an earlier date, I propose to mail the manuscript, or to hand it to Aannestad if he is still in England, during the second week in June. It is perfectly feasible to send it sooner, but I can always improve it so long as I keep it.

I much enjoyed seeing Aannestad.

Yours sincerely
Bertrand Russell

11th March 1931

Dear Norton

You will have seen that my brother died suddenly in Marseilles. I inherit from him a title, but not a penny of money, as he was bankrupt. A title is a great nuisance to me, and I am at a loss what to do, but at any rate I do not wish it employed in connection with any of my literary work. There is, so far as I know, only one method of getting rid of it, which is to be attainted of high treason, and this would involve my head being cut off on Tower Hill. This method seems to me perhaps somewhat extreme, but I am sure I can rely upon you not to make use of my title in the way of publicity.

Yours sincerely
Bertrand Russell

To Mr Runham Brown

21st March 1931

Dear Mr Runham Brown

Einstein's pronouncement on the duty of Pacifists to refuse every kind of military service has my most hearty agreement, and I am very glad that the leading intellect of our age should have pronounced himself so clearly and so uncompromisingly on this issue.

For my part I do not expect, much as I desire it, that any very large number of men will be found to take up the position of refusing to bear arms in war-time, nor do I think that a refusal on the part of two per cent would be sufficient to prevent war. The next war will, I think, be more fierce than the war which as yet is still called 'Great', and I think Governments would have no hesitation in shooting the pacifist two per cent. A more effective form of war resistance would be strikes among munition workers. But on the whole I expect more from international agreements than from the actions of individual pacifists. While, therefore, I agree with Einstein as to the duty of pacifists, I put a somewhat different emphasis upon the political and individual factors respectively.

There is one point upon which perhaps I disagree, on principle, with him and with many other Pacifists. If an international authority existed and possessed the sole legal armed forces, I should be prepared to support it even by force of arms.

Yours sincerely
Bertrand Russell

To Dr Steinbach

19th May 1931

Dear Dr Steinbach

I am afraid I have nothing very helpful to say about the English language. I notice that literary persons in America tend to study it as one studies a dead language, that is to say, it does not occur to them that the written word can be merely the spoken word transcribed. For my part, while I am willing to read good authors for the sake of their rhythms, and also to enrich my vocabulary, it would not occur to me to read them with any grammatical purpose.

I should define correct English in the year nineteen hundred and thirty-one as the habits of speech of educated people in that year, and I see no point in making a distinction between speech and writing. When once a distinction of this sort is allowed to creep in, one soon arrives at the condition of the literary Chinese. I knew a learned Chinese who was very keen on substituting the vernacular (as it is called) for the classical language. I asked him whether this movement made much progress; he replied that there are times when it does, and times when it does not. 'For example,' he said, 'it made great progress during the thirteenth century.' I do not know Chinese, but I inferred that classical Chinese corresponded to Latin, and that the vernacular corresponded to Chaucer. I do not wish this sort of thing to happen to those who speak English.

Yours very truly
Bertrand Russell

This and the following letter are the long and the short of it.

From and to Will Durant

44, North Drive
Great Neck, N.Y.
June 8th, 1931

Earl Bertrand Russell
Carn Voel, Porthcurno
Cornwall, England

Dear Earl Russell

Will you interrupt your busy life for a moment, and play the game of philosophy with me?

I am attempting to face, in my next book, a question that our generation, perhaps more than most, seems always ready to ask, and never able to answer—What is the meaning or worth of human life? Heretofore this question has been dealt with chiefly by theorists, from Ikhnaton and Lao-tse to Bergson and Spengler. The result has been a species of intellectual suicide: thought, by its very development, seems to have destroyed the value and significance of life. The growth and spread of knowledge, for which so many reformers and idealists prayed, appears to bring to its devotees—and, by contagion, to many others—a disillusionment which has almost broken the spirit of our race.

Astronomers have told us that human affairs constitute but a moment in the trajectory of a star; geologists have told us that civilization is a precarious interlude between ice ages; biologists have told us that all life is war, a struggle for existence among individuals, groups, nations, alliances, and species; historians have told us that 'progress' is a delusion, whose glory ends in inevitable decay; psychologists have told us that the will and the self are the helpless instruments of heredity and environment, and that the once incorruptible soul is only a transient incandescence of the brain. The Industrial Revolution has destroyed the home, and the discovery of contraceptives is destroying the family, the old morality, and perhaps (through the sterility of the intelligent) the race. Love is analyzed into a physical congestion, and marriage becomes a temporary physiological convenience slightly superior to promiscuity. Democracy has degenerated into such corruption as only Milo's Rome knew; and our youthful dreams of a socialist utopia disappear as we see, day after day, the inexhaustible acquisitiveness of men. Every invention strengthens the strong and weakens the weak; every new mechanism displaces men, and multiplies the horrors of war. God, who was once the consolation of our brief life, and our refuge in bereavement and suffering, has apparently vanished from the scene; no telescope, no microscope discovers him. Life has become, in that total perspective which is philosophy, a fitful pullulation of human insects on the earth, a planetary eczema that may soon be cured; nothing is certain in it except defeat and death—a sleep from which, it seems, there is no awakening.

We are driven to conclude that the greatest mistake in human history was the discovery of truth. It has not made us free, except from delusions that comforted us, and restraints that preserved us; it has not made us happy, for truth is not beautiful, and did not deserve to be so passionately chased. As we look upon it now we wonder why we hurried so to find it. For it appears to have taken from us every reason for existing, except for the moment's pleasure and tomorrow's trivial hope.

This is the pass to which science and philosophy have brought us. I, who have loved philosophy for many years, turn from it now back to life itself, and ask you, as one who has lived as well as thought, to help me understand. Perhaps the verdict of those who have lived is different from that of those who have merely thought. Spare me a moment to tell me what meaning life has for you, what help—if any—religion gives you, what keeps you going, what are the sources of your inspiration and your energy, what is the goal or motive-force of your toil; where you find your consolations and your happiness, where in the last resort your treasure lies. Write briefly if you must; write at leisure and at length if you possibly can; for every word from you will be precious to me.

Sincerely
Will Durant

Author of *The Story of Philosophy, Transition, The Mansions of Philosophy, Philosophy and the Social Problem,* etc.
Formerly of the Dept. of Philosophy, Columbia University; Ph.D. (Columbia); L.H.D. (Syracuse).

P.S. A copy of this letter is being sent to Presidents Hoover and Masaryk; the Rt. Hons. Ramsay MacDonald, Lloyd George, Winston Churchill, and Philip Snowden; M. Aristide Briand; Signors Benito Mussolini, G. Marconi and G. d'Annunzio; Mme. Curie, Miss Mary Garden and Miss Jane Addams; Dean Inge; and Messrs. Josef Stalin, Igor Stravinsky, Leon Trotzky, M. K. Gandhi, Rabindranath Tagore, Ignace Paderewski, Richard Strauss, Albert Einstein, Gerhardt Hauptmann, Thomas Mann, Sigmund Freud, G. B. Shaw, H. G. Wells, John Galsworthy, Thomas Edison, Henry Ford and Eugene O'Neill.

The purpose in view is purely philosophical. I trust, however, that there will be no objection to my quoting from the replies in my forthcoming book *On the Meaning of Life,* one chapter of which will attempt to give some account of the attitude towards life of the most eminent of living men and women.

20th June 1931

Dear Mr Durant

I am sorry to say that at the moment I am so busy as to be convinced that life has no meaning whatever, and that being so, I do not see how I can answer your questions intelligently.

I do not see that we can judge what would be the result of the discovery of truth, since none has hitherto been discovered.

Yours sincerely
Bertrand Russell

From and to Albert Einstein

Caputh bei Potsdam
Waldstr. 7/8
den 14. Oktober 1931

Lieber Bertrand Russell!

Ich habe schon lange den Wunsch, Ihnen zu schreiben. Nichts anderes wollte ich dabei, als Ihnen meine hohe Bewunderung ausdrücken. Die Klarheit, Sicherheit, and Unparteilichkeit, mit der Sie die logischen, philosophischen und menschlichen Dinge in Ihren Büchern behandelt haben, steht nicht nur in unserer Generation unerreicht da.

Dies zu sagen hätte ich mich immer gescheut, weil Sie wie die objektiven Dinge so auch dies selber schon am besten wissen und keine Bestätigung nötig haben. Aber da löst mir ein kleiner Journalist, der mich heute aufsuchte, die Zunge. Es handelt sich da um ein internationales journalistisches Unternehmen (Cooperation) dem die besten Leute als Mitarbeiter angehören, und das sich die Aufgabe gestellt hat, das Publikum in allen Ländern in internationalem Sinne zu erziehen. Mittel: Artikel von Staatsmännern und Journalisten, welche einschlägige Fragen behandeln, werden systematisch in Zeitungen aller Länder veröffentlicht.

Herr Dr J. Révész geht in kurzem nach England, um für diese Sache zu wirken. Es würde nach meiner Ueberzeugung wichtig sein, wenn Sie ihm eine kurze Unterredung gewährten, damit er Sie in dieser Angelegenheit informieren kann. Ich richte eine solche Bitte nicht leichthin an Sie, sondern in der Ueberzeugung, dass die Angelegenheit Ihrer Beachtung wirklich wert sei.

In freudiger Verehrung
Ihr
A. Einstein

P.S. Einer Beantwortung dieses Briefes bedarf es nicht.

(Translation by Otto Nathan):

October 14, 1931

Dear Bertrand Russell

For a long time I have had the wish to write you. All I wanted to do, was to express my feeling of high admiration of you. The clarity, sureness, and impartiality which you have brought to bear to the logical, philosophical and human problems dealt with in your books are unrivalled not only in our generation.

I have always been reluctant to say this to you because you know about this yourself as well as you know about objective facts and do not need to receive any confirmation from outside. However, a little-known journalist who came to see me today has now given me an opportunity to open my heart to you. I am referring to an international journalistic enterprise (**Cooperation**) to which the best people belong as contributors and which has the purpose of educating the public in all countries in international understanding. The method to be used is to publish systematically articles by statesmen and journalists on pertinent problems in newspapers of all countries.

The gentleman in question, Dr J. Révész, will visit England in the near future to promote the project. I believe it would be important if you could grant him a short interview so he could inform you about the matter. I have hesitated to ask of you this favour, but I am convinced that the project really deserves your attention.

With warm admiration,

Yours
A. Einstein

P.S. There is no need to reply to this letter.

Telegraph House
Harting, Petersfield
7.1.35

Dear Einstein

I have long wished to be able to invite you for a visit, but had until recently no house to which to ask you. Now this obstacle is removed, & I very much hope you will come for a week-end. Either next Saturday (12th) or the 19th would suit me; after that I shall be for 6 weeks in Scandinavia & Austria, so if the 12th & 19th are both impossible, it will be necessary to wait till the second half of March. I can scarcely imagine a greater pleasure than a visit from you would give me, & there are many matters both in the world of physics & in that of human affairs on which I should like to know your opinion more definitely than I do.

Yours very sincerely
Bertrand Russell

From and to Henri Barbusse

Vigilia
Miramar par Théoule
(Alpes-Maritimes)
10 *février* 1927

Cher et éminent confrère

Permettez-mois de joindre un appel personnel à celui que vous trouverez ci-inclus et auquel je vous demande de bien vouloir adhérer. Votre nom est un de ceux qui s'imposent dans une ligue de grands honnêtes gens qui se lèveraient pour enrayer et combattre l'envahissante barbarie du fascisme.

J'ai rédigé cet appel spontanément, sans obéir à aucune suggestion d'ordre politique ou autre. Je n'ai écouté que le sentiment de la solidarité et la voix du bon sens: le mal n'est pas sans remède; il y a 'quelque chose à faire'; et ce qu'on peut faire surtout et avant tout devant les proportions effrayantes qu'a prises le fascisme, c'est de dresser une force morale, de mobiliser la vraie conscience publique, et de donner une voix explicite à une réprobation qui est répandue partout.

Je dois ajouter que, sur la teneur de cet appel, j'ai échangé des vues avec Romain Rolland, qui est de tout coeur avec moi, et qui estime comme moi qu'une levée des esprits libres, qu'une protestation des personnes éclairées et respectées, est seule susceptible, si elle est organisée et continue, de mettre un frein à un état de choses épouvantable.

Je tiens enfin à vous dire que i'ai l'intention de créer très prochainement une revue internationale: Monde, *qui aura pour but de diffuser de grands principes humains dans le chaos international actuel, de lutter contre l'esprit et la propagande réactionnaires. Cette publication peut devenir, sur le plan intellectuel, artistique, moral et social, une importante tribune, si des personnalités comme vous le veulent bien. Elle servira de véhicule à la voix du Comité, et donnera corps à sa haute protestation.*

Je vous serais reconnaissant si vous me disiez que vous acceptez d'être considéré comme un collaborateur éventuel de Monde.

Je vous serais également obligé de me répondre au sujet de l'appel par une lettre dont je pourrais faire état le cas échéant, en la publiant en son entier ou en extraits. Croyez à mes sentiments de haute considération dévouée.

Henri Barbusse

*Sylvie
Aumont par Senlis
(Oise)
12 décembre* 1932

Mon cher Russell

Le Comité Tom Mooney voulant profiter du changement de gouvernement aux Etats-Unis pour arriver à la solution de l'affaire Tom Mooney, au sujet de laquelle de nouvelles révélations viennent encore de se produire, a décidé l'envoi au Président Roosevelt de la lettre ci-jointe qui bien que conçue en termes officiels et très déférents, quoique fermes, nous parait susceptible d'apporter réellement un terme au scandaleux martyre de Tom Mooney et de Billings.

Je vous demande de bien vouloir y apposer votre signature et de me la renvoyer d'urgence.

Croyez à mes sentiments amicaux.

Henri Barbusse
Je vous envoie d'autre part une brochure éditée par le Comité Tom Mooney.

47 Emperor's Gate
S.W.7
16th December 1932

Dear Barbusse

I am at all times willing to do anything that seems to me likely to help Mooney, but I have a certain hesitation about the draft letter that you have sent me.

You will, of course, remember that in the time of Kerensky the Russian Government made an appeal to President Wilson on the subject, and that he, in consequence, had the Mooney case investigated by a number of eminent legal authorities who reported favourably to Mooney. The State of California, however, pointed out that the President had no right to interfere with State administration of justice.

I do not think there is very much point in appealing to the President Elect, as he will merely take shelter behind his lack of legal power. In any case it would be no use presenting the letter until after he becomes President, which will, I think, be on March 4th. There is no doubt also that at this moment

American public opinion is not feeling particularly friendly to either your country or mine, and I doubt whether we can usefully intervene until passions have cooled.

> *Yours sincerely*
> *Bertrand Russell*

This letter shows that I was not always impetuous.

From Count Michael Károlyi

The White Hall Hotel
70 Guildford St, W.C.1
5th Feb. 1935

My dear Russell

I want to thank you for the brilliant letter you wrote for the defence of Rákosi.[1] The trial is still on, and the final sentence may come any day now. If he does not get a death sentence it will be due in very great part to your intervention. I fear in this case however, that he will be imprisoned for life. Of course, we will try to save him even so—perhaps we can succeed in getting him exchanged for something or other from the Soviet government.

The last time I saw you, you invited me to spend a week-end with you. If I am not inconveniencing you I should like to come and see you, not this Sunday, but any other time which would suit you.

There are so many things to talk over with you—please let me know.

My new address is as above, and my telephone number is Terminus 5512.

> *Yours very sincerely*
> *M. Karolyi*

From Gerald Brenan, author of
The Spanish Labyrinth and other books

June 1st 1935
Churriana
[Malaga]

Dear Bertie

I see that I have to say something really very stupid indeed to draw a letter from you. My letter was written late at night, when ones thoughts and fears tend to carry one away, and I regretted it afterwards. I spent the next day in penance reading an account of de Montfort's campaign.

It is easy enough to *sympathise* with the destructive desires of revolutionaries: the difficulty in most cases is to agree that they are likely to do any good. What I really dislike about them are their doctrinaire ideas and their spirit of intolerance. The religious idea in Communism, which is the reason for its success, (the assurance it gives of Time that is God, being on ones side) will lead in the end perhaps to a sort of Mohammedan creed of brotherhood & stagnation. The energy and combativeness of Christian nations comes, I

---

[1] Mátyás Rákosi, a Hungarian communist, re-arrested upon his release from a long prison sentence. His life was saved but he was again imprisoned. In 1940 Russia obtained him in exchange for Hungarian flags captured in 1849. Later, Rákosi became Deputy Prime Minister of Hungary.

suspect, from the doctrine of sin, particularly Original Sin and the kind of struggle that must go on for redemption (or for money). But for Augustine's Manichaeanism we should have been a more docile but less interesting lot. I am opposed to this Communist religion, because I think that Socialism shd be a matter of administration only. Any religious ideas that get attached to it will be impoverishing, unless of course they are treated lightly, as the Romans treated the worship of Augustus or the Chinese treated Confucianism. But that of course may [not] be the case.—Anyhow since one has in the end to accept or reject these things en bloc, I shall support Communism when I see it is winning—and I shall *always* support it against Fascism.

Out here every day brings news of the disintegration of the Popular Front. Moderate Socialists, Revolutionary Socialists and Syndicalists are all at loggerheads. Disorders go on increasing and I think that the most likely end is dictatorship. I incline to think that the best thing for the country would be a Dictatorship of the moderate left (present government with Socialists) for, say, ten years. I understand that the agricultural unemployment cannot be solved until large areas at present unirrigated have been made irrigateable. Dams have been begun, but many more are wanted and fifteen years must elapse till they are ready. The plan is for the Govt to control investments & direct them upon these dams, repaying the lenders by a mortage on the new irrigated land.

The weather is delicious now and every moment of life is a pleasure. Besides health and weather—which is Nature's health—very little matters. It would be nice if you rented a house out here & brought out some of your books. If everything in Spain is uncertain—what about the rest of Europe?

With love from us both to you & Peter

ever yrs
Gerald Brenan

Public opinion in England seems alarmingly warlike. I favour the dropping of sanctions and conclusion of a Mediterranean pact, which would be a check to Mussolini. But then we must be ready to go to war if he takes a Greek island.

In England the importance of Austria's not going Nazi is always under-estimated. *The Times* refuses to look at Central Europe at all. The English are priggish about everything beyond Berlin—Vienna—Venice. I suspect that you think as I do.

From Mrs Gerald Brenan

Bell Court
Aldbourne, Marlborough
[Nov. 1938]

My dear Bertie
I thought of you very much in those really horrible days—which must have been dreadful to you going further & further away from your children and

leaving them behind in such a world. It is the kind of thing you might dream of in an evil nightmare—but it was one of those modern nightmares in which you are still awake.

I share your difficulties. I am and always shall be a pacifist. But sometimes they seem to 'cry Peace Peace when there is no peace'. What a world we live in.

Power is having wonderful reviews, I see, and is a best seller. I am so glad. I hope to read it soon.

We have had an Anarchist from Holland staying with us, the Secretary of the A.I.T. He was a charming & very intelligent man, & had been a good deal in Spain with the C.N.T.

He was a great admirer of yours. He said that he had recently written an article on Anarchism for an Encyclopedia. In the Bibliography at the end he included 'All the works of Bertrand Russell' because, he explains, though they are not actually Anarchist they have 'the tendency' as old Anarchists say.

I was pleased—for whatever Anarchist parties are in practice 'the tendency' I'm sure is right. We went to Savernake Forest one day. The autumn leaves were beginning to fall but the day was warm & bright. I wished for you & Peter & John & Kate. Perhaps we will walk there again another day.

I hope you & Peter are as happy as it is possible to be so far from home & in such days.

With love to you both

> *Yours ever*
> *Gamel*

> Bell Court
> Aldbourne, Marlborough
> [Winter 1938–9]

My dear Bertie

I was so glad to get your letter and to think that you will be coming home now before so very long and we shall see you again.

Yes, we must somehow meet more often. We must have picnics in Savernake Forest—and find some charming place to come together half way between Kidlington and Aldbourne. Gerald and I are going to take to bicycles this summer, so we can meet anywhere.

I am sure America is very difficult to be in now. I was afraid you and Peter would find it trying in many ways—the tremendous lionizing must be very exhausting and very tiresome in the end however well they mean.

Longmans Green are going to bring out my book some time in the late spring I think. I am glad, for I think in a small way it is a useful book. It is such a painful picture of the war state of mind. It is to be called *Death's Other Kingdom*, from T. S. Eliot's line 'Is it like this in Death's other kingdom?'

Gerald and I have both read *Power* with great interest and great admiration. It has made a great impression, I gather, not only from the reviews, but from the fact that almost every intelligent person I meet happens somehow in some connection to mention it.

I can understand how you long to be in England. And I am so glad that you will soon be coming home.

With much love to you all,

Yours
Gamel

I am delighted to learn the real provenance of my name—but I am not sure how I feel about its nearness to Camel.

From Mrs Bernard Berenson
The Mud House
Friday's Hill, Haslemere
July 28, 1936

My dear Bertie

Might I motor over & call upon you and your wife on Thursday or Friday of this week, or sometime next week?

I've been very ill, and one of the results of illness is to make me understand what things have been precious in my life, and you were one of the most precious. I do not want to die without seeing you again & thanking you for so many things.

Yours affectionately
Mary Berenson

To and from Lion Fitzpatrick
Telegraph House
Harting, Petersfield
21.12.36

Dear Lion

It was very disappointing that I was ill just when we were coming to you— it was gastric flu, brief but incapacitating. We look forward to seeing you towards the end of January.

As Alys is going to stay with you, I wonder whether you could say some little word of a friendly sort from me. I am the more anxious for this because Mrs Berenson said a number of very critical things about Alys, to which I listened in stony silence; & I dare say she went away saying I had said them. I don't want to make mischief, so that there would be no point in mentioning Mrs Berenson to Alys; but I should be sorry if Alys thought that I said or felt unfriendly things about her.

Yours
B R

The Warden's Lodgings
All Souls College, Oxford
Dec. 28. 36

Dear Bertie

All right. I'll try to do that. But it isnt easy to inform Alys about you. She likes to think she knows everything about you. At bottom she is intensely interested in you but she still seems raw even after all these years. I expect she cares quite a lot about you still. People *are* queer. If they are without humour they either dry up or get rather rancid. I feel that to be able to regard yourself as somewhat of a joke is the highest virtue.

I'll ask (?) [illegible word] over when Alys & Grace Worthington and after them the Wells go—It will be in Feb. I am afraid unless I could come in between visits. But I generally have to go to bed then—oh Lord how unadaptable the English are and how unimpressionable the U.S. (?) [illegible word]. These people here are Scottish & Ulster. Much more flexible breed.

I have a rather miserable spot in my sub-conscious about your book on philosophy. I do wish you could get it out of you before you die—I think it would be important!—after all that is what you ought to be doing—not pot boilers. Bill Adams (the son of the Warden here) has been listening to you somewhere on physics and says your brain is the clearest in England— (Is this great praise in a country where brains are nearly all muddled and proud of it sir?)

My regards to Lady Russell—I hope she is well—I write to her later—

Lion

Lion Fitzpatrick, the writer of the preceding letter, was a close friend of Alys's and later also of mine. 'Lion' was a nickname given to her on account of her mane of black hair. Her father had been a Belfast business man, who, owing to drink, had first gone bankrupt and then died. She came to England penniless, and was employed by Lady Henry Somerset on philanthropic work in Somerstown (St Pancras). I met her first on June 10, 1894, at a Temperance Procession which I attended because of Alys. We quarrelled about the Mission to Deep Sea Fishermen, concerning which I made some disparaging remark. Shortly afterwards she followed the example of Bernard Shaw by standing for the St Pancras Vestry (which corresponded to what is now the Borough Council). She lived up a back staircase in a slum, and as I had my Cambridge furniture to dispose of, I gave some of it to her.

Meanwhile, through Alys, she came to know a young man named Bobby Phillimore, who had proposed to Alys but been refused. He was at Christchurch, and was the son of Lord Phillimore, a very rich Liberal Law Lord and a close friend of Mr Gladstone. Bobby, I think under Logan's influence, became Socialist and a poet. He was the original of the poet in Shaw's *Candida*. He decided that he wanted to marry Lion, but he was not going to repeat the mistake of precipitancy which he had committed with Alys. So he got himself elected to the St Pancras Vestry and carefully prepared his approaches. Shortly after Alys and I were married, when we were living in Berlin, I got a letter from Lion asking my advice as to whether she should accept him. I wrote back at once giving twelve reasons against. By return of post I got a letter from her saying that she had accepted him.

In the following spring, when Alys and I were staying with her sister at Fiesole, Lion and Bobby came to see us on their return from their honeymoon in North Africa. I then for the first time learned why she had accepted him.

After she had resolutely refused him for some time, he developed heart trouble, and eminent medical men gave it as their opinion that if she persisted he would die. His father pleaded with her, but in vain. Finally, in response to impassioned requests from Lord Phillimore, Mr Gladstone, though eighty and nearly blind, climbed her slummy staircase in person to urge her to abandon the role of Barbara Allen. This was too much for her, and she accepted her love-sick swain.

So far, so good—a pleasant King Cophetua story. But in Fiesole, after her honeymoon, she told a surprising sequel. Alys and I noticed at once that she had become profoundly cynical, and amazingly obscene in her conversation, so we naturally pressed her as to what produced such a change. She told us that, as soon as she and Bobby were married, he told her he had deceived the doctors, and had nothing the matter with his heart;[1] further that, though he had been determined to marry her, he did not love her and never had loved her. I believe the marriage was never consummated.

Bobby's father owned Radlett, at that time a picturesque country village; he owned also a rather beautiful country house between Radlett and Elstree. He gave Bobby the house and a free hand in managing the estate. The poet and the Socialist receded into the background, and were replaced by a very hard-headed business man, who proceeded to develop Radlett by putting up vast numbers of cheap, ugly, sordid suburban villas, which brought in an enormous profit. Years later he really did become ill. His wife nursed him devotedly for about three years, at the end of which he died. After his death she told me she would marry any man who would promise to be always ill, because she had grown so used to nursing that she did not know how to fill her days without it.

She did not, however, marry again. She published anonymously a book which had a considerable success, called *By an unknown disciple*. She had an abortive affair with Massingham. She took a great interest in psychical research. Being left a rich widow, she devoted a large part of her income to support of the Labour Party. I saw little of her in her last years, because she demanded that one should treat seriously things that I regard as nonsense— sentimental religiosity, second sight, the superior intuitions of the Irish, and so on. But I regretted these obstacles, and tried to see her without either quarrels or insincerity.

To W. V. Quine, the Harvard logician

Telegraph House
Harting, Petersfield
6-6-35

Dear Dr Quine

Your book [*System of Logistic*] arrived at a moment when I was over-worked and obliged to take a long holiday. The result is that I have only just finished reading it.

I think you have done a beautiful piece of work; it is a long time since I have had as much intellectual pleasure as in reading you.

---

[1] However, he died of heart disease some years later.

Two questions occurred to me, as to which I should be glad to have answers when you have time. I have put them on a separate sheet.

In reading you I was struck by the fact that, in my work, I was always being influenced by extraneous philosophical considerations. Take e.g. descriptions. I was interested in 'Scott is the author of Waverley', and not only in the descriptive functions of PM.[1] If you look up Meinong's work, you will see the sort of fallacies I wanted to avoid; the same applies to the ontological argument.

Take again notation (mainly Whitehead's): we had to provide for the correlators in Parts III and IV. Your α_β for our $R|S$ would not do for three or more relations, or for various forms (such as $R||S$) we needed.

I am worried—though as yet I cannot put my worry into words—as to whether you really have avoided the troubles for which the axiom of reducibility was introduced as completely as you think. I should like to see Induction and Dedekindian continuity explicitly treated by your methods.

I am a little puzzled as to the status of classes in your system. They appear as a primitive idea, but the connection of α with $\hat{x}(\phi x)$ seems somewhat vague. Do you maintain that, if $\alpha = \hat{x}(\phi x)$, the prop. $x\alpha$, is identical with ϕx? You must, if you are to say that all props are sequences. Yet it seems obvious that 'I gave sixpence to my son' is not the *same* as 'my son is one of the people to whom I gave sixpence'.

And do you maintain that an infinite class can be defined otherwise than by a defining function? The need of including infinite classes was one of my reasons for emphasizing functions as opposed to classes in PM.

I expect you have good answers to these questions.

In any case, I have the highest admiration for what you have done, which has reformed many matters as to which I had always been uncomfortable.

Yours very truly
Bertrand Russell

To G. E. Moore

Telegraph House
Harting, Petersfield
Feb. 8, 1937

Dear Moore

I have become very desirous of returning to purely philosophic work; in particular, I want to develop the ideas in my paper on 'The Limits of Empiricism', & to investigate the relation of language to fact, as to which Carnap's ideas seem to me very inadequate. But I am in the unfortunate position of being legally bound to pay between £800 & £900 a year to other people, & having only £300 a year of unearned income. I cannot therefore work at philosophy unless I can get some academic job. I suppose there is no possibility at Cambridge? I should be very glad if there were, as my desire to get back to philosophy is very strong.

Yours
Bertrand Russell

[1] *Principia Mathematica.*

Telegraph House
Harting, Petersfield
Feb. 18, 1937

Dear Moore

Thank you for your letter, which shows the position to be much as I supposed. I think perhaps, at the moment, it is hardly worth proceeding in the matter, as the chance of success seems small, & there are other possibilities elsewhere. I am very grateful to you for being willing to recommend me, & if other things fail I will write to you again. In the meantime, I think it will be best to do nothing.

The Leverhulme Fellowships are settled in June; till then, I shall not know. In any case they only last two years.

Yours
Bertrand Russell

From Desmond MacCarthy   25, Wellington Square
                                          S.W.3
                                          March 16. 37

Dear Bertie

I am relieved that you thought my review likely to wet the public appetite: that is what I tried to do. I did not write it well: I wrote it too quickly and only had time to make perfunctory corrections, but I think it will persuade people that *The Amberley Papers* are very interesting. I went to Trinity Commem: and dined in Hall on Sunday night. I found the review was working there.

What I am pleased about is that I got G. M. Younge to write about it in the *Observer*. He wanted to write about it in the S. T. & I got him, by grabbing the book from him, to offer his comments to Garvin.

I don't expect that you hope for a large sale, but I think it may have a very respectable one & go on selling.

I am interested to hear that you have sold Telegraph House, & long to hear particulars. I am afraid the price was not not [*sic*] good or you would have written with more elation. It does not mean—does it that your worst money worries are at an end? Do you remember what a fuss Schopenhauer made about having to pension the woman he pushed down stairs for the term of her natural life? And he had only a brown poodle dependent on him, (Its name was Butz) and you have never pushed a woman down stairs. Do you remember his triumphant entry in his diary after many years, *Obit anus, abit onus?* I look forward to getting *two* postcards from you, soon, with these words on them.

It is of the utmost importance that you should have leisure to write your book clearing up the relation of grammar and philosophy and many things beside. Is it true that you could manage on £500 a year till you can write those post-cards? Your admirers ought to be able to raise that. Would you object to being pensioned? I shouldn't if my prospects were as good as yours of writing something valuable.

Time is getting short now. I don't mean that death is necessarily near either of us, but the slow death is near; the softening and relaxing of the faculty of attention which in its approach feels so like wisdom to the victim.

I met Shaw not long ago & he talked about his latest works, which exhibit all his astonishing aptitudes—except grip. I had an impulse to say (but I thought it too unkind) 'Aren't you afraid though of letting out the deadly secret—that you can no longer *care*?' I guessed the nature of that secret from having observed what was threatening me. But with you & me it is still only a threat—You, especially, can still care, for your power of feeling has always been stronger than mine. Still, time is short. We are all (and I mean also people neither of us know) [anxious] that you should philosophise, and write your book before the power to write it begins to be insensibly sucked away in the fat folds of that hydra, old age.

I stayed with Moore and we were happy—grey-beards at play, most of the time. He made me read a paper by Wisdom on Definition but I didn't get the hang of it. It was Wittgensteinian. I wanted to talk about myself and make Moore talk about himself, but we didn't care enough to get over the discomfort of leaving the pleasant shore of memories. But damn it I'll do it next time (This isn't the first time though, I've said that). Do please send me word when you are *next* in London & come to lunch or in the morning or in the afternoon, or to dinner—any time. We cd put you up. Dermod is a ships doctor, his room is empty. And I will come to you for a visit in May after my Leslie Stephen lecture. Give my affectionate & best wishes to 'Peter' for a happy delivery—

Yours, always
Desmond

CHAPTER VI

AMERICA. 1938–1944

IN AUGUST 1938, we sold our house at Kidlington. The purchasers would only buy it if we evacuated it at once, which left us a fortnight in August to fill in somehow. We hired a caravan, and spent the time on the coast of Pembrokeshire. There were Peter and me, John and Kate and Conrad, and our big dog Sherry. It poured with rain practically the whole time and we were all squashed up together. It was about as uncomfortable a time as I can remember. Peter had to prepare the meals, which she hated doing. Finally, John and Kate went back to Dartington, and Peter and Conrad and I sailed for America.

In Chicago I had a large Seminar, where I continued to lecture on the same subject as at Oxford, namely, 'Words and Facts'. But I was told that Americans would not respect my lectures if I used monosyllables, so I altered the title to something like 'The Correlation between Oral and Somatic Motor Habits'. Under this title, or something of the sort, the Seminar was approved. It was an extraordinarily delightful Seminar. Carnap and Charles Morris used to come to it, and I had three pupils of quite outstanding ability—Dalkey, Kaplan, and Copilowish. We used to have close arguments back and forth, and succeeded in genuinely clarifying points to our mutual satisfaction, which is rare in philosophical argument. Apart from this Seminar, the time in Chicago was disagreeable. The town is beastly and the weather was vile. President Hutchins, who was occupied with the Hundred Best Books, and with the attempt to force neo-Thomism on the philosophical faculty, naturally did not much like me, and when the year for which I had been engaged came to an end was, I think, glad to see me go.

I became a professor at the University of California at Los Angeles. After the bleak hideousness of Chicago, which was still in the grip of winter, it was delightful to arrive in the Californian spring. We arrived in California at the end of March, and my duties did not begin until September. The first part of the intervening time I spent in a lecture tour, of which I remember only two things with any vividness. One is that the professors at the Louisiana State University, where I lectured, all thought well of Huey Long, on the ground that he had raised their salaries. The other recollection is more pleasant: in a purely rural region, I was taken to the top of the dykes that enclose the Mississippi. I was very tired with lecturing, long journeys, and heat. I lay in the grass, and watched the majestic river, and gazed, half hypnotized, at water and sky. For some ten minutes I experienced peace, a thing which very rarely happened to me, and I think only in the presence of moving water.

In the summer of 1939, John and Kate came to visit us for the period of the school holidays. A few days after they arrived the War broke out, and it became impossible to send them back to England. I had to provide for their further education at a moment's notice. John was seventeen, and I entered him at the University of California, but Kate was only fifteen, and this seemed young for the University. I made enquiries among friends as to which school in Los Angeles had the highest academic standard, and there was one that they all concurred in recommending, so I sent her there. But I found that there was only one subject taught that she did not already know, and that was the virtues of the capitalist system. I was therefore compelled, in spite of her youth, to send her to the University. Throughout the year 1939–40 John and Kate lived with us.

In the summer months of 1939 we rented a house at Santa Barbara, which is an altogether delightful place. Unfortunately, I injured my back, and had to lie flat on my back for a month, tortured by almost unendurable sciatica. The result of this was that I got behindhand with the preparations for my lectures, and that throughout the coming academic year I was always overworked and always conscious that my lectures were inadequate.

The academic atmosphere was much less agreeable than in Chicago; the people were not so able, and the President was a man for whom I conceived, I think justly, a profound aversion. If a lecturer said anything that was too liberal, it was discovered that the lecturer in question did his work badly, and he was dismissed. When there were meetings of the Faculty, the President of the University used to march in as if he were wearing jack-boots, and rule any motion out of order if he did not happen to like it. Everybody trembled at his frown, and I was reminded of a meeting of the Reichstag under Hitler.

Towards the end of the academic year 1939–40, I was invited to become a professor at the College of the City of New York. The matter appeared to be settled, and I wrote to the President of the University of California to resign my post there. Half an hour after he received my letter, I learned that the appointment in New York was not definitive and I called upon the President to withdraw my resignation, but he told me it was too late. Earnest Christian taxpayers had been protesting against having to contribute to the salary of an infidel, and the President was glad to be quit of me.

The College of the City of New York was an institution run by the City Government. Those who attended it were practically all Catholics or Jews; but to the indignation of the former, practically all the scholarships went to the latter. The Government of New York City was virtually a satellite of the Vatican, but the professors at the City College strove ardently to keep up some semblance of academic freedom. It was no doubt in pursuit of this aim that they had recommended me. An Anglican bishop was incited to protest against me, and priests lectured the police, who were practically all Irish Catholics, on my responsibility for the local criminals. A lady, whose daughter attended some section of the City College with which I should never be brought in contact, was induced to bring a suit, saying that my presence in that institution would be dangerous to her daughter's virtue. This was not a suit against me, but against the Municipality of New York.[1] I endeavoured to be made a party to the suit, but was told that I was not concerned. Although the Municipality was nominally the defendant, it was as anxious to lose the suit as the good lady was to win it. The lawyer for the prosecution pronounced my works 'lecherous, libidinous, lustful, venerous, erotomaniac, aphrodisiac, irreverent, narrow-minded, untruthful, and bereft of moral fiber'. The suit came before an Irishman who decided against me at length and with vituperation. I wished for an appeal, but the Municipality of New York refused to appeal. Some of the things said against me were quite fantastic. For example, I was thought wicked for saying that very young infants should not be punished for masturbation.

A typical American witch-hunt was instituted against me,[2] and I became taboo throughout the whole of the United States. I was to have been engaged in a lecture tour, but I had only one engagement, made before the witch-hunt had developed. The Rabbi who had made this engagement broke his contract, but I cannot blame him. Owners of halls refused to let them if I was to lecture, and if I had appeared anywhere in public, I should probably have been lynched by a Catholic mob, with the full approval of the police. No newspaper or magazine would publish anything that I wrote, and I was suddenly deprived of all means of earning a living. As it was legally impossible to get money out of England, this produced a very difficult situation, especially as I had my three children dependent upon me. Many liberal-minded professors protested, but they all supposed that as I was an earl I must have ancestral estates and be very well off. Only one man did anything

[1] Information about this suit will be found in *The Bertrand Russell Case*, ed. by John Dewey and Horace M. Kallen, Viking Press, 1941; and also in the Appendix to *Why I am Not a Christian*, ed. by Paul Edwards, Allen & Unwin, 1957.

[2] The Registrar of New York County said publicly that I should be 'tarred and feathered and driven out of the country'. Her remarks were typical of the general public condemnation.

practical, and that was Dr Barnes, the inventor of Argyrol, and the creator of the Barnes Foundation near Philadelphia. He gave me a five-year appointment to lecture on philosophy at his Foundation. This relieved me of a very great anxiety. Until he gave me this appointment, I had seen no way out of my troubles. I could not get money out of England; it was impossible to return to England; I certainly did not wish my three children to go back into the blitz, even if I could have got a passage for them which would certainly have been impossible for a long time to come. It seemed as if it would be necessary to take John and Kate away from the University, and to live as cheaply as possible on the charity of kind friends. From this bleak prospect I was saved by Dr Barnes.

The summer of 1940 offered for me an extraordinary contrast between public horror and private delight. We spent the summer in the Sierras, at Fallen Leaf Lake near Lake Tahoe, one of the loveliest places that it has ever been my good fortune to know. The lake is more than 6000 feet above sea-level, and during the greater part of the year deep snow makes the whole region uninhabitable. But there is a three-months' season in the summer during which the sun shines continually, the weather is warm, but as a rule not unbearably hot, the mountain meadows are filled with the most exquisite wild flowers, and the smell of the pine trees fills the air. We had a log cabin in the middle of pine trees, close to the lake. Conrad and his nursery governess slept indoors, but there was no room for the rest of us in the house, and we all slept on various porches. There were endless walks through deserted country to waterfalls, lakes and mountain tops, and one could dive off snow into deep water that was not unduly cold. I had a tiny study which was hardly more than a shed, and there I finished my *Inquiry into Meaning and Truth*. Often it was so hot that I did my writing stark naked. But heat suits me, and I never found it too hot for work.

Amid all these delights we waited day by day to know whether England had been invaded, and whether London still existed. The postman, a jocular fellow with a somewhat sadistic sense of humour, arrived one morning saying in a loud voice, 'Heard the news? All London destroyed, not a house left standing!' And we could not know whether to believe him. Long walks and frequent bathes in many lakes helped to make the time endurable, and, by September, it had begun to seem that England would not be invaded.

I found in the Sierras the only classless society that I have ever known. Practically all the houses were inhabited by university professors, and the necessary work was done by university students. The young man, for instance, who brought our groceries was a young man to whom I had been lecturing throughout the winter. There were also many students who had come merely for a holiday, which could be enjoyed very cheaply as everything was primitive and simple. Americans understand the management of tourists much better than Europeans do. Although there were many houses close to the lake, hardly one could be seen from a boat, since all were carefully concealed in pine trees; and the houses themselves were built of pine logs, and were quite inoffensive. One angle of the house in which we lived was made of a live and growing tree; I cannot imagine what will happen to the house when the tree grows too big.

In the autumn of 1940 I gave the William James lectures at Harvard. This engagement had been made before the trouble in New York. Perhaps Harvard regretted having made it, but, if so, the regret was politely concealed from me.

My duties with Dr Barnes began at the New Year of 1941. We rented a farmhouse about thirty miles from Philadelphia, a very charming house, about two hundred years old, in rolling country, not unlike inland Dorsetshire. There was an orchard, a fine old barn, and three peach trees, which bore enormous quantities of the most delicious peaches I have ever tasted. There were fields sloping down to a river, and pleasant woodlands. We were ten miles from Paoli (called after the Corsican patriot), which was the limit of the Philadelphia suburban trains. From there I used to go by train to the Barnes Foundation, where I lectured in a gallery of modern French paintings, mostly of nudes, which seemed somewhat incongruous for academic philosophy.

Dr Barnes was a strange character. He had a dog to whom he was passionately devoted and a wife who was passionately devoted to him. He liked to patronize coloured people and treated them as equals, because he was quite sure that they were not. He had made an enormous fortune by inventing Argyrol; when it was at its height, he sold out, and invested all his money in Government securities. He then became an art connoisseur. He had a very fine gallery of modern French paintings and in connection with the gallery he taught the principles of aesthetics. He demanded constant flattery and had a passion for quarrelling. I was warned before accepting his offer that he always tired of people before long, so I exacted a five-year contract from him. On December 28th, 1942, I got a letter from him informing me that my appointment was terminated as from January 1st. I was thus reduced once again from affluence to destitution. True, I had my contract, and the lawyer whom I consulted assured me that there was no doubt whatever of my getting full redress from the courts. But obtaining legal redress takes time, especially in America, and I had to live through the intervening period somehow. Corbusier, in a book on America, tells a typical story about Barnes's behaviour. Corbusier was on a lecture tour, and wished to see

Dr Barnes's gallery. He wrote for permission, which Dr Barnes always accorded very grudgingly. Dr Barnes replied that he could see it at nine o'clock on a certain Saturday morning, but at no other time. Corbusier wrote again saying that his lecture engagements made that time impossible and would not some other time be suitable. Dr. Barnes wrote an exceedingly rude letter saying it was then or never. To this Corbusier sent a long answer, which is printed in his book saying that he was not averse from quarrels, but he preferred to quarrel with people who were on the other side in matters of art, whereas he and Dr Barnes were both in favour of what is modern, and it seemed a pity that they should not agree. Dr Barnes never opened this letter, but returned it, with the word '*merde*' written large on the envelope.

When my case came into court, Dr Barnes complained that I had done insufficient work for my lectures, and that they were superficial and perfunctory. So far as they had gone, they consisted of the first two-thirds of my *History of Western Philosophy*, of which I submitted the manuscript to the judge, though I scarcely suppose he read it. Dr Barnes complained of my treatment of the men whom he called Pither-gawras and Empi-Dokkles. I observed the judge taking notice, and I won my case. Dr Barnes, of course, appealed as often as he could, and it was not until I was back in England that I actually got the money. Meanwhile he had sent a printed document concerning my sins to the Master and each of the Fellows of Trinity College, to warn them of their folly in inviting me back. I never read this document, but I have no doubt it was good reading.

In the early months of 1943 I suffered some financial stringency, but not so much as I had feared. We sublet our nice farmhouse, and went to live in a cottage intended for a coloured couple whom it was expected that the inhabitants of the farmhouse would employ. This consisted of three rooms and three stoves, each of which had to be stoked every hour or so. One was to warm the place, one was for cooking, and one was for hot water. When they went out it was several hours' work to get them lighted again. Conrad could hear every word that Peter and I said to each other, and we had many worrying things to discuss which it was not good for him to be troubled with. But by this time the trouble about City College had begun to blow over, and I was able to get occasional lecture engagements in New York and other places. The embargo was first broken by an invitation from Professor Weiss of Bryn Mawr to give a course of lectures there. This required no small degree of courage. On one occasion I was so poor that I had to take a single ticket to New York and pay the return fare out of my lecture fee. My *History of Western Philosophy* was nearly complete, and I wrote to W. W. Norton, who had been my American publisher, to ask if, in view of my difficult financial position, he would make an advance on it. He replied that because of his affection for John and Kate, and as a kindness to an old friend, he would advance five hundred dollars. I thought I could get more elsewhere, so I approached Simon and Schuster, who were unknown to me personally. They at once agreed to pay me two thousand dollars on the spot, and another thousand six months later. At this time John was at Harvard and Kate was at Radcliffe. I had been afraid that lack of funds might compel me to take them away, but thanks to Simon and Schuster, this proved unnecessary. I was also helped at this time by loans from private friends which, fortunately, I was able to repay before long.

The *History of Western Philosophy* began by accident and proved the main source of my income for many years. I had no idea, when I embarked upon this project, that it would have a success which none of my other books have had, even, for a time, shining high upon the American list of Best Sellers. While I was still concerned with ancient times, Barnes had told me that he had no further need of me, and my lectures stopped. I found the work exceedingly interesting, especially the parts that I knew least about beforehand, the early Mediaeval part and the Jewish part just before the birth of Christ, so I continued the work till I had completed the survey. I was grateful to Bryn Mawr College for allowing me the use of its library which I found excellent, especially as it provided me with the invaluable work of the Rev. Charles who published translations of Jewish works written shortly before the time of Christ and in a great degree anticipating His teaching.

I was pleased to be writing this history because I had always believed that history should be written in the large. I had always held, for example, that the subject matter of which Gibbon treats could not be adequately treated in a shorter book or several books. I regarded the early part of my *History of Western Philosophy* as a history of culture, but in the later parts, where science becomes important, it is more difficult to fit into this framework. I did my best, but I am not at all sure that I succeeded. I was sometimes accused by reviewers of writing not a true history but a biased account of the events that I arbitrarily chose to write of. But to my mind, a man without a bias cannot write interesting history—if, indeed, such a man exists. I regard it as mere humbug to pretend to lack of bias. Moreover, a book, like any other work, should be held together by its point of view. This is why a book made up of essays by various authors is apt to be less interesting as an entity than a book by one man. Since I do not admit that a person without bias exists, I think the best that can be done with a large-scale history is to admit one's bias and for dissatisfied readers to look for other writers to express an opposite bias. Which bias is nearer to the truth must be left to posterity. This point of view on the writing of history makes me prefer my *History of Western Philosophy* to the *Wisdom of the West* which was taken from the former, but ironed out and tamed—although I like the illustrations of *Wisdom of the West*.

The last part of our time in America was spent at Princeton, where we had a little house on the shores of the lake. While in Princeton, I came to know Einstein fairly well. I used to go to his house once a week to discuss with him and Gödel and Pauli. These discussions were in some ways disappointing, for, although all three of them were Jews and exiles and, in intention, cosmopolitans, I found that they all had a German bias towards metaphysics, and in spite of our utmost endeavours we never arrived at common premises from which to argue. Gödel turned out to be an unadulterated Platonist, and apparently believed that an eternal 'not' was laid up in heaven, where virtuous logicians might hope to meet it hereafter.

The society of Princeton was extremely pleasant, pleasanter, on the whole, than any other social group I had come across in America. By this time John was back in England, having gone into the British Navy and been set to learn Japanese. Kate was self-sufficient at Radcliffe, having done extremely well in her work and acquired a small teaching job. There was therefore nothing to keep us in America except the difficulty of obtaining a passage to England. This difficulty, however, seemed for a long time insuperable. I went to Washington to argue that I must be allowed to perform my duties in the House of Lords, and tried to persuade the authorities that my desire to do so was very ardent. At last I discovered an argument which convinced the British Embassy. I said to them: 'You will admit this is a war against Fascism.' 'Yes', they said; 'And', I continued, 'you will admit that the essence of Fascism consists in the subordination of the legislature to the executive'. 'Yes,' they said, though with slightly more hesitation. 'Now,' I continued, 'you are the executive and I am the legislature and if you keep me away from my legislative functions one day longer than is necessary, you are Fascists.' Amid general laughter, my sailing permit was granted then and there. A curious difficulty, however, still remained. My wife and I got A priority, but our son Conrad only got a B, as he had as yet no legislative function. Naturally enough we wished Conrad, who was seven years old, and his mother to travel together, but this required that she should consent to be classified as a B. No case had so far occurred of a person accepting a lower classification than that to which they were entitled, and all the officials were so puzzled that it took them some months to understand. At last, however, dates were fixed, for Peter and Conrad first, and for me about a fortnight later. We sailed in May 1944.

LETTERS

To Charles Sanger's wife

'The Plaisance'
On the Midway at Jackson
Park—Chicago
Nov. 5, 1938

My dear Dora

Thank you for your letter, which, after some wanderings, reached me here. I quite agree with you about the new war-cry. I was immensely glad when the crisis passed, but I don't know how soon it may come up again. Here in America, nine people out of ten think that we ought to have fought but America ought to have remained neutral—an opinion which annoys me. It is odd, in England, that the very people who, in 1919, protested against the unjust frontiers of Czechoslovakia were the most anxious, in 1938, to defend them. And they always forget that the first result of an attempt at an armed defence would have been to expose the Czechs to German invasion, which would have been much worse for them than even what they are enduring now.

I had forgotten about Eddie Marsh at the Ship in 1914, but your letter reminded me of it. Everybody at that time reacted so characteristically.

Ottoline's death was a very great loss to me. Charlie and Crompton and Ottoline were my only really close friends among contemporaries, and now all three are dead. And day by day we move into an increasingly horrible world.

Privately, nevertheless, my circumstances are happy. John and Kate are everything that I would wish, and Conrad Crow (now 19 months old) is most satisfactory. America is interesting, and solid, whereas England, one fears, is crumbling. Daphne[1] must have had an interesting time in Belgrade.

I shall be home early in May, and I hope I shall see you soon there. All good wishes,

Yours ever
Bertrand Russell

To W. V. Quine

212 Loring Avenue
Los Angeles, Cal.
16 Oct., 1939

Dear Dr Quine

I quite agree with your estimate of Tarski; no other logician of his generation (unless it were yourself) seems to me his equal.

I should, consequently, be very glad indeed if I could induce the authorities here to find him a post. I should be glad for logic, for the university, for him, and for myself. But inquiries have shown me that there is no possibility whatever; they feel that they are saturated both with foreigners and with logicians. I went so far as to hint that if I could, by retiring, make room for him, I might consider doing so; but it seemed that even so the result could not be achieved.

[1] The Sangers' daughter.

I presume you have tried the East: Harvard, Princeton, Columbia, etc. Princeton *should* be the obvious place. You may quote me anywhere as concurring in your view of Tarski's abilities.

Yours sincerely
Bertrand Russell

From an anonymous correspondent   Newark, N.J.
                                                 March 4, 1940

Bertrand Russell

Just whom did you think you were fooling when you had those hypocritically posed 'family man' pictures taken for the newspapers? Can your diseased brain have reached such an advanced stage of senility as to imagine for a moment that you would impress anyone? You poor old fool!

Even your publicly proved degeneracy cannot overshadow your vileness in posing for these pictures and trying to hide behind the innocence of your unfortunate children. Shame on you! Every decent man and woman in the country loathes you for this vile action of yours more than your other failings, which, after all, you inherited honestly enough from your decadent family tree. As for your questions and concern regarding Church and State connections in this country—just what concern has anything in this country got to do with you? Any time you don't like American doings go back to your native England (if you can!) and your stuttering King, who is an excellent example of British degenerate royalty—with its ancestry of barmaids, and pantrymen!

Or did I hear some one say you were thrown out of that country of liberal degeneracy, because you out-did the royal family. HAW!

Yours
Pimp-Hater

P.S.—I notice you refer to some American Judge as an 'ignorant fellow'. If you are such a shining light, just why are you looking for a new appointment at this late date in your life? Have you been smelling up the California countryside too strongly?

From Aldous Huxley   Metro-Goldwyn-Mayer
                                           Pictures
                                      Culver-City, California
                                      19.III.40

Dear Bertie

Sympathy, I'm afraid, can't do much good; but I feel I must tell you how much I feel for you and Peter in the midst of the obscene outcry that has broken out around your name in New York.

Ever yours
Aldous H.

Press statement by the Student Council, College of the City of New York
March 9, 1940

To the Editor

The appointment of Bertrand Russell to the staff of the City College has brought forth much discussion in the press and has evoked statements from various organizations and individuals. We do not wish to enter any controversy on Prof. Russell's views on morals and religion; we feel that he is entitled to his own personal views.

Prof. Russell has been appointed to the staff of the City College to teach mathematics and logic. With an international reputation, he is eminently qualified to teach these subjects. He has been lecturing at the University of California and has been appointed visiting professor at Harvard University before he comes to the City College in February 1941. The student body, as well as the faculty, are of the opinion that the addition of Prof. Russell to the faculty cannot but help to raise the academic prestige and national standing of our college.

Nobody questioned public school teachers or City College instructors about their belief on the nature of the cosmos—whether they were Catholics, Protestants, Jews, atheists or worshippers of the ancient Greek Pantheon—when they were appointed. The American public education system is founded on the principle that religion has nothing to do with secular education and theoretically the religious beliefs of teachers have nothing to do with their jobs. Religious groups are free to expound their views. Why not educators?

By refusing to yield to the pressure being brought to bear and by standing firm on the appointment of Prof. Russell, the Board of Higher Education will be saving City College an academic black eye and doing its duty to the community in the highest sense.

We wish to stress again in the words of President Mead that Prof. Russell has been appointed to the City College to teach mathematics and logic and not his views on morals and religion.

City College has long been subject to attack from various sources seeking to modify or destroy our free higher education; the attack on Bertrand Russell is but another manifestation of this tendency.

> *Executive Committee*
> *Student Council*
> *The City College*

To Bernard Goltz,
Secretary, the Student
Council, C.C.N.Y.   March 22, 1940

Dear Mr Goltz

I am very happy to have the support of the student council in the fight. Old York was the first place where Christianity was the state religion, and it was there that Constantine assumed the purple. Perhaps New York will be the last place to have this honor.

> *Yours sincerely*
> *Bertrand Russell*

To William Swirsky,
a student at C.C.N.Y.

212 Loring Avenue
West Los Angeles, California
March 22, 1940

Dear Mr Swirsky

Thank you very much for your letter, and for the enclosures from *The Campus*. I am very glad indeed that the students do not share Bishop Manning's views about me; if they did it would be necessary to despair of the young. It is comforting that the Board of Higher Education decided in my favor, but I doubt whether the fight is at an end. I am afraid that if and when I take up my duties at the City College you will all be disappointed to find me a very mild and inoffensive person, totally destitute of horns and hoofs.

Yours gratefully
Bertrand Russell

From M. F. Ashley-Montagu

The Hahnemann Medical
College and
Hospital of Philadelphia
31 March 1940

Dear Professor Russell

I owe you so much that I feel I could never adequately repay you for the part which your writings have played in my own intellectual development. Having acquired my share of inhibitions under the English 'system' of miseducation, I have since 1930 gradually relieved myself of what used to be termed 'a natural reluctance' to address people to whom I had not been formally introduced. At this rather trying period in your life I want to reassure you. It was really Mrs Russell's remark (as reported in *The New York Times*) which is responsible for precipitating this letter. This *is* a strange land, but you are not strangers here. Your friends here number millions, and as you have obviously known for a long time, this is really the most humane, and fundamentally the most decent land in the world. That is why there is every hope, every reason to believe, that the decision of a single jurist will ultimately be faithfully evaluated for what it is worth, and your appointment to the faculty of City College maintained. When situations such as yours are given a thorough airing I have noted that justice is practically always done. It is only under the cloaca of local departmental privacy that injustice succeeds and may prosper, I have on more than one occasion suffered the consequences of such private tyranny, but you are in far different case. There are many of us who, both as individuals and as members of societies for the preservation of academic and intellectual freedom, will fight your case, if necessary, to the last ditch. I can predict, with a degree of probability which amounts to certainty that despite the barking of the dogs of St Ernulphus, common decency will prevail.

I can well realise how full your mailbag must be, so please don't attempt to acknowledge this letter. Your sense of humour will look after you, and you can leave the rest to us.

With all good wishes,

Ever yours sincerely
M. F. Ashley-Montagu
Associate Professor of Anatomy

To Mr Harry W. Laidler,
of the League for Industrial Democracy

April 11, 1940

Dear Mr Laidler

The undersigned members of the Department of Philosophy at U.C.L.A. are taking the liberty to answer your letter of inquiry addressed to Miss Creed. We have all attended lectures or seminars conducted by Mr Russell on this campus, and have therefore first hand knowledge of the character and the content of his teaching here. We find him to be the most stimulating teacher we have known, and his intellectual influence upon the student is remarkable. The general effect of his teaching is to sharpen the student's sense of truth, both by developing his desire for truth and by leading him to a more rigorous application of the tests of truth. Also unusual is the influence of Mr Russell's moral character upon the student. It is impossible to know Mr Russell without coming to admire his complete fairness, his unfailing and genuine courtesy, and his sincere love of people and of humanity.

We may add that there has not been any criticism of Mr Russell's teachings on this campus. This Department, in recommending Mr Russell's appointment, was aware that there would be some criticism on the part of outsiders of such action by the University. But in no case has there been any objection based upon Mr Russell's work here. In inviting Mr Russell to join us we did so in the faith that the individual instructor is entitled to his individual opinion on political, moral and other social issues, and that unorthodox opinions in such matters are no ground for banning an individual from public life.

You may use this letter in any way you think fit.

Yours sincerely
Hans Reichenbach
Isabel P. Creed
J. W. Robson
Hugh Miller, Acting Chairman

From and to William Ernest Hocking,   16 Quincy Street
Professor of Philosophy,   Cambridge, Massachusetts
Harvard University   April 30, 1940

Dear Russell

I answered part of your letter of April 14 by telegram: 'No possible objection to engagement at Newark'.

For the other part, which called equally for an answer—the part in which you expressed the 'hope that Harvard doesn't mind too much'—I thought it best to wait until I could send you something tangible.

The enclosed clipping from Sunday's *Boston Herald* gives a statement issued Saturday evening by our governing body ('The President and Fellows', commonly dubbed 'The Corporation'), standing by the appointment. It will also give you a hint of the kind of attack which instigated the statement. The page from Monday's *Crimson* shows more of the inside.

Please consider what I say in comment as purely personal. Individual members of the department have taken action, as you have noticed; but the department has formulated no attitude, and I am speaking for myself alone.

It would be foolish for me to pretend that the university is not disturbed by the situation. Harvard is not a 'state university' in the sense that it draws its major support from legislative grants (as in Indiana, Michigan, etc.). But it is a state institution, with certain unique provisions for its government set into the constitution, so that political interference with our working is legally possible. The suit promised by Thomas Dorgan, legislative agent for the City of Boston, has some footing in the law of the Commonwealth, though the University is prepared to meet it. But beyond that, there are possibilities of further legislation which might be serious for an institution already an object of dislike on the part of certain elements of the public.

As to the suit itself, the university is not proposing to contest it on the ground of 'freedom of speech' or 'freedom of teaching' (for this would make the university appear as protagonist of a claim of right on your part to teach your views on sex-morals at Harvard, a claim certainly uncontemplated in our arrangements and probably untenable at law). The university is simply holding the ground of the independence of our appointing bodies from outside interference. This is a defensible position, if we can show that we have exercised and are exercising that independence with a due sense of responsibility to our statutory obligations. This line will explain the emphasis in the university's statement on the scope of your lectures, and on the restriction of your teaching to advanced students; under the circumstances we shall have to abide by this limitation.

(The number of lectures mentioned in the university's statement was taken from the words of the founding bequest, which reads 'not less than six': in practice the lectures have run to ten or twelve, partly, I suppose, because of the shift to a biennial plan.)

We are all terribly sorry that this hue and cry has arisen, both because of the distress to you, and because it gives capital prominence to what (I presume) we were both considering background stuff, in which we are definitely not interested. For myself, I am equally sorry that you are making the issue one of freedom of speech in the New York situation. For if you lose, you lose; and if you win, you lose also. And the colleges will lose, too: for the impression already in the public mind will be deepened, that the colleges insist on regarding all hypotheses as on the same level,—none are foolish and none are immoral: they are all playthings of debate for a lot of detached intellects who have nothing in common with the intuitions of average mankind. Personally I am with the average man in doubting whether all hypotheses are on the same level, or can escape the invidious adjectives.

Largely because of this, I have had, so far, nothing to say in public on this question. I have been cultivating the great and forgotten right of the freedom of silence, which it is hard to maintain in this country. If I were talking, I should agree in the main with the first paragraph of the editorial in the *New*

York Times of April 20, which you have doubtless seen, and whose refrain is that 'mistakes of judgment have been made by all the principals involved'.

Your scheme of lecture titles has come, and it looks splendid to me,—many thanks. I shall write again when the department has had a chance to look it over.

Sincerely yours
Ernest Hocking

212 Loring Avenue
Los Angeles, Cal.
May 6 1940

Dear Hocking

Thank you for your letter. It makes me wish that I could honourably resign the appointment to the William James lectures, but I do not see how I can do so without laying myself open to the charge of cowardice and of letting down the interests of the whole body of teachers.

I almost wish, also, that the President and Fellows had not re-affirmed the appointment, since as you say, and as appears in the newspaper quotation you sent me, the opposition has considerable basis in law. From my point of view it would be better to be dismissed now, with financial compensation, than to be robbed both of the appointment and of compensation after long anxiety and distress.

I did not seek the appointment, and I am not so fond of the role of martyr as to wish continuously and without respite to suffer for a cause which concerns others so much more than me. The independence of American universities is their affair, not mine.

Some one seems to have misled you as to the line that I and the Board of Higher Education in New York have taken about my appointment there. I have never dreamed of claiming a right to talk about sexual ethics when I am hired to talk about logic or semantics; equally, a man hired to teach ethics would have no right to talk about logic. I claim two things: 1. that appointments to academic posts should be made by people with some competence to judge a man's technical qualifications; 2. that in extra-professional hours a teacher should be free to express his opinions, whatever they may be. City College and the Board of Higher Education based their defense solely on the first of these contentions. Their defense was therefore identical with that which you say is contemplated by Harvard.

The principle of free speech was raised by other people, in my opinion rightly. I am afraid that Harvard, like the New York Board, cannot prevent popular agitation based on this principle; though it is of course obvious that in both cases the official defense of the appointment is rightly based on the independence of duly constituted academic bodies and their right to make their own appointments.

I ask now, in advance, that I may be officially notified of any legal proceedings taken against the University on account of my appointment, and allowed to become a party. This was not done in the New York case, because of the hostility of the Corporation Counsel, who handled their defence. I cannot endure a second time being slandered and condemned in a court of law without any opportunity of rebutting false accusations against which no one else can adequately defend me, for lack of knowledge.

I hope that Harvard will have the courtesy to keep me informed officially of all developments, instead of leaving me to learn of matters that vitally concern me only from inaccurate accounts in newspapers.

I should be glad if you would show this letter to the President and Fellows.

Yours sincerely
Bertrand Russell

To the Editor of the *Harvard Crimson*   212 Loring Avenue
Los Angeles, Cal.
May 6 1940

Dear Sir
I hope you will allow me to comment on your references in the *Harvard Crimson* of April 29 to the recent proceedings concerning my appointment to the City College of New York.

You say 'Freedom of speech will not be the point under argument, as was the case in the proceedings against City College of New York, when the latter based an unsuccessful defense of its Russell appointment on the assertion that Russell should be permitted to expound his moral views from a lecture platform'.

In fact freedom of speech was not the defense of City College and the New York Board of Higher Education. The Board and College based their defense on the principle of academic freedom, which means simply the independence of duly constituted academic bodies, and their right to make their own appointments. *This, according to your headline, is exactly the defense contemplated by the Corporation of Harvard.* Neither the Board of Higher Education nor the faculty of City College at any time made the claim that I 'should be permitted to expound my moral views from a lecture platform'. On the contrary, they stated repeatedly and with emphasis that my moral views had no possible relevance to the subjects I had been engaged to teach.

Even if I were permitted to expound my moral views in the classroom, my own conscience would not allow me to do so, since they have no connection with the subjects which it is my profession to teach, and I think that the classroom should not be used as an opportunity for propaganda on any subject.

The principle of freedom of speech has been invoked, not by the New York Board of Higher Education as their legal defense, but by many thousands of people throughout the United States who have perceived its obvious relation to the Controversy, which is this: the American constitution guarantees to everyone the right to express his opinions whatever these may be. This right is naturally limited by any contract into which the individual may enter which requires him to spend part of his time in occupations other than expressing his opinions. Thus, if a salesman, a postman, a tailor and a teacher of mathematics all happen to hold a certain opinion on a subject unrelated to their work, whatever it may be, none of them should devote to oratory on this subject time which they have been paid to spend in selling, delivering letters, making suits, or teaching mathematics. But they should all equally be allowed to express their opinion freely and without fear of penalties in their spare time, and to think, speak and behave as they wish, within the law, when they are not engaged in their professional duties.

This is the principle of free speech. It appears to be little known. If therefore anyone should require any further information about it I refer him to the United States Constitution and to the works of the founders thereof.

Yours faithfully
Bertrand Russell

To Kingsley Martin,   212 Loring Avenue
editor of the *New Statesman*   Los Angeles, Cal.
                         May 13 1940

Dear Kingsley Martin

Thanks for your kind paragraph about my New York appointment. We still hope to appeal, but the Mayor and corporation counsel, from respect for the Catholic vote, are doing their best to prevent it. A similar fuss is promised over my appointment to give the William James lectures at Harvard in the autumn.

Actually I am being overwhelmed with friendship and support, but in this country the decent people are terrifyingly powerless and often very naive. This fuss is serving a useful purpose in calling attention to the sort of thing that happens constantly to people less well known.

The news from Europe is unbearably painful. We all wish that we were not so far away, although we could serve no useful purpose if we were at home.

Ever since the war began I have felt that I could not go on being a pacifist; but I have hesitated to say so, because of the responsibility involved. If I were young enough to fight myself I should do so, but it is more difficult to urge others. Now, however, I feel that I ought to announce that I have changed my mind, and I would be glad if you could find an opportunity to mention in the *New Statesman* that you have heard from me to this effect.

Yours sincerely
Bertrand Russell

To Professor Hocking from John Dewey   1 West 89th St. N Y City
                                    May 16th, 40

Dear Hocking

I have seen a copy of your letter to Russell and I cannot refrain from saying that I am disturbed by one portion of it—especially as coming from you.

Of course I do not feel qualified to speak from the Harvard point of view or to give advice on the matter as far as it is Harvard's administrative concern. But I am sure of one thing: Any weakening on the part of Harvard University would strengthen the forces of reaction—ecclesiastical and other—which are already growing too rapidly, presumably on account of the state of fear and insecurity now so general. I don't think it is irrelevant to point out that the

N Y City Council followed up its interference in the City College matter with a resolution in which they asked for the dismissal of the present Board of Higher Education and the appointment of a new one—the present Board being mainly La Guardia's appointments and sticking by the liberal attitudes on acct of which they were originally appointed—in spite of the Mayor's recent shocking cowardice. Tammany and the Church aren't now getting the educational plums they want and used to get. In my opinion (without means of proof) the original attack on Russell's appointment, and even more so the terms of McGeehan's decision were *not isolated* events. The reactionary catholic paper in Brooklyn, *The Tablet*, openly expressed the hope that the move might be the beginning of a movement to abolish all municipal colleges in Greater New York—now four in number. A policy of 'appeasement' will not work any better, in my judgment, with this old totalitarian institution than it has with the newer ones. Every weakening will be the signal for new attacks. So much, possibly irrelevant from your point of view, regarding the Harvard end of the situation.

The point that disturbed me in your letter was not the one contained in the foregoing gratuitous paragraph. That point is your statement of regret that Russell raised the issue of freedom of speech. In the first place, he didn't raise it; it was raised *first* by McGeehan's decision (I can't but wonder if you have ever seen that monstrous document), and then by other persons, originally in New York institutions but rapidly joined by others throughout the country, who saw the serious implications of passively sitting by and letting it go by default. As far as the legal side is concerned the issue has been and will be fought on a ground substantially identical with that you mention in the case of the Harvard suit. But the educational issue is wider, much wider. It was stated in the courageous letter of Chancellor Chase of N Y University in a letter to the *Times*—a letter which finally evoked from them their first editorial comment—which though grudging and ungracious did agree the case should be appealed. If men are going to be kept out of American colleges because they express unconventional, unorthodox or even unwise views (but who is to be the judge of wisdom or lack of wisdom?) on political, economic, social or moral matters, expressing those views in publications addressed to the general public, I am heartily glad my own teaching days have come to an end. There will always be some kept prostitutes in any institution; there are always [the] more timid by temperament who take to teaching as a kind of protected calling. If the courts, under outside group pressures, are going to be allowed, without protest from college teachers, to confine college faculties to teachers of these two types, the outlook is dark indeed. If I express myself strongly it is because I feel strongly on this issue. While I am extremely sorry for the thoroughly disagreeable position in which the Russells have been personally plunged, I can't but be grateful in view of the number of men of lesser stature who have been made to suffer, that his case is of such importance as to attract wide attention and protest. If you have read McGeehan's decision, I suppose you would feel with some of the rest of us that no self-respecting person would do anything—such as the *Times* editorial suggested he do—that would even remotely admit the truth of the outrageous statements made—statements that would certainly be criminally libellous if not protected by the position of the man making them.

But over and above that I am grateful for the service Russell renders the teaching body and educational interests in general by taking up the challenge—accordingly I am going to take the liberty of sending a copy of this letter to Russell.

> *Very sincerely yours*
> *John Dewey*

Dear Mr Russell

The above is self-explanatory—I know how occupied you are and it needs no reply.

> *Sincerely, & gratefully yours*
> *John Dewey*

From Alfred North Whitehead   1737 Cambridge St.
                                           Cambridge, Mass.
                                           April 26, 1940

Dear Bertie

Evelyn and I cannot let this occasion pass without telling you how greatly we sympathize with you in the matter of the New York appointment. You know, of course, that our opinions are directly opposed in many ways. This note is just to give you our love and deep sympathy in the personal troubles which have been aroused—

With all good wishes from us both.

> *Yours ever*
> *Alfred Whitehead*

Controversy over my appointment to C.C.N.Y. did not end in 1940.

From *The Times*, November 23rd and 26th, 1957, on the publication of *Why I am Not a Christian*:

To the Editor of *The Times*   10, Darlington Street, Bath
Sir

In a letter to *The Times* which you published on October 15, Lord Russell complains that in 1940 Protestant Episcopalians and Roman Catholics in New York City prevented him from denying in court what he terms their 'libels'.

The official record of the decision declaring him ineligible for the professorship in question makes it clear that his counsel submitted a brief on his behalf which was accepted by the court. His subsequent application to re-open the case was denied by the court on the grounds, among others, that he gave no indication of being able to present new evidence which could change the decision, which was unanimously upheld by two Courts of Appeal.

He could also have brought an action for libel against anyone for statements made out of court, but he failed to do this.

In these circumstances is it fair to state, as Lord Russell does, that Protestant Episcopalians and Roman Catholics prevented him from denying in court the charges which were largely based on his own writings?

Yours truly
Schuyler N. Warren

To the Editor of *The Times*
Plas Penrhyn
Penrhyndeudraeth
Merioneth.

Sir

In your issue of November 23 you publish a letter from Mr Schuyler N. Warren which shows complete ignorance of the facts. I shall answer his points one by one.

First as to 'libels'. I wrote publicly at the time: 'When grossly untrue statements as to my actions are made in court, I feel that I must give them the lie. I never conducted a nudist colony in England. Neither my wife nor I ever paraded nude in public. I never went in for salacious poetry. Such assertions are deliberate falsehoods which must be known to those who make them to have no foundation in fact. I shall be glad of an opportunity to deny them on oath.' This opportunity was denied me on the ground that I was not a party to the suit. The charges that I did these things (which had been made by the prosecuting counsel in court) were not based on my own writings, as Mr Warren affirms, but on the morbid imaginings of bigots.

I cannot understand Mr Warren's statement that *my* counsel submitted a brief on my behalf. No counsel representing me was heard. Nor can I understand his statement that two Courts of Appeal upheld the decision, as New York City refused to appeal when urged to do so. The suggestion that I could have brought an action for libel could only be made honestly by a person ignorant of the atmosphere of hysteria which surrounded the case at that time. The atmosphere is illustrated by the general acceptance of the prosecuting counsel's description in court of me as: 'lecherous, libidinous, lustful, venerous, erotomaniac, aphrodisiac, irreverent, narrow-minded, untruthful, and bereft of moral fiber.'

Yours truly
Russell

From and to Schuyler N. Warren
10, Darlington Street
Bath
10th January, 1958

Dear Lord Russell

I am writing with regard to your letter which appeared in the *Times* on November 26th. In this letter dealing with the controversy and subsequent litigation over your appointment as a Professor of Philosophy in the college in the City of New York you contradicted statements made by me in a letter that was published in the *Times* on November 23rd.

I enclose photostats of both decisions of the Supreme Court for your information, one revoking your appointment and the second denying your application to reopen the case. I also enclose copy of the letter from Mr. Charles H. Tuttle, then as now, a member of the Board of Higher Education.

In view of your denials that no counsel representing you was heard, and that no appeal was made on your behalf, the enclosed decisions confirm the correctness of my statements. In the appendix of the volume *Why I am Not a Christian,* Professor Edwards mentions Mr Osmund K. Fraenkel as having been your Attorney and of his unsuccessful appeals to the Appellate Division and to the Court of Appeals.

> *Very truly yours*
> *Schuyler N. Warren*

> Plas Penrhyn
> 13 January, 1958

Dear Mr Warren

Your letter of January 10 with the enclosed photostats does not bear out your stated view as to what occurred in my New York case in 1940. The appeal which you mentioned was not an appeal to the substance of the case, but on whether I should be allowed to become a party. You have not quite grasped the peculiarity of the whole affair. The defendants wished to lose the case—as at the time was generally known—and therefore had no wish to see McGeehan's verdict reversed on appeal. The statement that I was kept informed of the proceedings is perhaps in some narrow legal sense defensible, but I was held in Los Angeles by my duties there, the information as to what was happening in New York was sent by surface mail, and the proceedings were so hurried-up that everything was over before I knew properly what was happening. It remains the fact that I was not allowed to become a party to the case, that I was unable to appeal, and that I had no opportunity of giving evidence in court after I knew what they were saying about me. Mr Fraenkel, whom you mention, was appointed by the Civil Liberties Union, not by me, and took his instructions from them.

> *Yours truly*
> *Russell*

From Prof. Philip P. Wiener

> The City College
> New York 31, N.Y.
> Department of Philosophy
> Oct. 4, 1961

To the Editor of the New York Times

For myself and many of my colleagues I wish to express our distress at the unfairness and the poor taste shown by your Topics' editor's attempted comical rehashing of the Bertrand Russell case. It is well known that the educated world on moral grounds condemned Judge McGeehan's character assassination of one of the world's greatest philosophers, and that the courts did not allow Russell to enter the case. Now that this great man is almost ninety years old and fighting for the preservation of humanity (though some of us do not agree with his unilateral disarmament policy[1]), we believe your columnist owes him and the civilized world an apology.

Philip P. Wiener
Professor and Chairman

289 Convent Avenue
New York City
Dec. 8, 1940

Dear Professor Russell

After having enjoyed your timely lecture before the P.E.A[2]. and friendly chat at the Penn. R.R. terminal, I reported to my colleagues that we had indeed been filched of a great teacher who would have brought so much of light and humanity to our students that the harpies of darkness and corruption might well have cringed with fear of a personality so dangerous to their interests. John Dewey is working on an analysis of the McGeehan decision in so far as it discusses your books on education. That will be Dewey's contribution to the book to be published by Barnes. Our department has offered to co-operate with the editors, but we have not yet heard from Horace Kallen, who appears to be directing the book.

The Hearst papers link your appointment to City College with that of the communists named by the State Legislative Committee investigating subversive political activities of city college teachers, in order to condemn the Board of Higher Education and recommend its reorganization under more reactionary control. You may have noticed in yesterday's N.Y. Times that President Gannon of Fordham University recommended that 'subversive philosophical activities' in the city colleges be investigated!

I noted with interest your plan to devote the next four years to the history of philosophy. I always regarded your work on Leibniz next in importance only to your Principles of Mathematics and Principia Mathematica. If you made similar analytical and critical studies from primary sources of the most influential philosophers—even if only a few—e.g. Plato, Aristotle, Aquinas, Hobbes, Hume, Kant and Hegel, you would have contributed to the critical history of philosophy what only a philosopher equipped with modern instruments of analysis and a direct knowledge of the texts could do. This would be philosophically significant as a union of analytical and historical methods of investigating pervasive ideas like that of freedom (which exists mainly as an idea).

I should like to have a chance to discuss this matter with you, since the whole subject lies close to my chief interest and activity connected with the Journal

[1] I advocated unilateral disarmament at this time only for Britain.
[2] Progressive Education Association.

of the History of Ideas. I may be in Philadelphia for the Amer. Philosophical Assoc. Symposium, Dec. 28, 1940, and should like to phone you if you are free that evening or the next day (Sunday, Dec. 29).

Yours sincerely
Philip P. Wiener

P.S.—Professor Lovejoy might be free to come along to see you if I knew when you were free to talk history of philosophy.

To and from Robert Trevelyan

212 Loring Avenue
Los Angeles, Cal., U.S.A.
22.12.39

Dear Bob

Ever since I got your letter a year ago I have meant to write to you, but I felt like God when he was thinking of creating the world: there was no more reason for choosing one moment than for choosing another. I have not waited as long as he did.

I am established here as Professor of Philosophy in the University of California. John and Kate came out for the summer holidays, and stayed when the war came, so they are having to go to the university here. John has a passion for Latin, especially Lucretius; unfortunately your Lucretius is stored in Oxford with the rest of my books. (I had expected to come back to England last spring.)

Thank you very much for the list of misprints.

I wonder what you are feeling about the war. I try hard to remain a pacifist, but the thought of Hitler and Stalin triumphant is hard to bear.

C.A. [Clifford Allen]'s death must have been a great sorrow to you. I do not know what his views were at the end.

Americans all say 'you must be glad to be here at this time', but except for the children's sake that is not how we feel.

Much love to both you and Bessie from us both. Write when you can—it is a comfort to hear from old friends.

Yours ever affectionately
Bertrand Russell

The Shiffolds
Holmbury St Mary, Dorking
11 Febr. 1940

Dear Bertie

It was very nice hearing from you the other day, and to know that all is well with Peter and you and the children (I suppose they are hardly children any longer now). We are fairly all right here—at present at any rate. Bessie keeps quite cheerful, though her eye is no better. I read to her in the evening now, instead of her reading to me.

We are very glad the children are staying in America. I hope it won't be for ever, though. At present things look pretty hopeless. I have sent you a copy of my Lucretius for John, as it might be a help to him. I have also sent my Poems and Plays, as a Christmas present. Of course, I don't expect you to read them from the beginning to the end: in fact, my advice, is, if you feel you must read in them at all, that you should begin at the end, and read backwards (not line by line backwards, but poem by poem), until you get exhausted.

I don't think I shall write much more poetry. If I do, it will perhaps be Whitmaniac, in form, I mean, or rather in formlessness; though no one had a finer sense of form than W. W., when he was inspired, which he was as much as or more than most poets. I have quite come back to my old Cambridge love of him, of his prose as well as his poetry. His *Specimen Days* seems to me (especially the part about the Civil War) one of the most moving books I know. I've been reading another American book, which will hardly be popular in California, I mean *Grapes of Wrath*. It may be unfair and exaggerated about the treatment of the emigrants, I can't tell about that; but it seems to me a rather great book, in an epic sort of way. We are now reading aloud Winifred Holtby's *South Riding*, which also seems to me very nearly a great book, though perhaps not quite.

I am bringing out a book of translations of Horace's *Epistles* and two Montaigne essays, which I will send you some time this year, unless the Cambridge Press is bombed, which hardly seems likely. I have a book of prose too getting ready; but that will hardly be this year. I cannot think of a title— it is a 'Miscellany', but all the synonyms (Hotch potch, Olla Podrida etc.) sound undignified, and some of the material is highly serious. Bessie won't let me call it 'A Faggot of sticks', as she says that suggests it only deserves to be burnt.

Bessie is, I believe, intending to write to you soon, and after that I hope another year won't pass before we hear from you again. We have had the Sturge Moores here since the war began. He is rather an invalid now. We had a pleasant visit from G. E. M. in August. He is lecturing at Oxford to large audiences. Francis Lloyd says a lot of Dons go, and are amused or shocked. She seems to get a lot out of his lectures. We have also an Italian boy, a Vivante, a nephew of L. de Bosis, to whom I teach Latin and Greek. He's just got a scholarship at Pembroke Oxford. It is clear to me now I ought to have been a school-master.

Much love to you both from B. and me.

Yours ever affectionately
Bob

212 Loring Avenue
Los Angeles, Cal., U.S.A.
19 May 1940

Dear Bob

Thank you very much for the fine volumes of your works, which arrived safely, and which I am delighted to have.

At this moment it is difficult to think of anything but the war. By the time you get this, presumably the outcome of the present battle will have been decided. I keep on remembering how I stayed at Shiffolds during the crisis of the battle of the Marne, and made you walk two miles to get a Sunday paper. Perhaps it would have been better if the Kaiser had won, seeing Hitler is so much worse. I find that this time I am not a pacifist, and consider the future of civilization bound up with our victory. I don't think anything so important has happened since the fifth century, the previous occasion on which the Germans reduced the world to barbarism.

You may have seen that I am to be hounded out of teaching in America because the Catholics don't like my views. I was quite interested in this (which involves a grave danger of destitution) until the present battle began— now I find difficulty in remembering it.

Yes, I have read *Grapes of Wrath*, and think it a very good book. The issue of the migrant workers is a burning one here, on which there is much bitter feeling.

John and Kate are settling in to the university here, and Conrad (just 3) is flourishing and intelligent. We are all desperately homesick, and hope to return as soon as it is financially feasible.

Give my love to Bessie and tell her it will be very nice to hear from her. John was *most* grateful for Lucretius.

> *Yours affectionately*
> Bertrand Russell

> The Shiffolds
> 3 May 1941

My dear Bertie

We were so glad to hear from you about you and yours. I put in this line just before the post goes. Yes Plato was a comic poet. He did also apparently write some none too serious pseudo-philosophical dialogues, which got taken too seriously. Some scholars say there were two Platos; but scholars will say anything.

I am sending you a small book of Leopardi translations. I should never have started them but for you asking me to do that passage from the Ginestra, so you may look upon yourself as their 'onlie begetter'.

Bessie keeps fairly well, though she is getting rather blinder. I go on trying to work, and have lately been translating more Montaigne, not being able to write poetry. Much love to you and all yours.

> *Yours ever*
> Bob

> Little Datchet Farm
> Malvern R.D.1.
> Pennsylvania
> 20 August 1941

My dear Bob

I was delighted to have your Leopardi translations, which I thought *very* good. I am glad to think I had a share in bringing them about.

A very short time after writing to you, I came across an allusion to Plato the comic poet. He had been till then completely unknown to me.

How does George enjoy his new dignity?[1] I have only seen him once since August 4, 1914. In old Butler's days I once stayed at the Lodge and slept in Queen Anne's bed. Is it still there?

What led you to Montaigne? Do you disapprove of Florio? I was pleased to find that 'Lead kindly Light', vulgarly attributed to Newman, was really written by Cleanthes in the 3rd century B.C. There are whole chunks of the New Testament in the Stoics.

I enclose a letter to Bessie. I hope her eyesight won't go on getting worse.

Yours ever
Bertrand Russell

The Shiffolds
Holmbury St Mary, Dorking
2 October 1941

My dear Bertie

It was a great pleasure to hear from you again. Bessie no doubt will be writing or has written. She is very well, except for her eyes. I am now reading to her Nevinson's memoirs in the evening, which are not at all bad. We read a Willa Cather novel, which we both liked. I have not written much poetry lately, but what I have written I shall soon be sending you in a volume with some old ones, as all my collected poems were burnt in Longman's fire. There are two or three quasi-philosophical poems among them, perhaps rather too Santayanaish to meet with your approval. I have lately been reading his book on the *Realm of Spirit*, which, though sometimes a bit wordy, pleases me more than most philosophy—but then I'm not a philosopher. I wish I could understand your last book, but it is rather too difficult for me. I liked, though, your little book of essays (most of which I knew before), and felt in agreement with most of what you say.

As to Montaigne, I wonder whether you have ever compared Florio with the French; if so I think you would see why I think it worthwhile translating him again—though I am only doing the Essays, or parts of Essays, I like best. I also am writing some prose myself, short essays and reminiscences; also I want to write about a few of my friends, who are dead such as Tovey, C. A., Goldie and Roger.[2] So you see I can't do you yet; but I may come to living friends if they don't disappear soon enough. George[3] did not want to be Master, but his *nolo episcopari* was brushed aside by Churchill, and now he enjoys being Master a lot. The Lodge has been done up, as it was in fearful disrepair, and now is quite pleasant and well-furnished. I slept in the Junior Judge's room. Queen Anne's bed is still there, though I think the bed-tester is gone. We enjoyed our three days visit there. George is cheerful when in company, but often sinks into gloom when alone. He feels the world he cared for is at an end. I don't quite feel like that myself, at least not often. He has written a book on Social England, leaving out wars and politics etc. What I

[1] He had become Master of Trinity.
[2] Donald Tovey, Clifford Allen, Goldie Dickinson, Roger Fry.   [3] His brother.

saw was quite good. It will be out soon I suppose. His son Humphrey has written a book on Goethe, which will be very good when it comes out (by which I don't mean that 'coming out' will make it good, though perhaps that's true too). Flora Russell and her sister called last week, and they talked affectionately of you, and Flora said you had written to her, which had evidently pleased her a lot. She is getting older and is rather crippled. I haven't seen Desmond[1] since July, but hope he will come to see us soon. He is getting older, and had a bad illness this spring, but he is as charming as ever. We liked Virginia Woolf's Life of Roger very much.

Well, you must write to us again before long, and then we will write to you. I do hope you are both well, and that you both like America fairly well. G. E. Moore, it seems, likes America and Americans very much. I am very glad he is staying there this winter. I hope the children are both* well. I suppose they are hardly children now. Much love to you both from

Yours affectionately
R. C. Trevelyan

*Conrad is an infant, not a child; but I hope he is well too.

Little Datchet Farm
Malvern, R.D.1
Pennsylvania
9 July 1942

My dear Bob

For the last 6 months I have been meaning to write to you and Bessie, but have kept on putting it off for a moment of leisure. How very sad that your Collected Poems were burnt in Longman's fire. I am all the more glad that my copy is intact. I love getting your poems—if you don't get thanks, please attribute it to enemy action.

I haven't read Santayana on the *Realm of Spirit*, as I had just finished writing on him when it appeared. I was glad to find he liked what I wrote on him. Philosophers in this country lack something I like, and I have come to the conclusion that what they lack is Plato. (Not your friend the comic poet.) I can't free myself of the love of contemplation *versus* action.

Did you realize that at a certain time Thales and Jeremiah were both in Egypt, probably in the same town? I suggest your composing a dialogue between them.

I wrote to George about the possibility of my son John going to Trinity after the war, and what would be his standing if he did; he wrote a very kind answer, showing he had taken a good deal of trouble. John is at Harvard, and he is to be allowed to complete his course there (which ends in February) before returning to England to join the British forces. For a long time this was in doubt; we were very glad when it was settled. He will presumably be in England in March. He knows a great deal of history, and reads both Latin and Greek for pleasure. I am ploughing through my history of philosophy from

[1] Desmond MacCarthy.

Thales to the present day. When Scotus Erigena dined *tête-a-tête* with the King of France, the King asked 'what separates a Scot from a sot?' 'Only the dinner-table' said the philosopher. I have dined with 8 Prime Ministers, but never got such a chance. Goodbye, with all good wishes.

Yours affectionately
Bertrand Russell

The Shiffolds
Holmbury St Mary, Dorking
3 January 1942 [1943]

My dear Bertie

I have long owed you a letter. Your last letters to us were written to us in July. For nearly two months I have been in hospital, as a consequence of my bravery in crossing Hyde Park Corner diagonally during the blackout and so getting knocked over. It might have been much worse; for now, after a month at home, I can walk about much as usual, though I easily get tired. You were only knocked over by a bicycle; I by an army-taxi. An army-lorry would have been more honourable, though perhaps less pleasant.

Ted Lloyd was to have come to tea today, but has influenza, so only Margaret and John came.[1] I expect you know Ted is going East. It seems he is sorry not to come back to America. We hope to see him next Sunday and then we shall hear from him about you both. I am very glad you are writing some sort of history of philosophy and philosophers. No one could do it better than you. You will no doubt trace the influence of Jeremiah upon the cosmology of Thales. Yes, a dialogue between them might be well worth doing; but at present I know almost nothing of Jeremiah and his little book. By the way, if you want a really first-rate book on the Greek Atomists, you should have a look at Cyril Bailey's *Greek Atomists* (Clarendon Press) 1928. But I dare say you know it. It seems to me he really does understand Epicurus, which our friend Benn never[2] did. Bailey is, I think very good too about Leucippus, Democritus etc.

I have not written any poetry for nearly two years; and not much prose; though I am bringing out a book of Essays and Dialogues some time this year, which I will send you, if I can manage to get it to you. All the mental effort I have been able to make lately is a little easy 'mountaineering', by which I mean translating Montaigne—not all of him, but the less dull parts. Sometimes he can be really good. For instance, I have just translated a famous sentence of his: 'When all is said, it is putting an excessively high value on one's conjectures, to cause a man to be roasted alive on account of them.'

If you can get hold of a copy, you should read Waley's translation of *Monkey*, a 15th century Chinese fairy story about Buddhism, Taoism, and human nature generally, a superbly Rabelaisian, Aristophanic, Biblical, Voltairian book. It came out last summer (Allen & Unwin).

When John comes over here, I hope we may have some opportunity of seeing

[1] His wife, my cousin Margaret Lloyd, my Uncle Rollo's daughter, and her eldest son John.
[2] A. W. Benn, the classical scholar.

him. We still take in the *Manch. Guardian*, so have seen your and P's letters, with which we are quite in agreement.

We wish you could have spent Christmas here with us. Perhaps next Christmas?—but hardly so soon I fear.

There's an amusing Life of B. Shaw by Hesketh Pearson, but mostly written by G.B.S. himself. Yet I got a little tired of Shaw before I came to the end. Raymond Mortimer's Essays are not at all bad (*Channel Packet*). There's a good review of the *Amberley Papers*; but I expect you have seen that. It's just on dinner-time, so I must stop. Much love to you both from Bessie and me,

Yours affectly
Bob

Desmond was quite ill this autumn; but he seems fairly well again now.

To and from Gilbert Murray
The West Lodge
Downing College, Cambridge
3.3.37

Dear Gilbert

Thank you for your letter. C.A. lies in his throat. The speech was against armaments, & it is nonsense to suggest that Tory Peers are against armaments.

Spain has turned many away from pacifism. I myself have found it very difficult, the more so as I know Spain, most of the places where the fighting has been, & the Spanish people, & I have the strongest possible feelings on the Spanish issue. I should certainly not find Czecho-Slovakia more difficult. And having remained a pacifist while the Germans were invading France & Belgium in 1914, I do not see why I should cease to be one if they do it again. The result of our having adopted the policy of war at that time is not so delectable as to make me wish to see it adopted again.

You feel 'They ought to be stopped'. I feel that, if we set to work to stop them, we shall, in the process, become exactly like them & the world will have gained nothing. Also, if we beat them, we shall produce in time some one as much worse than Hitler as he is worse than the Kaiser. In all this I see no hope for mankind.

Yours ever
B.R.

Yatscombe
Boar's Hill, Oxford
Jan. 5th. 1939

My dear Bertie

A man has written to the Home University Library to say that there ought to be a book on the Art of Clear Thinking. There is plenty written about theoretic logic, but nothing except perhaps Graham Wallas's book about the actual practice of clear thought. It seems to me that the value of such a book would depend entirely on the writer; I found Wallas's book, for instance, extremely suggestive and helpful, and I think that if you felt inclined to write something, it might make a great hit and would in any case be of real value. It might be a little like Aristotle's *Sophistici Elenchi*, with a discussion of the ways in which human thought goes wrong, but I think it might be something more constructive. I wonder if the idea appeals at all to you.

I read *Power* the other day with great enjoyment, and a wish to argue with you about several points.

Give my respects to your University. Once when I was in New York, there was a fancy dress dinner, to which people went as celebrated criminals. One man was dressed as a trapper, but could not be identified till at the end of the evening he confessed he was the man who discovered Chicago.

Yours ever
G. M.

University of Chicago
January 15th 1939

My dear Gilbert

Thank you for your letter of January 5th. I think a book about how to think clearly might be very useful, but I do not think I could write it. First, for external reasons, that I have several books contracted for, which I am anxious to write and which will take me some years. Secondly—and this is more important—because I haven't the vaguest idea either how I think or how one ought to think. The process, so far as I know it, is as instinctive and unconscious as digestion. I fill my mind with whatever relevant knowledge I can find, and just wait. With luck, there comes a moment when the work is done, but in the meantime my conscious mind has been occupied with other things. This sort of thing won't do for a book.

I wonder what were the points in *Power* that you wanted to argue about. I hope the allusions to the Greeks were not wholly wrong.

This University, so far as philosophy is concerned, is about the best I have ever come across. There are two sharply opposed schools in the Faculty, one Aristotelian, historical, and traditional, the other ultra-modern. The effect on the students seems to me just right. The historical professors are incredibly learned, especially as regards medieval philosophy.

I am only here till the end of March, but intellectually I enjoy the place very much.

Yours ever
B. R.

212, Loring Avenue
Los Angeles
21.4.40

My dear Gilbert

It is difficult to do much at this date in America for German academic refugees.[1] American universities have been very generous, but are by now pretty well saturated. I spoke about the matter of Jacobsthal to Reichenbach, a German refugee who is a professor here, and whom I admire both morally and intellectually. He knew all about Jacobsthal's work, which I didn't. The

[1] Murray had appealed to me on behalf of a German anti-Nazi Professor named Jacobsthal.

enclosed is the official reply of the authorities of this university. I must leave further steps to others, as I am at the moment unable to save my own skin. In view of the German invasion of Norway, I suppose it is only too likely that Jacobsthal is by now in a concentration camp.

Yes, I wish we could meet and have the sort of talk we used to have. I find that I cannot maintain the pacifist position in this war. I do not feel sufficiently sure of the opposite to say anything publicly by way of recantation, though it may come to that. In any case, here in America an Englishman can only hold his tongue, as anything he may say is labelled propaganda. However, what I wanted to convey is that you would not find me disagreeing with you as much as in 1914, though I still think I was right then, in that this war is an outcome of Versailles, which was an outcome of moral indignation.

It is painful to be at such a distance in war-time, and only the most imperative financial necessity keeps me here. It is a comfort that my three children are here, but the oldest is 18, and I do not know how soon he may be needed for military service. We all suffer from almost unbearable home-sickness, and I find myself longing for old friends. I am glad that you are still one of them.

Please give my love to Mary even if she doesn't want it. And do write again, telling me something of what you feel about the whole ghastly business.

Yours ever
Bertrand Russell

July 29th, 1940

My dear Bertie

I was very glad to get your letter, though I feel greatly distressed by it. I should have thought that the obviously unjust attack on you as a teacher would have produced a strong and helpful reaction in your favour; there was quite a good article about it in the *Nation* (American). I still hope that it may have the result of making your friends more active.

I do not suppose you are thinking of coming back here. It would be easy enough if you were alone, but children make all the difference. I suppose this country is really a dangerous place, though it is hard for the average civilian to realise the fact; life goes on so much as usual, with no particular war hardship except taxes, only news every day about battles in the air and a general impression that we are all playing at soldiers. I am inclined to think that one of the solid advantages of the English temperament is that we do not get frightened or excited beforehand as Latins and Semites do, we wait till the danger comes before getting upset by it. I suppose this is what people call lack of imagination.

One development that interests me is this: assuming that the war is in a sense a civil war throughout the world, or a war of religions or what they now call ideolog'es, for a long time it was not quite clear what the two sides were: e.g. some people said it was Communism or Socialism against Fascism, others that it was Christianity against ungodliness. But now, as far as ideas are concerned, it is clearly Britain and America with some few supporters against the various autocracies, which means Liberalism v Tyranny. I found Benes saying much the same the other day; he had been afraid that the war would come on what he called a false issue, of Communism v. Fascism. Now he thinks it is on the right one.

If ever I can be of any use to you, please let me know.

Yours ever
Gilbert Murray

(As from) Harvard University
Cambridge, Mass. U.S.A.
September 6th 1940

Dear Gilbert

Thank you very much for your letter of July 29. My personal problems have been solved by a rich patron (in the eighteenth-century style) who has given me a teaching post with little work and sufficient salary. I cannot return to England, not only on account of my children, but also because I could not earn a living there. Exile at such a time, however, is infinitely painful. Meanwhile, we have spent the summer in a place of exquisite beauty, like the best of the Tyrol, and I have finished a big book, *An Inquiry into Meaning and Truth*— Hume plus modern logic. Sometimes I think the best thing one can do is to salvage as much as possible of civilization before the onset of the dark ages. I feel as if we were living in the fifth century.

I quite agree with what you say about the war of ideologies. The issue became clear when Russia turned against us. Last time the alliance with the Czar confused the issue.

Sympathy in this country is growing more and more emphatic on our side. My belief is that, if we pull through this month, we shall win. But I am not optimistic as to the sort of world that the war will leave.

Yours ever
Bertrand Russell

(Permanent address)
Little Datchet Farm
Malvern, R.D.1. Pa; U.S.A.
January 18th 1941

My dear Gilbert

I was very glad to get your good letter of October 23. I am now established in a small country house 200 years old—very ancient for this part of the world— in lovely country, with pleasant work. If the world were at peace I could be very happy.

As to the future: It seems to me that if we win, we shall win completely: I cannot think the Nazis will survive. America will dominate, and will probably not withdraw as in 1919; America will not be war-weary, and will believe resolutely in the degree of democracy that exists here. I am accordingly fairly optimistic. There is good hope that the militaristic régime in Japan will collapse, and I do not believe China will ever be really militaristic. Russia, I think, will be the greatest difficulty, especially if finally on our side. I have no doubt that the Soviet Government is even worse than Hitler's, and it will be a misfortune if it survives. There can be no permanent peace unless there is only one Air Force in the world, with the degree of international government that that implies. Disarmament alone, though good, will not make peace secure.

Opinion here varies with the longitude. In the East, people are passionately pro-English; we are treated with extra kindness in shops as soon as people notice our accent. In California they are anti-Japanese but not pro-English; in the Middle West they were rather anti-English. But everywhere opinion is very rapidly coming over to the conviction that we must not be defeated.

It is rather dreadful to be out of it all. I envy Rosalind [his daughter] as much as I admire her.

I am giving a 4-year course of lectures on history of philosophy in relation to culture and social circumstances, from Thales to Dewey. As I can't read Greek, this is rather cheek; but anyway I enjoy it. I divide it into 3 cycles, Greek, Catholic, Protestant. In each case the gradual decay of an irrational dogma leads to anarchy, and thence to dictatorship. I like the growth of Catholicism out of Greek decadence, and of Luther out of Machiavelli's outlook.

I remember your description of Sophocles (which you afterwards denied) as 'a combination of matricide and high spirits'. I remember, also, when I besought you to admit merit in 'hark, hark the lark' you said it ought to go on 'begins to bark'. I disagree with you about Shakespeare; I don't know enough about Sophocles to have an opinion. At the moment, I am full of admiration for Anaximander, and amazement at Pythagoras, who combined Einstein and Mrs Eddy. I disapprove of Plato because he wanted to prohibit all music except Rule Britannia and The British Grenadiers. Moreover, he invented the Pecksniffian style of the *Times* leading articles.

Do write again. Goodbye.

Yours ever
Bertrand Russell

Little Datchet Farm
Malvern, R.D. 1
Pennsylvania
June 18th 1941

Dear Gilbert

Thank you very much for your letter of 23 April, which reached me safely. I humbly acknowledge my error about quadruplicity! I agree with everything you say in your letter, and particularly with what you say about the 'Christian tradition'; I have been feeling the attraction of conservatism myself. There are, however, some things of importance to note. First: the tradition in question is chiefly represented in this country by the Catholic Church, which, here, has none of the culture one associates with that body historically. (On this, Santayana writes convincingly.) The Church lost much at the Reformation, more when intellectual France turned free-thinking; it has not now the merits it had. Generally, a conservative institution ceases to be good as soon as it is attacked.

I should regard Socialism in its milder forms as a natural development of the

Christian tradition. But Marx belongs with Nietzsche as an apostle of disruption, and unfortunately Marxism won among socialists.

The Romantic Movement is one of the sources of evil; further back, Luther and Henry VIII.

I don't see much hope in the near future. There must first be a World-State, then an Augustan age, then slow undramatic decay. For a while, the yellow races may put vigour into the Hellenic–Roman tradition; ultimately, something new may come from the negroes. (I should like to think St Augustine was a negro.)

It seems to me that everything good in Christianity comes from either Plato or the Stoics. The Jews contributed bad history; the Romans, Church Government and Canon Law. I like the Church of England because it is the most purely Platonic form of Christianity. Catholicism is too Roman, Puritanism too Judaic.

Life here, with the job I have, would be very pleasant if there were no war. The country is like inland Dorsetshire; our house is 200 years old, built by a Welshman. My work is interesting, and moderate in amount. But it all seems unreal. Fierceness surges round, and everybody seems doomed to grow fierce sooner or later. It is hard to feel that anything is worth while, except actual resistance to Hitler, in which I have no chance to take a part. We have English friends who are going back to England, and we envy them, because they are going to something that feels important. I try to think it is worth while to remain civilized, but it seems rather thin. I admire English resistance with all my soul, but hate not to be part of it. Goodbye. Do write again.

Yours ever
Bertrand Russell

Little Datchet Farm
Malvern, R.D. 1
Pennsylvania
March 23rd 1942

My dear Gilbert

I have had a letter of yours on my desk for a shamefully long time, but I have been appallingly busy. You wrote about physics and philosophy. *I* think the effect of physics is to bolster up Berkeley; but every philosopher has his own view on the subject. You wrote also about post-war reconstruction. I think the irruption of Japan has changed things. Anglo–American benevolent imperialism won't work: 'Asia for the Asiatics' must be conceded. The only question is whether India and China shall be free or under Japan. If free, they will gravitate to Russia, which is Asiatic. There will be no cultural unity, and I doubt whether Russia and U.S.A. can agree about any form of international government, or whether, if they nominally do, it will have any reality. I am much less hopeful of the post-war world than before Japan's successes.

In my survey of the history of culture—alternatively, 'Sin, from Adam to Hitler'—I have reached Charlemagne. I find the period 400–800 AD very important and too little known. People's conscious thoughts were silly, but their blind actions founded the institutions under which England still lives—e.g.

Oxford, and the Archbishops. There were many lonely men in those days— Archbishop of Canterbury Theodore, educated at Athens, trying to teach Greek to Anglo-Saxons; English St Boniface and Irish St Virgil disputing, in the wilds of the German forests, as to whether there are other worlds than ours; John the Scot, physically in the 9th century, mentally in the 5th or even 4th. The loss of Roman centralization was ultimately good. Perhaps we need 400 years of anarchy to recover. In a centralized world, too few people feel important.

Very interesting struggles are going on in this country. The Government is compelled to control the capitalists, and they, in turn, are trying to get the trade unions controlled. There is much more fear here than in England of 'planned economy', which is thought socialistic and said to lead to Fascism; and yet the necessities of the war compel it. Everybody in Washington realizes that a great deal of planning will be necessary after the war, but the capitalists hope then to get back to laissez-faire. There may be a good deal of difficulty then. There is a great deal of rather fundamental change going on here, which is worth studying. But I wish I could be at home.

All good wishes,

Yours ever
Bertrand Russell

Little Datchet Farm
Malvern, R.D. 1
Pennsylvania
9 April 1943

My dear Gilbert

Thank you for your letter of March 13, which arrived this morning; also for your earlier letter about Barnes. He is a man who likes quarrels; for no reason that I can fathom, he suddenly broke his contract with me. In the end, probably, I shall get damages out of him; but the law's delays are as great as in Shakespeare's time. Various things I have undertaken to do will keep me here till the end of October; then (D.V.) I shall return to England—Peter & Conrad too, if the danger from submarines is not too great. We can't bear being away from home any longer. In England I shall have to find some means of earning a livelihood. I should be quite willing to do Government propaganda, as my views on this war are quite orthodox. I wish I could find a way of making my knowledge of America useful; I find that English people, when they try to please American opinion, are very apt to make mistakes. But I would accept any honest work that would bring in a bare subsistence for 3 people.

It is not growing fanaticism, but growing democracy, that causes my troubles. Did you ever read the life of Averroes? He was protected by kings, but hated by the mob, which was fanatical. In the end, the mob won. Free thought has always been a perquisite of aristocracy. So is the intellectual development of women. I am sorry to hear Mary has to do the housework. My Peter's whole time is absorbed in housework, cooking, & looking after Conrad; she hardly ever has time to read. The eighteenth & nineteenth centuries were a brief interlude in the normal savagery of man; now the world has reverted to its

251

usual condition. For us, who imagined ourselves democrats, but were in fact the pampered products of aristocracy, it is unpleasant.

I am very sorry to hear about Lucy Silcox[1]; if you see her, please give her my love & sympathy.

Our reason for coming home is that we don't want to send Conrad to an American school. Not only is the teaching bad, but the intense nationalism is likely to cause in his mind a harmful conflict between home & school. We think submarines, bombs, & poor diet a smaller danger. But all this is still somewhat undecided.

I shall finish my big History of Philosophy during the summer—you won't like it, because I don't admire Aristotle.

My John is in England, training for the navy. Kate is still at College, at Radcliffe. She wants, after the war, to get into something like Quaker Relief work—She specializes in German, & is unable to feel prescribed hatreds.

Give my love to Mary—It would be a real happiness to see you again—old friends grow fewer.

Yours ever
Bertrand Russell

From Sir Ralph Wedgwood, the brother of Col. Josiah [Jos] Wedgwood who was later Lord Wedgwood of Barlaston.

Aston House
Stone, Staffordshire
29.7.41

Dear Russell

Jos has now returned safely to this country, and the first thing he did was to tell me that he had seen you, and send me your letter to him as corroborative evidence. It set me thinking of Cambridge days of long ago,—a thing that I find myself rather apt to do now that I have passed the limit of 65 which I had always hoped would be the term of my active life. This was to be the really good time of life, when one's conscience being satisfied, and work done, one could pick up old tastes, and perhaps find old friends. Besides, I have been reading your last book of essays, and that alone made me want to write to you to tell you what a delight they are. Many of them are new to me, and I cannot decide whether I like the new or the old best—only I am sure they are most enjoyable of all when read together.

I *should* like to meet you again, and to make the acquaintance of your wife. Are you ever likely to be in England again? Not until after the war I suppose in any event. Nor shall I be in America before that (speaking wishfully) happy event. So many of our friends have gone—and some have become altogether too reactionary! George Moore is the only one who goes on unchanged, and I expect you have seen him in America. He too seems likely to stay there for the duration, but he is a great loss to Cambridge. I stayed a night last month with the new Master of Trinity at the Lodge—not so formidable as it sounds. He is a dear, but one has to avoid so many subjects like the plague. However we discussed old days, and listened to the nightingales,—

---

[1] A well-known liberal schoolmistress.

and so escaped shipwreck. Desmond McCarthy I used to see from time to time, but war-time puts an end to all such social meetings—everybody is left to work or chafe in his own compartment. If you can find time, do write and tell me about yourself. I shall ask Jos all about his visit to you when I see him: he was rather ominously silent in his letter about his visit to U.S.A. as a whole. I am afraid the Wheeler episode has rather embittered it all for him. Goodbye, and best wishes.

> *Yours fraternally*
> *Ralph Wedgwood*

To Ely Culbertson, the Bridge expert

January 12 1942

Dear Culbertson

After a great deal of thought, I have come to more or less definite opinions about international government and about your scheme.

As regards international government, I think it far and away the most important question at present before the world. I am prepared to support any scheme which seems to me likely to put a large preponderance of armed force on the side of international law; some would please me more than others, but I should support whichever had a good chance of being adopted. The matter will ultimately be decided by Roosevelt, Stalin, and Churchill (or his successor); or perhaps without Stalin. Roosevelt and Churchill will be much influenced by public opinion in their own countries, but also by their officials. They are almost certain to modify any scheme they adopt.

I feel, in these circumstances, that my job is to advocate the *principle* of international government, not this or that special scheme. Special schemes are very useful, in order that the thing can be done, but I should not wish to get into controversy as between one scheme and another.

You are, as you must know, extraordinarily persuasive, and I thought I could throw in my lot publicly with you, but reflection has led me, very regretfully, to the conclusion that my points of disagreement are too important for this. The most important are the following.

(1) Your plan of regional federations with leader States has difficulties. You yourself make France and Italy equal in the Latin Federation; South Americans would resent acknowledged inferiority of status to that of the U.S.; Germany ought not to be put above the smaller Teutonic countries, which are much more civilized, and much more favourable to a World Federation.

(2) I cannot agree to your suggestion as regards India. I have been for many years an advocate of Indian freedom, and cannot abandon this just when it has a good chance of realisation.

(3) I don't like your fixing the quotas of military power 'for ever', or even for 50 years; 25 years is the utmost that would seem to me wise. This is part of a wider objection, that you have not, to my mind, a sufficient mechanism for *legal* change, yet this is essential if violence is to be made inattractive.

You may say that the points I do not like in your scheme make it more likely to be adopted. I do not think so. It seem to me that that nucleus of any practicable plan will be Anglo–American cooperation, and that a number of small countries will quickly join themselves on as satellites. One might hope the same of China and of a resurrected France. I expect therefore, at first, a Federation from which ex-enemy countries will be excluded, and from which Russia will probably hold aloof. As for the ex-enemy countries, there should be no difficulty about Italy, which is not deeply Fascist. Japan, I think, will disintegrate, and need armies of occupation to keep order; behind these armies, a new civilisation could be introduced. Germany, no doubt, will take a considerable time, but could, I think, be brought in within 20 years. As for Russia, one must wait and see.

The upshot is that I don't think we can get *everything* in the Peace Treaty. Better a nucleus of Powers in genuine agreement, and then a gradual growth, always assuming that the nucleus, at the time of the peace, has overwhelming military superiority, and the means of keeping it for some time.

As I said before, I favour *any* plan of international government that is not too like Hitler's, and I should be very glad if yours were adopted, though I still prefer the one I outlined in the *American Mercury*. I should still be very glad, if you desire it, to go over any work of yours, with a view to criticisms *from your point of view*. There might be details that could advantageously be modified. I should also, as soon as your scheme is public, speak of it as having very great merits, whenever I had occasion to talk or write on international government. But I cannot be paid by you for any public appearance, as I find this would involve too much sacrifice of intellectual independence.

I am very sorry about this, both because I found the prospect of working with you very attractive, and because it will diminish my opportunities for advocating international government. For both these reasons I was anxious to throw in my lot with you, and thought I could; but I am not good at subordinating my judgment to anybody else, and if I tried to do so I feel that it wouldn't answer.

The above applies in particular to a possible lecture at Columbia Teachers' Training College about which I wrote.

I should be very sorry indeed if anything I have said in this letter impaired our personal relations. Our talks have been a great intellectual stimulus to me, and I should like to hope that, by bringing up objections, I might be of some reciprocal use to you. Apart from all that, I should like to feel that there is a real friendship between us.

> *Yours sincerely*
> *Bertrand Russell*

My wife asks me to send her regards.

From Pearl Buck, author of *The Good Earth* and other books

R.D. 3
Perkasie,
Pennsylvania
October 23, 1942

My dear Mr Russell

I was so impressed with your attitude the other Sunday that I have been thinking of whether I might not write you.

Then Wednesday Lin Yutang spoke of your letter in PM, which he thought very fine indeed. I have not yet seen it myself—I shall try to get a copy—but he told me enough about it to make me feel that indeed I must write you.

I have for a long time—for many months, in fact—been deeply perturbed because of the feeling toward England in the minds of many Americans. I knew it was certain to rise over the India situation. I think I knew that years ago when I was in India, and saw for myself what would be inevitable if war came, and even then war seemed pretty clearly ahead.

You may ask why I have taken my share in discussions about India, if I deplored any lack of warmth between our two countries. I have done so in spite of my devotion to England, because as an American it has seemed to me my duty to do all I could, first, to see if something could not be devised to bring India wholeheartedly into the war effort, and second, because I knew there must be some sort of strong reassurance to China that we were not all thinking along the same old lines. For the latter reason I have welcomed the excellent stand that the English have taken in regard to American color segregation in our armed forces in England.

Now I feel that what has been done in India is done and the question ahead is no longer to discuss who was right and who was wrong there but to plan together, all of us, how to cope with the disaster ahead. I hope that you will read, if you have not already done so, Edgar Snow's article in the current *Saturday Evening Post*, entitled 'Must We Beat Japan First?' It is so grave that all of us must take thought together.

This alienation between Americans and English, it seems to me, must not be allowed to continue. I don't think we will get over India, especially as our losses of men in the Far East grow more severe, as they must, since India will not be mobilized to help us. I fear both the professional anti-English persons and those who have been alienated by the failure to bring India wholeheartedly into the war. I fear even more those who will grow angry when they see what the loss of India will cost us.

I don't think that Americans are particularly pro-Indian—if at all—I know I am not. But there is just something in the average American that heartily dislikes the sort of thing that has been going on in India, and this in spite of our equally wrong behavior to our own colored folk. We are, of course, full of contradictions, but there it is. What can be done to mend the situation between our two countries?

I think of one thing which ought not to be too difficult. Granting that Churchill cannot and will not change, it would help a great deal if we could see another kind of Englishman and see him in some numbers and hear him speak. As you know, the liberal English opinion has been fairly rigidly censored. Here in America we have not been allowed to hear dissenting voices in England and the sort of official Englishman we have here, and all his propaganda, does little or nothing to mend the rift in the common man.

What can we do, English and Americans together, who know the necessity of human equality, to make known our unity of thought and purpose?

The time has come for us to find each other and to stand together for the same sort of world. We cannot yield to each other's faults and prides, but we can speak together against them, and together determine a better way and so reaffirm before our enemies and before our doubting allies everywhere the essential unity of our two peoples.

Very sincerely yours
Pearl S. Buck

My views at that time on India were that it would be necessary to persuade the British Government to renew negotiations with India. It was difficult, however, to see how this could be done while Churchill remained in power. Also, India leaders should be persuaded to end the civil disobedience movement and cooperate in negotiations. Possibly the latter could be done through Nehru. I took for granted that India should be free of all foreign domination, whether British or other.

From and to Mrs Sidney Webb   Passfield Corner
                                                Liphook, Hants.
                                                December 17th 1942

My dear Bertrand

I was so glad to see in that remarkable book—*I meet America*—by W. J. Brown M.P. that you were not only intent on winning the war but wished to reconstruct the world after the war. We were also very much interested that you had decided to remain in the U.S.A. and to encourage your son to make his career there rather than in Great Britain. If you were not a peer of the realm and your son a possible great statesman like his great grandfather I should think it was a wise decision but we want you both back in Great Britain since you are part and parcel of the parliamentary government of our democracy. Also I should think teachers who were also British Peers were at some slight disadvantage in the U.S.A. so far as a public career is concerned as they would attract snobs and offend the labour movement? But of course I may be wrong.

Sidney, I am glad to say, is very well and happy though of course owing to his stroke in 1938 he is no longer able to take part in public affairs. I go on writing, writing, writing for publication. But I am old and tired and suffer from all sorts of ailments from swollen feet to sleepless nights.

I send you our last booklet which has had a great sale in Great Britain and is being published by the New York Longman firm. Probably you will not agree with it but I think you will be interested and Bernard Shaw's Preface is amusing. Like ourselves the Bernard Shaws are very old and though Shaw goes on writing Charlotte is a hopeless invalid and rather an unhappy one. Shaw is writing a book—*What's What to the Politicians*. He has been writing it for many months and would have gone on writing a longer and longer book if he had not been pulled up by the shortness of paper.

Whether you stay in the U.S.A. or not I do hope you and your two clever young people will pay a visit to Great Britain and that we shall have the pleasure of seeing you and your wife. Pray give her my greetings; I wonder how she likes America.

Your affectionate friend
Beatrice Webb
(Mrs. Sidney Webb)

P.S. I don't think you know our nephew Sir Stafford Cripps—but he represents a new movement growing up in Gt Britain, which combines the Christian faith . . . [words missing]—which might interest you. He left the Cabinet over India!

Little Datchet Farm
31 Jan 1943

My dear Beatrice

Thank you very much for your letter of Dec. 17. I was delighted to have news of you and Sidney, and to know that he is well. I am sorry you suffer from 'ailments'. I suppose it is inevitable after a certain age—to which I shall soon attain.

I don't know what gave W. J. Brown the idea that I meant to settle in America. I have never at any time thought of doing such a thing. At first I came for 8 months, then jobs came in my way. Then, with the war, I thought it better for Conrad (now aged 5) to be here. But all these reasons are nearing their end.

John (Amberley) is finished with Harvard, and returning to England in a few days, to go into the Navy if he can, and, if not, the Army. My daughter Kate is at Radcliffe; she always does as well as possible in everything she studies. Her hope, after the war, is to get into some kind of relief work on the Continent. I myself am kept here for the moment by various engagements, but I may come home fairly soon, leaving Peter and Conrad here till the end of the war.

I was much disappointed that India rejected Cripps' offer. People here are ignorant about India, but have strong opinions. I have been speaking and writing to try to overcome anti-English feeling as regards India, which in some quarters is very strong.

Thank you very much for your most interesting booklet on Russia. Whether one likes the régime or not, one can't help immensely admiring the Russian achievement in the war.

I do hope to see you again when I get back to England. Peter sends greetings and thanks for your message.

Yours affectionately
Bertrand Russell

From Dr & Mrs A. N. Whitehead

1737 Cambridge St.
Cambridge, Mass.
Jan. 3. 1944

Dear Bertie

We have just read—in the minutes of the Trinity Council—that you have been re-elected to a Fellowship and Lectureship. The minutes also emphasised that the election was unanimous. Our warmest congratulations. It is exactly what ought to have happened.

Yours ever
Alfred and Evelyn Whitehead

INDEX

259

260

265

266